WOMEN OF YORK

Claire Shaw

First Edition 2021

ISBN 978 1 8380086 4 2

British Library Cataloguing-in-Publication Data
A catalogue record for this book is available from the British Library.

Published by Destinworld Publishing Ltd.
www.destinworld.com

Cover design by Ken Leeder

CONTENTS

Prologue   1

Chapter One   Cartimandua: Traitor or Survivor?   5

Chapter Two   Roman Women of York: Diversity   17

Chapter Three   Queen Ethelburga: Game of Thrones   35

Chapter Four   The Naughty Nuns of the Priory of St Clements   43

Chapter Five   Margaret Clitherow: The Martyr of York   49

Chapter Six   Jennet Preston: Executed for Witchcraft   57

Chapter Seven   Mary Tuke and Mary Anne Craven:

                      The Queens of Confectionary   69

Chapter Eight   Elizabeth Montagu and Sarah Scott: Contrasting Lives   77

Chapter Nine   Women of the Bar Convent   95

Chapter Ten   Anne Fairfax: Sole Survivor   101

Chapter Eleven   Anne Lister and her Secret Lovers   137

Chapter Twelve   Mary Ellen Best: Forgotten Artist   147

Chapter Thirteen Benefactresses of York   161

Chapter Fourteen Prostitutes of York: Contagious Diseases Act   167

Epilogue   201

Bibliography   203

Prologue

WHEN I MOVED to York in 2009 the first notable woman from history who I encountered was Anne Fairfax. On a visit to the impressive Fairfax House, while admiring the beautifully ornate floral wallpaper of her bedroom, I noticed hanging over the mantelpiece, the portrait of a striking young woman. I was shocked when the room guide informed me that the lady, enveloped her sumptuous yellow gown, was the only surviving child of nine siblings. All her brothers and sisters, as well as her mother, had died of smallpox in the eighteenth century, leaving her and her father to face the future alone.

I began to wonder what it must have been like to be the daughter of a Viscount who had experienced bereavement on such a huge and tragic scale. It was some years later that I was able to buy a copy of Gerry Webb's 'Fairfax of York' and discovered the story of Anne's life in more intriguing detail. Shocked once more, I learnt of what she had gone through in later life at the hands of a predatory relative who had tried to swindle her out of her inheritance. As I mused upon Anne's life, I began to wonder about all the other women who had lived in the city that was once the capital of the north.

Although it is becoming somewhat of a cliché that King George VI famously said that the history of York is the history of England, he did have a point. And if this is the case, then where is all the evidence of the lives of the women of York? If York holds the key to the history of England, then what does this tell us about the history of women's lives?

Today in York there is a statue of Mr Leeman outside the train station due to his contribution to the advent of York as the railway city. There is another statue of the Victorian artist, William Etty, high on a plinth outside York Art Gallery. Where are all the statues of the women of York, I asked myself? My admiration York's grand architecture led me to the conclusion that the great city had been designed completely by men, such as John Carr or Lord Burlington. While admiring their contribution, the same question continued in my mind. Where were all the women who had contributed to the history of York?

There were a few clues in the names of streets and alleys. Lady Peckitt's yard turned out to be named after the wife of a mayor who had lived in the house above the yard, and that was about all there was to know about her. Mad Alice, who once gave her name to Lund's Court, didn't even exist upon further investigation. Even the city's most famous criminal, Dick Turpin, was a man. The male names of the numerous generations of the Terrys and the Rowntrees have become practically synonymous with York, and for good reason. Their philanthropic legacy continues to this day. Yet this still did not answer my question – where were all the women?

Gradually, as I ambled along York's ancient streets, enchanted by the layers of history that jostled beside each other, I began to happen upon the odd blue plaque, dedicated to a mysterious woman. Intrigued, I went home and searched the internet for more information. Often the facts were frustratingly difficult to unite into a coherent picture, failing to provide answers to the most basic questions such as 'what had life been like for women in York over the various centuries?' and 'what do the lives of the women of York tell us about the city itself?'

As a by-product of the research for a book of historic walks of York clues to the lives of more women began to surface, oftentimes in the context of the men who they had married. Some leads arrived at frustratingly dead ends. Although Elizabeth of York had the right surname, she spent the majority of her life in London. She was once imprisoned in Sheriff Hutton by her uncle, Richard III, but that was about as near as she ever got to the city. Even though there is a stained glass window in York Minster dedicated her marriage to Henry VI, commemorating the end of the War of the Roses, she wasn't married in York, but at Westminster Abbey. I had to return to the drawing board.

Eventually, I was able to draw up a list of eleven women who had some connection to the city of York. I was then able to group together other women thematically. I decided that to gain entry into the book, it was not necessary to have been born in York, although many were, but that the woman at least had some connection with the city. Jennet Preston was hung in York in 1596 under the false allegation of being a witch. Dying in York meant Jennet had a definite place in the book.

As the writing progressed, certain themes began to emerge. Women like Mary Tuke and Mary Craven became successful entrepreneurs because the men in their lives had died and they had had to pick up the reigns of their businesses due to economic adversity. Moreover, Mary Tuke battled against sexist laws designed to end her career. Religion was a huge factor in many women's lives, with one woman, Margaret Clitherow, heroically dying for her beliefs in order to protect her children.

There were several rebels against orthodoxy and many of the women made huge personal sacrifices to be allowed the freedoms that we take for granted today. Sometimes the woman's mere survival, when the odds were stacked against her, was enough to make her of heroic proportions. Many women were extremely charitable and tried to benefit their fellow citizens, believing in the need for education of both women and men. There were also some interesting surprises along the way, such as when writing about Elizabeth Montagu, I discovered the life of her practically forgotten, but equally as interesting sister, Sarah Scott.

Another pattern that emerged was that the vast majority of the women were from the middle and upper classes, due to better documentation of their lives in archives and in letters. However, the day before I left York in 2020, I found a book called 'Prostitutes of York' in a second-hand bookshop in Micklegate. Dating from 1974, it was a little-known, but groundbreaking study of the heartbreaking lives that over a thousand prostitutes had led in Victorian York, written by Frances Finnegan. It painted a shocking picture of what I had come to believe was a genteel cathedral city. It was as though destiny had put the book in my hands so that the lives of many desperate working class women, victims of a society that failed to help them, would be remembered and recorded with the help of the author of the study.

Prologue

As I wrote 'Women of York', many of my questions were answered, but still more questions emerged. Rather than trying to answer the questions myself, I have made a list in the epilogue for you to ponder, dear reader. Perhaps they may be of interest to a reading group. However, you choose to read the book – alone, in a reading group, from cover to cover, dipping in a chapter at a time, I hope that it goes some way to answering the fundamental question - where are the women of York and therefore the women of England?

CHAPTER ONE

Cartimandua

Traitor or Survivor?

QUEEN CARTIMANDUA RULED over the ancient British tribe of the Brigantes and they are the principal reason why the city of York was founded by the Romans in AD 71. When the Emperor Claudius invaded Britain in AD 43, he was not met with much resistance and eleven of the native British kings immediately surrendered to him. Although it is not known whether Cartimandua was among the eleven surrendering monarchs, she would have been equally as overawed as her fellow countrymen by the might and power of the Roman military machine. However, instead of resisting the overwhelming power of the Romans, Cartimandua decided to develop a cooperative relationship with the brutal invaders, as did several other local Celtic tribal leaders.

While the Romans concentrated on defeating the Celtic tribes in the south of the province, they decided that it would be beneficial to use Cartimandua's large kingdom of Brigantia as a buffer zone between the wild northern province of

Caledonia (Scotland) and the rebellious southern tribal areas. Using buffer zones was a tactic often employed by the Romans in their gradual conquest of provinces and their purpose was to prevent them being challenged on multiple fronts at any one time. With a relatively small number of highly trained soldiers, the Romans disliked splitting their forces and so weakening their military effectiveness.

In return for becoming a 'client queen', Cartimandua could expect to receive financial subsidies from Rome, which she could use to benefit her people, as well as military protection should she ever be attacked. She would have also enjoyed easier access to luxury goods that the Romans imported, as well as finding new outlets for any products that the Brigantes made, such as hides and furs.

The Iron Age hill fort complex at Stanwick in North Yorkshire is thought to be the seat of Cartimandua's court. Arguments for this theory are that it was ideally located to control the northern Brigantes. The three-kilometre square area is surrounded by earthworks, some of which reach a height of more than five metres in places. From excavations by Haselgrove et al in 1990, it has been suggested that the first settlement was comfortably organised and enjoyed luxury items from the south, such as rare Samian ware and uncommon varieties of amphora and volcanic glass that were hardly known outside Italy. Perhaps these products were given to Cartimandua in diplomatic exchanges, rather than as normal trade goods.

By the mid first century AD Stanwick was at the height of its prosperity at a time when Brigantia was a kingdom friendly to Rome and it is possible that Cartimandua and her husband, Venutius, were based there. The large imposing north-western entrance seems to have been designed to impress as much as protect. High-status imports have added to the prestige of the place, suggesting that it could have been a 'palatial' dwelling complex.

Of greater benefit to Cartimandua than luxury goods, her relationship with Rome would have allowed her to keep her hereditary throne and tribal lands, as well as her other assets and her sovereignty over her people. The Roman historian Tacitus (AD 56 – AD 120), the main source of information about Cartimandua, tells us that she was 'a princess of noble birth'. The alternative to cooperation with the Romans was the possibility of defeat in battle, confiscation of property, annexation of land and ultimately enslavement or death.

Prasutagus, king of the Iceni tribe in the region of East Anglia also decided to take the same pragmatic course of action as Cartimandua and became a client king of the Romans. It was not until his death and the subsequent rape of his daughters by Roman soldiers, combined with the public flogging of his wife, Boudicca, that the relationship between Rome and the Iceni faltered and Boudicca led her famous, devastating rebellion against the Romans.

Although Cartimandua's decision to foster positive relations with the Romans brought peace and prosperity to her kingdom, it did not please all her subjects. The Brigantes was a large and loose confederation of disparate tribes which banded together for mutual benefit and protection. With such a large population to control and to satisfy, there were more possibilities for dis-satisfied factions to form within her own tribe, with their own agendas and rivalries.

While there were other monarchs with cooperative relationships with Rome, Frere in his 1987 work, 'Britannia' describes Cartimandua's situation as unique:

'Cartimandua was in a class by herself, for her Brigantian kingdom lay beyond the frontiers of the province and was not really under Roman control save at the cost of special military effort'.

Upon invading Britain, Claudius had ordered that all weapons be removed from conquered territories. Not only those hostile to Rome had to lay down their arms, but those bound by treaty also. For people from a warrior culture, many would have seen this as an affront to their dignity, as well as their identity. They would have been subjected to frequent searches and the experience would have been degrading and humiliating to a proud people. Naturally, the ancient Britons would have felt resentment towards their new rulers.

A mere four years after Emperor Claudius' invasion of Britain, some of the disaffected Brigantes are known to have rebelled against Cartimandua's decision to ally with the Romans. In AD 47 or 48 there was an uprising amongst the disgruntled factions of the Brigantes and Cartimandua decided to play her ace card and call on the Romans for the support that they promised in return for her cooperation.

The size of the Brigantian territory and the number of prominent nobles involved in the uprising would have meant that rival elements, each with their own interests, aims and agendas would have been inherent in such a vast kingdom. As the leader of a large number of individual sub-tribes, it would have been a challenge for her to enforce a common policy. There may have been some sympathy amongst her people for the Welsh and southern tribes who were in conflict with the Romans.

The reputation of the Brigantes as difficult to rule even reached the Roman senator and writer, Seneca (4 BC – 64 AD), who described them as being ordered to submit to Roman authority in his work, 'Apocolocyntosis'.

In her book, 'Cartimandua, Queen of the Brigantes', Nikki Howarth goes so far as to suggest that the Druids, the religious leaders of the Celtic tribes, may have encouraged opposition to Cartimandua's alliance with Rome. The Druids had been forced into exile on the sacred island of Anglesey (Mona) in Wales and were fearful of their own fate at the hands of the Romans. As it turned out their fears were justified. The governor of Britannia, Suetonius Paulinus, advanced on their stronghold in AD 60 and massacred them all. Tacitus records that Paulinus' troops crossed the Menai Straits in the face of cursing Druids and fanatical women, who were prepared to fight to the death.

Upon Cartimandua's call for assistance, the new governor of the province, Ostorius Scapula, rushed back from his campaign against the Deceangli in Wales. Tacitus tells us that an entire legion was employed to put down the rebellion, showing the extent of the unrest. After the defeat the Brigantians, the ringleaders were executed. However, it was decided to show mercy to those with lesser involvement or possibly a pragmatic decision on the part of Cartimandua to avoid sowing the seeds of future conflict.

For the next three years or so, Cartimandua continued to rule the Brigantes. Today it may seem strange to us that a woman was able rule over a diverse and sometimes troublesome group of people. Cartimandua's authority was accepted because she was a hereditary ruler. Tacitus describes her as ruling over the Brigantes 'by virtue of her illustrious birth'. It may have been the case that her predecessor unified the diverse tribes of Brigantia and therefore her lineage may have been considered as particularly powerful. Unfortunately, in approximately AD 51, she was faced with one of the most difficult situations of her monarchy. Caractacus, one of the leaders of the Catuvellauni tribe near Hertfordshire, fled his battle with the Romans, escaping to Cartimandua's territory, whereupon he requested sanctuary from her.

Caractacus' tribe, the Catuvellauni was powerful and was ruled by the descendents of the war leader, Cassivellaunus, who had led resistance to Caesar's invasion in BC 55. Cunobelin was the king of the dynasty from the early first century and his sons, Togodumnus and Caractacus began a programme of territorial expansion into the southern kingdom of the Arebates. Togodumnus and Caractacus resisted the Roman presence, even though they had a lot to lose in doing so. Once they had annexed the neighbouring kingdom of the Arebates, they now faced the wrath of Rome. After a number of encounters, Togodumnus was killed and Caractacus withdrew to the west.

Caractacus saw that all his possible south-eastern allies had been crushed by the Roman invasion or had to decided to pay homage to Rome. His only option was to retreat to Wales. There the Catuvellaunian rebel prince was able to win the support of the Silures, who were hostile to Rome. The Silures were the strongest and most successful opponents to the Romans in Britain. They used their natural terrain and the knowledge of their lands to their advantage in strategic battle strategies. Tacitus describes how their fierceness was strengthened by their belief in the military abilities of their leaders.

In around AD 51 Caractacus took a defensive position in the steep hills of Snowdonia, behind a river with no easy crossing. The Roman cavalry struggled to pass the slopes which had been blocked with piled stones. Equally, the horses were ineffective in the densely wooded terrain. However, eventually the Roman infantry won through and defeated Caractacus' warriors in a pitched battle. His wife and daughter were captured and another brother surrendered. Abandoning his wife and his family to their fate, he fled north to the lands of the Brigantes.

Several historians have speculated as to why Caractacus decided to flee to Cartimandua's lands. Undoubtedly, he would have known about her reciprocal arrangement with the Romans. Some suggest that they knew each other through trade links. The Catuvellauni would have had the power to supply or withhold high-status goods and luxury items to the leaders of other British tribes pretty much at will. A more romantic theory comes from the Triads of Welsh literature which name Cartimandua as Aregwedd Foeddawg and claim that she and Caractacus were second cousins. In the Scottish 'The Buik of Cronicilis of Scotland', it is stated that Cartimandua was Caractacus' stepmother, which seems highly unlikely. There may have been familial links between the two tribes, but there is no evidence to prove it. It is equally as possible that neither individual had anything to do with the other prior to Caractacus' surprise arrival in Brigantia.

What happened next has served to blacken the name of Cartimandua for two thousand years. She has been called variously a 'quisling', a 'traitor', a 'collaborator' and a betrayer of a fellow ruler. Some sources suggest that she even had Caractacus clapped in irons when she handed him over to the Romans.

Even though Cartimandua's decision to proffer up Caractacus benefitted the

Romans, the Roman historian Tactitus in his 'Histories' described her behaviour as the 'treacherous capture of king Caractacus'. Modern writers have used the disparaging adjective 'quisling' to describe Cartimandua, which originates from a Norwegian politician called Vidkun Quisling who helped the Nazis capture his own country during World War Two.

It is time now that this judgement of Cartimandua's decision to offer up Caractacus to the Romans be reassessed. If we look at the definition of the adjective 'traitor' it means 'one who is disloyal to or who betrays their nation'. The problem with the application of this description to Cartimandua is that she was not part of a 'nation' in the modern sense of the word. The Celtic tribes of Britain were a collection of disparate groups of people, who often not only did not show allegiance to each other, but actually made war against each other, often for economic gain in the form of territorial rights. As we have already seen, Caractacus had no qualms about annexing the land of the Arebates.

The king of the Iceni, Prasutagus, had a cooperative relationship with the Romans and it wasn't until he died and left his kingdom to his two daughters that the relationship with Rome broke down. Even Caractacus would have enjoyed the benefits of friendship with Rome while his father was alive.

Knowing that Cartimandua had a client-queen relationship with Rome, one is forced to question Caractacus' motives in fleeing to Brigantia in the first place. Perhaps his objective was not just sanctuary under Cartimandua's aegis. Perhaps his presence was much more of a threat to her sovereignty. He had been content to abandon his wife and daughter to their fate at the hands of the Romans. Was he seeking reinforcements from among the Brigantes to help him liberate them and continue his rebellion against the invaders? What if Caractacus wanted to usurp Cartimandua and take her throne for himself so that he could command the Brigantes to continue his fight against the Romans? It is likely that he would have known about the earlier uprising. Did he want to exploit the discontent factions in Cartimandua's kingdom and persuade them to his cause? Perhaps Caractacus' motives were not as innocent as they first appear. Whatever his choices, Caractacus' presence in Cartimandua's realm put her and her people in extreme danger.

In the event Cartimandua's choices in the situation were very limited. The alternative to giving Caractacus up to the Romans was to help him and furnish him with warriors. Had Cartimandua taken this course of action she would have brought disaster down upon herself and her people at the hands of the ruthless Romans who would never countenance defeat. Her kingdom, her lands and her assets would have been confiscated; she would have been stripped of her birthright and the legacy that her ancestors had built. Ultimately, her people would have been killed or enslaved. She herself would have at best been paraded in irons through the streets of Rome, a warning to other tribal leaders not to rebel. At worst she would have been enslaved or killed herself.

Whatever Caractacus' motives for fleeing to Cartimandua, he clearly hadn't considered the invidious position that he would put her in. Having abandoned his wife and daughter to their fate at the hands of the Romans, it seems that his reasons were purely personal and selfish. If there was any more unrest amongst the Brigantes, it could give the Romans the excuse to appropriate her lands. If

Cartimandua had joined forces with Caractacus, they would have both been annhiliated by the Romans' superior power. She did the only thing that a wise and pragmatic political leader could do in such circumstances. She handed over the rebel leader to his enemy. Conveniently, at the same time, Cartimandua would reassure Rome of her loyalty and strengthen her position.

Fortunately, for Caractacus things did not end as badly as they could have done. He and his family were taken to Rome and paraded through the streets in a triumphal procession before the people, important dignitaries and even the Emperor Claudius himself. Tacitus records that he gave a rousing speech to the gathered crowd. Claudius was so impressed that he and his family were released from their bonds and allowed to live on in exile in Italy, whereupon they disappear from the record into the sands of time.

Unfortunately, Cartimandua, back in misty, wild Britannia at the head of a tribe of quarrelsome Brigantes was unable to forget her monumental decision so easily. It is likely that the next revolt that she faced led by her husband, Venutius, had something to do with her decision to hand over Caractacus. According to Tacitus the rift between Venutius and Cartimandua was so deep that they divorced. There have been many suggestions that this was because she was having an affair with Venutius' armour-bearer, Vellocatus. Although she did ultimately marry Vellocatus, the reason for Venutius taking up arms against Cartimandua is more likely to have been because he did not agree with her political choices.

Venutius had been happy to go along with Cartimandua's cooperative relationship with Rome while they were married. However, something changed to make him rally the Brigantes that were already hostile to Cartimandua's politics and attack Cartimandua's forces. Again, Cartimandua looked to the Romans for military aid. The new governor of Britannia, Didius Gallus, sent auxiliary troops to Brigantia. There they met with sustained resistance and there were several skirmishes. Finally, the Romans met with success after sending possibly the 9th Legion Hispana, commanded by Caesius Nasica. Ultimately, Venutius and his forces were defeated by Roman troops coming to the aid of the queen.

Venutius was allowed to flee to his own people, believed to be the Carvetti based around modern Cumbria. Meanwhile Cartimandua took Venutius' brother and relatives hostage, an insurance policy against future attacks from her rebel consort. Cartimandua did not request that the Romans hunt him down. Perhaps she decided not to pursue Venutius as she knew how popular he was amongst her people and to sacrifice him could have caused more unrest.

It is unlikely that Venutius would have been able to rally forces against Cartimandua due to her choice of consort, Vellocatus. Cartimandua was a hereditary queen and even Tacitus acknowledges that the Celtic peoples accepted female monarchs as their rulers. As such Venutius was inferior in standing to Cartimandua and was her consort, rather than her king. Their marriage may have been a political one to cement an alliance between rival tribes. Cartimandua's choice of lover was her own decision. Perhaps Venutius had enjoyed the taste of power that being Cartimandua's consort had given him and he decided that he wanted more control of the Brigantes than his inferior status allowed. Before the incident with Caractacus, Venutius was happy to be the friend of Rome.

For twelve years Venutius disappears from the record until AD 69. This was a particularly notorious year in Roman history as a civil war broke out in Rome caused by opposition to Emperor Nero's rule. There was so much political strife that the year has come to be known as 'The Year of the Four Emperors'. It is likely that Venutius noticed the reduction of Roman troops in Britannia as many were recalled home to help stabilise the unrest. Consequently, it was this year that Venutius decided to attack Cartimandua once more.

It is possible that Venutius' attack was linked to Cartimandua taking Vellocatus as her second husband at this time. Tacitus tells us that Vellocatus was Venutius' armour-bearer and that in elevating him to the position of royal companion, Cartimandua made a reckless decision and 'this scandal immediately shook the royal house to its foundations'. There has been much speculation that the scandal was caused by Vellocatus' servile status. However, in antiquity the position of armour-bearer was a prestigious one and it is still listed as one of the Great Offices of the Royal Household of Scotland. Although it is a ceremonial role in modern times, historically it was very influential. It does seem possible that in the warrior culture of the Brigantes, a great fighter may have been an acceptable consort for a queen, even if he did not have noble blood.

Others have suggested that Vellocatus many have been a Roman and therefore her choice of consort was deeply unpopular with her people, leading some of them to join forces with Venutius in his attempt to overthrow her. It is possible that Cartimandua had been granted Roman citizenship herself by this point for her continued loyalty to the Roman Empire. It has been speculated that Cartimandua' relationship with Vellocatus may have been a shrewd move on her part to deprive Venutius of a potential spy and capable ally. Perhaps Vellocatus had men loyal to him who she could use if her throne was ever threatened again by Venutius. It is likely that there were political motivations to her decision to make him her official consort. After all she had ruled alone for over a decade and could have taken him as her lover, had she chosen to do so.

In 'Histories' Tacitus describes the situation in Brigantia in AD 69:

> 'These dissensions, and the continual rumours of civil war, raised the courage of the Britons. They were led by one Venutius, who, besides being naturally high spirited, and hating the name of Rome, was fired by his private animosity against Queen Cartismandua. Cartismandua ruled the Brigantes in virtue of her illustrious birth; and she strengthened her throne, when, by the treacherous capture of king Caractacus, she was regarded as having given its chief distinction to the triumph of Claudius Caesar. Then followed wealth and the self-indulgence of prosperity. Spurning her husband Venutius, she made Vellocatus, his armour-bearer, the partner of her bed and throne. By this enormity the power of her house was at once shaken to its base. On the side of her husband were the affections of the people, on that of the adulterer, the lust and savage temper of the Queen'.

As has already been noted, although Cartimandua was loyal to Rome throughout her life and Venutius was the rebel, not only does the Roman historian

Tacitus ignore this fact, but proceeds to portray Cartimandua as greedy, corrupt, sexually promiscuous, an adulterer, lustful, violent and vengeful. 'Barbarian' queens were fascinating to the Romans because, although they recognised the intelligence of women, they did not approve of them wielding power in their own right. To Romans, women were most definitely second-class citizens and there seems to be some of this anti-female bias in Tacitus' chronicle. It is unlikely that Tacitus would have used the same adjectives to describe a male leader who had made the same choices as Cartimandua. While in his chronicle Tacitus gave Caractacus, a rebel against Rome, a rousing speech, Cartimandua is denigrated, even though all she was ultimately doing was trying to protect her hereditary birthright. Tacitus was equally as reticent about Boudicca's military prowess as a woman, describing her as being 'descended from mighty men'.

Venutius attacked with external forces at the same time as an internal Brigantian revolt. In serious danger, Cartimandua appealed to Rome for help once more. Vettius Bolanus sent Cartimandua a group of auxiliary infantry and cavalry, which were cohorts made up of mercenary soldiers from all over the Empire. Cartimandua was in such peril that she needed a crack company of legionary troops. It is likely that none was available due to the internal strife in Rome.

Whether Bolanus' decision was through inability or merely disinclination, according to Nikki Haworth in her book 'Cartimandua: Queen of the Brigantes', 'there is little doubt that the governor's choice of rescue party lost Cartimandua her throne. Had a legionary force been sent, it is likely that there would have been a very different result'.

There was a lot at stake for Venutius in this attack. Perhaps his relatives had died in the interim and so he did not need to worry about their safety. However, if he was defeated a second time, he may not have been treated as mercifully as the first time. We do not know how many rebels he managed to recruit, but it was no easy victory. The Roman auxiliary soldiers were met with 'desperate fighting' before they managed to rescue Cartimandua from her dangerous position. Had Venutius captured her, she would have at best been taken hostage, at worst killed. Nothing is known of Cartimandua's fate after she was extricated from danger, except that this was the end of a unique era in British history. The first ever hereditary British queen who we know about had been defeated and overthrown.

Venutius' control of the throne did not last long. After the initial euphoria of his victory, he would have come to realise the precariousness of his position. The dark shadow of Roman reprisals must have haunted him. The Brigantes would have been used to Cartimandua's influence with the Roman administration and perhaps they wanted reassurances that they were safe, like when under Cartimandua's rule. Now Venutius was in Cartimandua's position, he too would have come to know what it was like to try to control tribal factions, who may even have been plotting their own attempts to gain power. As a military man, Venutius would have been ill-prepared for the administration of Cartimandua's kingdom. He would not have been able to rely on the subsidies and assistance in times of bad harvest that Cartimandua had enjoyed. He may have come to realise, like many usurpers, that it was easier for him to be popular when it was not him taking the tough decisions. With Venutius on the throne, Rome had lost her major ally in the north.

The Romans did not know Venutius' future intentions. It was clear that his victory could not go unchallenged.

In AD 71 Vettius Bolanus was replaced by Petillius Cerealis, an experienced and ambitious soldier, who was determined to crush any rebellion in the expanding province, which returned the British contingent back to the same number as before the 'Year of the Four Emperors'. His first priority now was to make a direct strike against the Brigantes. Perhaps it was personal for Cerealis too. The Roman historian, Birley, tells us that Caesius Nasica who led the legion which defeated Venutius in his first rebellion in AD 51 was thought to be Cerealis' brother.

After marching west from Lincoln in AD 71 with 5000 soldiers from the Ninth Legion Hispana, plus a further 500 auxiliary troops, Cerealis set his men to work on a patch of land between the River Ouse and the River Foss. They were instructed to build a fortress of wooden palisades, which would later become known as Eboracum, the place of the Yew trees. The fortress later evolved into the city of York that we know today. In his book 'Roman York', Patrick Ottaway describes the thinking behind this choice of site:

'One reason for the choice of York as a fortress site must have been that it was ideally placed to allow the army to strike at centres of native resistance in the valleys of the Pennines and North York Moors'.

From this fortress, Cerealis' campaign against Venutius was swift and decisive. Tacitus tells us that:

'Petilius Cerealis at once struck terror into their hearts by attacking the state of the Brigantes...After a series of battles – some of them by no means bloodless- Petilius had overrun, if not actually conquered, the major part of their territory.'

It is unlikely that Venutius had occupied the hill fort of Stanwick as Cartimandua was thought to have done. Archaelogical evidence suggests that it was not a major stronghold at this time, capable of repelling the Romans. Perhaps after his initial success, he decided to march further north and try to gain more sympathisers on the way, particularly as he reached wild Scotland. A place in the Scottish lowlands identified as Venution has been suggested as a possible base for Venutius as he tried to fend off Roman attacks.

We do not know if there was ever a decisive showdown. Perhaps there was a series of battles instead. Like Cartimandua, we do not know his ultimate fate. If he had been captured in battle or killed in action, it is likely that his destiny would have been recorded and celebrated by chroniclers. However, it is possible that he simply died of natural causes. If he was married to Cartimandua in AD 43, then that would make him around fifty by AD 71. By the time that Julius Frontinus arrived in Britannia in AD 74 to replace Petillius Cerealis, Venutius was no longer considered a threat. Frontinus then turned his attention to the Silures in Wales. It was not until Agricola arrived four years later that the far north became a major focus once more.

Ultimately, Venutius' victory against Cartimandua was short-lived and doomed. His subsequent fight against the advancing Roman army was futile and the

Brigantian rebels were defeated and subdued by the forces of the governor Petilius Cerealis between AD 71 and AD 74.

So, what may have happened to Cartimandua after her overthrow? Although we do not know Cartimandua's final destiny, it is safe to say that the Romans were not willing to fight to reinstate her to her throne. If to her people she was seen as the human representation of the goddess Brigantia, her expulsion from the tribe would have been unsettling. Nevertheless, she was forced to leave her birthright.

One theory as to Cartimandua's fate is that she was housed in a purpose-built protected residence in Chester and that the building was abandoned in AD 79 when the queen died. However, the problem with this theory is that the building was not constructed until five years after Cartimandua's rescue and does not explain what happened to her in the interim.

She may have performed an honourable suicide like Cleopatra, or she may simply have died. However, she did have a new husband and the gratitude of Rome for many years of support. It is likely that she had been granted Roman citizenship before Venutius' rebellion. Had she continued to live in Britain, she would have been the continual target of hostilities and assassination attempts. It is therefore possible that like Caractacus, Cartimandua lived out the rest of her days in exile in Rome.

The historian Braund states that the Romans were willing 'to offer refuge to kings in flight from their kingdoms' as it 'was to add still further to imperial prestige'. There was a precedent for this when the Emperor Tiberius encouraged the defeated German king, Maroboduus, to fly to Rome and then proceeded to portray himself to the senate as saving Rome from a dangerous enemy by keeping the monarch in exile.

Haworth believes that Cartimandua is 'likely to have spent her remaining days settled comfortably in a privileged life in Italy somewhere – she was not the first exiled British royal to do so...' She imagines her being kept away from Caractacus, enjoying the Italian sunshine. She speculates that she may even have had children with Vellocatus. If she was with Vellocatus and he was a Roman, this would have facilitated her integration into Roman life and culture. Just maybe she lived happily ever after.

Unfortunately, throughout history Cartimandua has been portrayed as the adulterous betrayer of British royal men with Venutius and Caractacus being her stepping stones to material success. However, while Caractacus, Boudica and Venutius did not see a future for themselves in a Roman world, Cartimandua, on the other hand, must have thought that she did not have a future outside of it.

Cartimandua was forced to make some tough decisions to maintain her throne, but ultimately they paid off. She saw that her relationship with the Romans would bring new outlets for trade for Brigantian goods and new opportunities for increasing the wealth of her territory and her people. Under Cartimandua her people were not abused or enslaved, unlike those who resisted Rome. Perhaps had it not been for the key geographical position of her kingdom and its size, she may well have had to deal with the possibility of invasion. As it was, she took advantage of the political situation afforded by her geographical location and was so adept at political manoeuvring that she was able to stay in power for at least twenty-six years. She endured years of conflict, infighting and rivalry, so she must have been continually one step ahead of her enemies. Clearly, she was an astute and pragmatic politician.

Rome may have conquered Cartimandua's homeland, but it never treated her badly. She was a native Briton negotiating her way in a man's world. Eventually, both the Iceni and the Brigantes were devastated by death and slavery. A magnificent bronze statue of Boudica, Queen of the Iceni, resides just below Westminster Bridge, near to the Houses of Parliament in London. She stands with staff in hand at the helm of her moving chariot, her fearsome horses rearing up in front of her. Behind her, her two semi-naked daughters are protected by this heroic warrior queen. As the horses race forward, her arms are open, as though embracing her tragic destiny, her final defeat against the Romans in AD 61.

But where is the statue to Cartimandua, Queen of the Brigantes, the northern tribe of Celts, whose territory encompassed what was to later become the city of York? There is no statue of Cartimandua and many may not have even heard of her. History has done a lot to damn and erase Cartimandua. Those who research her discover the prevailing myths about her - that she was both sexually immoral and a traitor to her people. M. Aldhouse Green pulled no punches when he wrote of her, "sleek with prosperity and sexual gratification, a beast of a woman who played out her conquests in bed rather than on the battlefield".

If Cartimandua was in power when Claudius invaded in AD 43, her reign lasted at least twenty-six years until AD 69. It is facile to write off the legacy of a woman who commanded the respect of Rome for such a long period. She was a pragmatic politician and a wise ruler who saw that any attempt to defy Rome would be met with devastating consequences for her and her people. Under her rule, her people enjoyed relative peace and the financial benefits of a symbiotic relationship with Rome. She had to make some very difficult decisions during her reign, but she took them. She could be ruthless, taking hostages. However, she was never merciless. She preferred peace and diplomacy to war. Ultimately, she survived in a world dominated by brutal men. Perhaps this is her greatest achievement.

CHAPTER TWO

Roman Women of York

Diversity

JUST AS IN all the other parts of the Roman Empire, Roman York was a man's world. When Petillius Cerialis' Ninth Legion Hispana marched north from Lindum (Lincoln) in AD 71, his objective was to find a suitable location from which to base a campaign to subjugate the troublesome northern Celtic tribe of the Brigantes, now led by Venutius, the rebellious ex-husband of Cartimandua.

Cerialis' surveyors had located a piece of flat land in an ideal position for his encampment, nestled between the confluence of the rivers Ouse and Foss. Providing access to the North Sea via the Humber estuary, the river Ouse would prove invaluable for future import of supplies and men. After clearing the area of the native woodland, it was decided to name the new fortress after the trees that had been cut down to make way for the garrison - Eboracum - the place of the yews.

Working with speed and efficiency Cerialis' 5000 legionaries, supplemented by additional multi-national auxiliaries, dug a deep rectangular trench in the shape of a playing card. Re-using the excavated earth, they worked together to pack the soil into a defensive rampart. The felled trees were hewn to form spiked timber palisades to protect the battle-hardened soldiers inside, and to keep fearsome enemy warriors without. Captured native Britons may have been forced to carry out some of the heavy labouring tasks as well.

The troops knew exactly what to do. While they were part of the most efficient war machine that the world had ever seen, they had also regularly carried out regular military building drills to practice the essential skills of encampment. There was no time for innovative techniques at Eboracum. They built to a blueprint that worked. Roman legionaries were not just warriors, they were able to construct ships to cross the high seas, as well as fortresses. One of the reasons the Roman army was so successful was the fact that it was expert at entrenchment.

Built to a formulaic design that had been perfected and refined over centuries, the fortress of Eboracum arose on the exact same lines as practically every other Roman fortress. There were four points of entry and exit with watchtowers at intervals and weak points. Inside a grid of streets with names such as *via principalis* and *via decumana* were bisected by three areas for barrack blocks, the headquarters (*principia*), a meeting hall (*basilica*), the commander's house (*praetoria*), along with a brew house, granary, workshops and a bath house.

Occupying twenty-five hectares - the equivalent of fifty football pitches today - it would grow to contain everything necessary to maintain the legionaries, who enjoyed the benefits of precious Roman citizenship. This force was supplemented by a smaller number of auxiliary soldiers, who were drawn from subjects of conquered territories. On lower pay and with fewer rights, this non-citizen force would have had to stay in a smaller fort outside the main fortress, the remains of which have not been found to this day.

Without a large enough native population to ensure that the Roman Empire could fulfil its ambitions, it relied heavily on slave labour for both domestic work and huge infra-structure projects, such as road building. It is therefore likely that the soldiers were aided in the construction of the new fortress by prisoners of war, captured in battle and forced into slavery.

Did any women travel with the legion to found the fortress at Eboracum? While soldiers were housed in barracks, they would have been provided with communal cooking facilities and would have been expected to feed themselves, probably dining together in small groups, rather than all together like their modern military counterparts in a mess. However, it is likely that female camp followers were present to take care of menial tasks and other domestic chores to help the camp to survive.

For many years the consensus view has been that no women were allowed inside Roman fortresses, except the wives of the commanders. However, in 2005 Anna Salleh argued that women did live and work in Roman military forts, dispelling the notion that they were male-only domains. Hairpins, beads, perfume bottles and spindle wheels have been excavated and generally found in groups in different parts of a range of forts. The grouped locations of the objects suggest that women may have played an active role in the life of the encampment, either as shopkeepers, crafters or traders.

Sallah believes that forts 'might be better described as a functioning town with a market, rather than a sterile male-only province'. She suggests that 'women were well and truly integrated into the forts, playing "helpful" non-combatant roles of wives, mothers, craftspeople and traders.' Further evidence of a female presence in forts is the remains from one fort of 11 babies buried beneath a barracks. It is not clear whether these deaths were the result of still-birth, illness or infanticide. However, it is incontrovertible evidence of the presence of women in fortresses.

Startlingly in 1975, the skeleton of a human baby was found buried in the floor of an area of the *praetentura* discovered inside the fortress area of Eboracum. A 200m2 area of the fortress at Blake Street was excavated prior to its redevelopment of the area. The unusual discovery was made in the principal room of the stone-built residential range. Because children were not considered to be fully human, they did not have to be buried in the cemeteries outside the settled areas. Patrick Ottaway in 'Roman York' acknowledges that infant burials are 'not unknown' in a 'military context' but are 'rare'. He speculates that the child may have been a votive offering to encourage the gods to look favourably on the residents. He presumes that the infant died of natural causes and was not a sacrifice. Again, whatever the reason for the child's death, it is testament to the presence of women within the confines of the fortress, although we cannot be sure of the status of the mother. Was she the wife of one of the elite soldiers or was she the lover of a legionaire, present in the fortress due to her craft, trade or domestic role?

It is difficult to disagree with Salleh's view that the reason that forts were viewed as male-only domains for so many years is because of the 'elitist attitude' of 19th century military historians who believed that forts would be segregated because women disrupted military life.

While ordinary soldiers were not legally allowed to marry, away from the front soldiers did have common law wives. Centurions, in charge of a century of eighty men enjoyed private rooms at the end of the barrack block that they oversaw, where they could live with their families, if they so desired. The commander, who lived in the *praetorian*, was allowed to cohabit with his wife and family.

Hygiene was of paramount importance to the Romans and the wives of officers frequented the huge Roman baths inside the fortress of Eboracum. The authorities would have tried to ensure that the different sexes used the baths at alternate times or on different days, but they were not always successful. Inside a huge sewer which ran from the baths on the interior of the fort to what is now Church Street near the river Ouse, a gold earring and gold pendant fitting have been found, suggestive of a female bather. Slaves would have been forced to crawl along the sewer to clean it, and just like modern-day archaeologists, slaves may have come across pottery and bone counters in the silt, proof of the Romans' love of games and gambling.

The baths were a place to socialise as well as to get clean, the modern equivalent of a leisure centre. Evidence of bath houses has been found both inside the fortress and outside in the civilian settlement at Eboracum. If you were not clean in Roman times, you were viewed with disdain. There was not much excuse for dirtiness as a visit to the baths was free for children and slaves.

In the Roman world it was also standard practice for a fortress to be accompanied by an area of land outside called the *territorium*. Initially the *territorium* would have held supplies of timber and later stone for building purposes, as well as the provision of food for both animals and people. It would have been large enough to allow space for the grazing of the cavalry horses and mules and oxen used for transport. Although the location of the *territorium* at Eboracum is unknown, it is likely that over time this area developed into the civilian settlement that was eventually recognised as a *colonia* in AD 237. It is highly likely that female camp followers lived in the *territorium* and helped to service the fortress. Perhaps both male and female native Celtic Britons, whose settlements had taken over by the Romans, went there to seek a means to earn a living.

As the fortress of Eboracum became more permanent, Roman citizens from across the Roman world would be encouraged to settle there to help Romanise the area, spreading Roman culture and values. It is probable that citizens would have been personally attracted by the new possibilities that opening up a new northerly frontier provided, despite many Romans regarding Britannia like the poet Eumenius as the 'region in which the earth terminates'. For centuries Britannia had been viewed as a mysterious and wild land, inhabited by savages. But as the Roman military campaign became more successful, Roman citizens would have heard about the developments there and been interested in the possibilities for self-improvement that this new province could offer. As their status as Roman citizens entitled them to free movement within all the provinces of the Roman Empire, many may have seen Britannia as a new land of opportunity.

Inside the fortress superior officers could enjoy female company, whereas ordinary legionaries would have to wait 126 years to be able to marry legally. It was not until Emperor Septimius Severus, who arrived in Eboracum in AD 197, decided to alter the regulation and allow legionaries to marry. While this would have come as a great relief to the couples already in relationships, for the empire it was a pragmatic solution to an ever-growing problem. While not legally sanctioned, legionaries had begun to enter into common law marriages with women regardless, often of local origin, especially in peacetime. By legalising marriage, the wives would gain Roman citizenship, as would their offspring. Ever in need of manpower, the Roman army would be able to recruit the sons of veterans much more easily now that they had the highly valued Roman citizenship, which entitled them to more civil rights.

After nearly a decade of war, finally by AD 79 the Ninth Legion, under Agricola, had subdued the Brigantes. From this period onwards, the men of the fortress of Eboracum might have had a little more opportunity to form relationships with women. However, they were often busy on campaign to help defend the northern frontier. Meanwhile more and more people, both native Britons and Roman citizens from across the empire would arrive in Eboracum over time.

It is difficult to draw conclusions from archaeological evidence from the approximately one hundred burials found in York, often due to haphazard or absence of recording in previous eras. However, there is evidence to suggest that while many of the men were from the eastern Mediterranean, with a smaller proportion of men of African ancestry, many of the women were of a 'single, probably indigenous race', according to Royal Commission on the Historical Monuments of England. The Ninth Legion Hispana had been recruited in Roman Spain and the Sixth Legion Victrix, which replaced the ninth in around AD 120, had originally been raised in the Roman province of Gaul, modern France. Therefore, when multi-national Roman soldiers began to form relationships with local British women of Celtic extraction, a new Romano-British ethnicity was born.

The wooden fortress was rebuilt in stone in phases, probably starting in AD107-8 under the emperor Trajan when the south-west gate that overlooked the river Ouse was commemorated to him in a stone inscription. Rebuilding in stone was a massive undertaking and another phase took place probably before or during the time that the Emperor Septimius Severus lived in Eboracum with his family between AD 208 and AD 211. This project was either ordered by him or begun to impress him. Consequently, the defenses of Eboracum were probably not uniform in appearance, unlike the medieval walls, some of which trace the line of the fortress walls today.

As the fortress grew, a civilian settlement, providing residences for people who could provide services to the garrison, slowly evolved on the opposite side of the River Ouse. Testament to its size and importance, by AD 237 this residential area had been granted the status of a *colonia*, a title that by this time was mainly honorific and did not grant the inhabitants exemption from tax as had been the original intention. The expansion of the *colonia* is indicated by the raising of the south-west bank of the Ouse in around AD 275, either for the construction or reconstruction of a bridge over the river connecting the fortress to the *colonia*. It is estimated that at their height, provincial *coloniae* would not have exceeded a population of 3,000 inhabitants, in contrast to Londinium, which would have housed 10,000 residents. It is from the female burials of the women who lived in the *colonia* that we can glean the most information about what it must have been be a woman living in Roman York.

When a new road was being created between The Mount and South Bank in 1922, builders came across a tombstone dedicated to Julia Velva. The inscription reads,

'To the spirits of the departed and of Julia Velva: she lived most dutifully 50 years. Aurelius Mercurialis, her heir, had this set up, and in his lifetime made this for himself'.

The carved scene depicts a funeral banquet with fir cones on each corner of the stone, signifying life beyond the grave. Julia reclines on a couch, resting her head on her right hand, with a wine goblet in her left. In front of her is a table topped with a wine bowl and a loaf of bread. Perhaps this signifies the funeral banquet which would have taken place after the burial of a wealthy individual. It was also considered to be the height of good manners to dine while reclining in the Roman world. The dining room was the most important chamber in a Roman house and feasting and banqueting were an important part of Roman festivities and funerals.

To Julia's right sits a young woman in a wicker chair, holding a pet dove or a pigeon in her lap, symbolising childhood. On the left of the table stands a boy bearing a wine jug, a servant or a relative of Mercurialis. Patrick Ottaway, author of 'Roman York' believes that his inferior size suggests that he may have even been a slave. Beyond him sits Mercurialis, the dedicator of the memorial, who is bearded and wearing a tunic, cloak and boots. It is not clear whether Mercurialis was Julia Velva's husband. However, he clutches the scroll of her will in his right hand, suggesting that he was grateful to her for her legacy. While laws prohibited women from inheriting all of their husbands' fortune, clearly Julia Velva had achieved considerable material success in life to enable a man to be her heir.

The group is represented in what would have been a semi-public room in their house where they would receive clients and dispense patronage. Perhaps a good diet and lifestyle due to Julia's material success had enabled her to live to what was, in Roman times, the ripe old age of fifty. Ottaway calculates that between 75 - 80 percent of the population died before the age of 40. A large cemetery, near to Julia's tombstone found on The Mount, at Trentholme Drive was excavated at four different times in the 1950s and gave up 316 inhumation burials of an estimated total of one thousand. When the remains were examined, the very old were conspicuous by their absence. It was calculated that women were on average 1.55 metres tall (5 feet 1 inch), while men reached an average height of 1.7 metres (5 feet 7 inches). This is contrary to the popular belief that people in the past were less tall than they are today. It is only since the Second World War that there has been a slight increase in height, due to better nutrition.

As well as being a memorial to Julia Velva, her tombstone is a status symbol showing the wealth and standing of an elite family in Roman York. Roman law stated that the dead could not mix with the living and that burials had to take place outside the confines of the residential settlements. Numerous burial sites have been excavated around York, but perhaps the highest status burials were on what is now the area of The Mount. Like the Via Appia in Rome these roadside monuments may have lined the road from Eboracum to Calcaria (Tadcaster) and were a way of advertising the status of a family to travellers. Julia's tombstone was found at one of the most prominent elevated and eye-catching areas on this stretch of road. Originally, it would have been painted in vivid colours, having an even greater impact on the viewer, leaving them in no doubt as to the wealth and status of her family.

Nevertheless, the most interesting thing about Julia is her name. Velva is thought to be the feminine form of Velvor, a Celtic name found in Wales. Julia Velva's inscription is evidence of Romano-Celtic intermarriage in Eboracum and of the financial benefits that relationships with Romans could bring to the local Celtic population.

It is believed that the Trentholme Drive cemetery, near the Mount, but in a less prominent position, just away from the main road between Eboracum and Calcaria, was the final resting place of people of lower status. The bones of one female found here showed that she had developed 'squatting facets', the remodelling of bones at the front of the ankle, indicating that she had spent a lot of time squatting while cooking and tending the fires. While Julia Velva was praised for being 'dutiful' on her tombstone, it didn't matter what your financial status was in Roman times, you were subservient to men.

As time passed the fortress attracted a whole host of people - local, national and foreign, for the purposes of trade and commerce. It is likely that Hadrian stayed at Eboracum in AD 120 on his way north to build his famous wall. As the roots of Eboracum grew stronger, so did its importance. Testament to its significance was the fact that the Emperor Septimius Severus settled his court there for three years from AD 208-211, as a base to re-establish his control of the empire. The governor of Britain, Clodius Albinus, had begun an unsuccessful civil war against him. Severus arrived in York with his wife, eager to purge his administration of all those who had been loyal to this treacherous governor.

While in Britain, Severus decided to improve the administration of the province, splitting it into two. Londinium became the capital of Britannia Superior (Upper Britain) and Eboracum became the capital of Britannia Inferior (Lower Britain). By AD 211, the residents of Eboracum were living in a sophisticated regional capital where British grain would be exported from the banks of the River Ouse, while pottery and glass were offloaded and distributed around the province. Wealthy Eboracuns would not have to forego their favourite Roman foods, as merchant ships would bring a stock of wine and olives.

The Romans believed in an afterlife and that the soul was immortal. At death the soul would be judged before a tribunal in the Underworld. Those who had performed good deeds would be sent to the Elysian Fields. Those who had done ill would be sent to Tartarus. Therefore, an individual's prized possessions were placed in their grave with them to help them on their journey to the afterlife. A female burial found near the railway station contained three bronze dress fasteners, two bronze brooches, a jet hair pin under the skull and a fragmentary coin in her mouth. It was a well-known practice to place a coin in or on the mouth of the deceased.

Known as Charon's obol, the coin was the payment to Charon, the ferryman who conveyed the souls of the dead across the water that separated the world of the living from the Underworld. Relatives of the deceased were desirous that their loved one would have an unhindered passage into the next life. From the inscription on Deciminia's tombstone we do not know her age due to breakage. However, we do know that her father, Decimus, placed a silver denarius of Antoninus Pius with her remains. The bottom of the tombstone, with his expression of fatherly regret at her death, is also now lost to us.

In 1818 a female skeleton was found on Holgate Bridge with a plaited bracelet around her arm and silver earrings by her skull. She was also well-provided for on her journey to the Underworld with twenty-nine coins, dating chiefly from the time of the Emperor Constantine (r. AD 306 and AD 337), as well as some from the time of his son, the Emperor Crispus. Seventy-four years later a female burial was unearthed in the Walmgate area. Her coffin was of lead and was rich in graves goods. Amongst her seven necklaces, four jet pins, three jet necklaces, jet pendant medallion of a Gorgon, there was also a coin identifiable as one of Septimius Severus (r. AD 193- AD 211). Therefore, the practice of placing coins in the graves of the departed was an enduring one in the Roman Empire.

Not only was food important in the real life, it was also significant in the journey to the after-life. Flagons or cups containing drink and pots with food have been found in grave furniture. Eggs placed in urns as appropriate food for the dead are recorded from the Trenholme Drive. A cooking pot with a lattice decoration was re-used as cinerary urn. Remains of horse, ox, sheep, pig, red deer, birds and oysters have been found in graves, sometimes in pots, sometimes not. Clearly, loved ones were desirous that their dead relations would have enough sustenance to make the journey into the afterlife.

Many objects made of jet have been unearthed in excavations in York over the centuries. Items include beads, brooches, pendants, hairpins, bangles, anklets and rings. More intricate pieces include medallion pendants with human portraits and one with a Gorgon mask, which served to repel the evil eye. An abundant source of jet is to be found forty-five miles away at the east coast town of Whitby, where decomposed driftwood that has been subjected to heat and pressure over time, eventually forms jet. This mineraloid is dense in texture and deep black in colour. Easily cuttable, it is capable of attaining an appealing, polished finish. An added bonus for the superstitious Romans was that jet becomes electric when rubbed. Consequently, during antiquity it acquired an aura of magic that enhanced its value and endowed it with medicinal and fabulous properties.

Alongside the abundance of jet artefacts, there is some evidence to suggest that jet jewellery was carved in York. During the Railway excavations of 1873 several blocks of jet were unearthed, alongside some pieces that had been partially prepared to make pins. Due to the proximity to York of a large supply of the raw material and what appears to be a workshop, archaeologists have concluded that not only is it likely that jet objects were made for a local domestic market, but could also have been exported to the Rhineland, where good quality jet pieces have been discovered where there was no raw material available.

During the same excavations four jet pendants featuring Gorgons were also uncovered. Although the Gorgons, three sisters whose hair comprised venomous snakes, originated in Greek mythology, the Romans ardently admired Greek civilization. When the Romans conquered the Greeks, they assimilated many Greek ideas and beliefs into their culture. Roman appropriation of the Gorgon myth is attested to in York by the discovery of a huge mosaic from a townhouse (*mansione*) in the Toft Green area of the *colonia*. Now housed in the Yorkshire Museum and somewhat damaged, Medusa, the only mortal Gorgon, stares out from centuries past. For the rich homeowners who commissioned this mosaic floor, she would have been viewed as a protective amulet, her head of snakes powerful enough to combat evil spirits.

Although women in Roman York were very much second-class citizens to men, female deities were worshipped. Many stone inscriptions to the Mother Goddess have been unearthed. An altar found in Micklegate in 1752 reads, 'To the mother goddesses of Africa, Italy and Gaul, Marcus Minucius Mudenus, soldier of the Sixth Legion Victorious, pilot of the Sixth Legion, paid his vow joyfully, willingly and deservedly.' In the following century a limestone altar was found which read, 'Caius Julius Cresens to the mother goddesses matres of the home paid his vow deservedly and willingly.' The matres was a popular Celtic triad of goddesses, further evidence of the flexibility with which the Romans appropriated the beliefs of other cultures. It is also suggestive of how, over time, the Romans and the Celts began to form relationships and it is likely that by the fifth century there would be many people who would class themselves as Romano-British.

While the Romans worshipped female deities, Roman men had a contradictory attitude to women. They often idealized women, comparing them to goddesses, who were incredibly beautiful and powerful. However, real women had a harder time, running their households and raising their children. While Rome itself was sentimalised as the 'Mother' of the nation, for ordinary women, bearing children was seen as a wife's main job. Roman women were respected as mothers, but if a woman was not able to provide her husband with children, then this was adequate grounds for the husband to divorce her. Unfortunately, the reverse was not the case. Roman women had very few rights in law and were little better off than slaves. She could not inherit all her husband's property after he died, nor could she leave all her money to her children.

The man was always the head of the family, the *pater familias*, and he ruled the household, making decisions over the lives of his wife, his children, other relatives, servants and slaves. A man could even order the death of his wife or children. A child under two was entirely the property of its father, to be disposed of how he saw fit. If it was deformed, it was compulsory to put it to death. If the baby was unwanted or weak, he could order it to be abandoned or left outside to die, until the fourth century when Constantine I put an end to infanticide. Baby girls were more vulnerable to infanticide than boys. They would be 'assessed' for eight days before being accepted into the family, and only then given a name.

Roman men had three names - a first name (*praenomen*), a family name (*nomen*) and a private name (*cognomen*). Therefore, the standard bearer of the Ninth Legion, Lucius Duccius Rufinus, would have been of the Duccius clan. Although Lucius died at the tender age of 28, he may have had a daughter. If so, she would have taken the female form of his *praenomen* and been known as Lucia. If he had had two daughters, they may have been called Lucia Major and Lucia Minor, to be able to distinguish between the two. Clearly, this naming system did little to encourage women to develop a unique sense of self. Their identity would always be linked to that of their fathers. Luccius Duccius Rufinus' tombstone tells us that he came from Vienne in the Rhône Valley in Gaul. He is just one of the many Eboracan Romans who were of international origins.

Lucky daughters of wealthy fathers would be educated at home. Some girls went to school with their brothers, under the care of a nurse. Girls were allowed to go to the elementary school (*ludus*) where they were taught to read and write. Boys were able to continue their education onto the high school (*grammaticus*) to study for careers in the law and government. Intelligent girls may have carried on studying at home. However, the most important occupation of a woman was the spinning and weaving of cloth. On her wedding day, a Roman bride would carry a symbolic distaff and spindle, both for winding flax into wool. Distaffs have been discovered in burials at the Roman cemetery excavated at York Railway Station.

Since time immemorial, childbirth has been a risky business for women, and it was equally so in Roman times. Miscarriage could be fatal, and many women died in childbirth or from infections afterwards, and a great many children died as babies. Meanwhile many women bore more children than was good for their health. Yet it could be a personal tragedy for a married woman to be childless, as her husband could divorce her. An anonymous female burial was unearthed in 1846 in a field that now forms part of the gardens of the Bar Convent. Poignantly, she had a child beside her. Seven years later the skeleton of a woman with the skeleton of a child between her legs was found on Bishopgate Street. The placement of the child may suggest that the woman died in childbirth. Her stone coffin suggests some status and wealth, although no graves goods were found, except for a small coin.

While many women died in childbirth, many children never reached maturity. At the same time as the discovery of the tombstone of Julia Velva, the cremated ashes of a thirteen-year-old girl called Corelia Optata were found below an inscribed tombstone in the high status cemetery near the Mount. Commissioned by her father, the pain and devastation at losing his teenage daughter can still be felt to this day in the words he left for posterity:

'To the spirits of the departed Corelia Optata, 13 years old. Ye hidden spirits that dwell in Pluto's Acherusian Realms, whom the scanty ash and shade, the body's image seek after life's little day. I, the pitiable father of an innocent daughter, caught by cheating hop, lament her final end. Quintus Corellius Fortis, the father made this'.

The location of the burial and the inscribed stone suggest that Quintus must have been relatively wealthy. However, it is clear that this was little comfort to him in his devastation at the death of his teenage daughter, which led him to reach out to poetry to express his feelings. His reference to 'Pluto's Acherusian realms' refers to the Roman belief in the afterlife. All souls would travel with the ferryman Charon along the river Styx, also known as Acheron, to the Underworld. Having successfully passed the ferocious multi-headed dog, Cerberus, they would find themselves on the other side where Pluto presided. However, it was not guaranteed that the soul would be accepted by Pluto and able to pass on to the Elysian Fields where the spirit would be reborn. Less fortunate souls would either wander as lonely shadows for ever more, or worse, were persecuted by the three furies. Corelia's father was trying to ensure that her young soul had safe passage to the next life.

Corelia's ashes were found under her tombstone in a large green glass vessel, sealed with lead and it is the only complete cinerary vessel to be found in York. This dates the burial to the late 1st or 2nd century. Eventually cremation died out in favour of inhumation, but it is thought that there would have been some overlap in funerary traditions between AD 200 and AD 300.

Gaius Aeresuis Saenus, a veteran of the Sixth Legion Victrix, which arrived in Eboracum around AD 120 to replace the Ninth Legion Hispana, was more circumspect than Corelia's father about his emotions in bereavement. Against all the odds he had survived countless campaigns over a twenty-year period and was finally entitled to collect his hard-won earnings. Perhaps he had even been awarded a plot of fertile North Yorkshire land to farm in exchange for his loyal service, only to lose his entire family in retirement. His dedication found on the Mount in the 1859 cemetery excavation reads:

> 'To the spirits of the departed and of Flavia Augustina. She lived 39 years, 7 months, 11 days. Her son Saenius Augustinus lived 1 year, 3 days and her [daughter?] lived 1 year 9 months, 5 days. Gaius Aeresius Saenus, veteran of the Sixth Legion Victrix, had this set up for his beloved wife and himself'.

Although there is no outpouring of grief, unlike Corelia's father, his choice of 'beloved' to describe his dead wife shows the depth of his feelings for Flavia. The deaths of both his children under the age of 2 is evidence of the high infant mortality rate in Eboracum. His son, Saenius Augustinus, would never live to fulfil the ambition of the Roman Empire - to grow up farming the portion of land awarded to his father and then be recruited into the Roman army at an early age to follow in his father's footsteps, hopefully providing 25 years of service before retiring.

Aelia Severa did not outlive her husband for very long. Because her stone coffin was inscribed, it was not meant to be buried, but placed above ground in a mausoleum, although mausolea in Eboracum would not have been as elaborate as some of those still visible outside Rome and other Mediterranean cities. Surprisingly, it wasn't Aelia's husband who commissioned her dedication, but her husband's former slave.

> 'To the spirits of the departed and the honest lady Aelia Severa, once the wife of Caecilius Rufus. She lived 27 years 9 months and 4 days. Caelcilius Musicus his freedman placed this monument.'

The term 'honesta femina' is thought to apply to the wife or daughter of a decurion, who was a cavalry officer in command of a squadron (turma) of horsemen. Although Caracalla had extended Roman citizenship to all free people in the Roman society in AD 212, Aelia's tomb proves that Roman society was still as hierarchical as ever. As an honestiore, she was among the upper crust of citizens whose husbands occupied positions in government and administration. She and her husband, Caecilius Rufus, would have enjoyed privileges that the mass of the rest of the population of *humiliores* could only aspire to, as quite literally second-class citizens. The location of her burial in a high status cemetery, her connection to an elite member of the Roman army and the fact that her husband could afford a slave, all suggest that she lived a life of comparative luxury. Needless to say, this did not protect her from an early death. Aelia's and Caecilius' relationship to their slave Caecilius Musicus is an interesting one.

Although it is difficult to ascertain the quantity of individuals held in bondage in the Roman Empire, much less at Eboracum, slaves were used in both the cultivation of the land, building projects and as house slaves. Robert Knapp in his book 'Invisible Romans' estimates that fifteen percent of the Roman population were slaves. As the head of the domestic household, it would have been Aelia's job to ensure that the slaves did their work properly. After years of loyal service, a Roman could free his or her slaves, but it would come at a cost. The *vicesima libertatis* was a tax on owners who freed their slaves, with the owner forced to pay 5 percent of the slave's value to the government. Often slaves were freed upon the death of their owners and sometimes even became their heirs when no other relatives were available. The fact that the freedman, Caecilius Musicus, proudly set up the monument, suggests that not only had he gained his freedom on his masters' deaths, but had inherited a legacy also. His emotion at his new-found wealth and freedom can only be imagined! Perhaps Musicus had always been highly regarded. Some slaves could be given positions of trust within a household, such as tutor to the owner's children, which was the case with some well-educated slaves from conquered Greece. Caecilius' second name 'Musicus' suggests that he may have entertained the household as a musician and or been a music teacher.

Being a freedman or freedwoman did not entitle the individual to Roman citizenship, which would have to be granted separately. According to Knapp, house slaves would probably have lived in the 'hallways and under the stairs of great houses, pulling out their cots at night and putting them away during the day'. Unfortunately, slaves of both genders were often victims of the masters' and mistresses' sexual predations. However, women slaves were more vulnerable. In AD 500 Salvian wrote,

'Female slaves are forced unwilling to service their most shameless masters; these sate their lust on them, trapped as they are by their condition, unable to resist.' (On the Government of God. 7.4)

Although the Roman philosopher Musonius Rufus was described as an enlightened author he did write that, 'Every master has the full authority to use his slave as he might wish.' (Discourse 12.88).

Caecilius Musicus must have felt enormous relief on receiving his freedom in a world where the universal expectation was that 'slaves were available anytime, anyplace'.

The location of the forum, the social and administrative heart of any Roman city have not been located in York as yet, it is therefore not surprising that likewise, no evidence of a brothel has ever been uncovered. As the buildings that once housed brothels still stand today in Ephesus in Turkey and Pompey in Italy, it is more than likely that there was a brothel in the *colonia* in Eboracum. Eboracum was essentially and fundamentally a garrison town, and while Roman soldiers may have formed relationships with women of native Celtic British origin, due to their lifestyle it is highly likely that many did not seek long-term commitment.

One can only hope that if there was a brothel at Eboracum, it was not inhabited by captive slaves kidnapped from all corners of the empire, like the *Lupanare* at Pompey. Here two floors, each encompassing five small chambers containing a stone bed, were provided to cater to the sexual needs of poor men, such as visiting sailors to male slaves. Excavations of this site unearthed remnants of bottles of vinegar that the enslaved prostitutes like Abbia and Nika used to try to disinfect themselves in an attempt to prevent pregnancy and sexually transmitted diseases, which in those days, without antibiotics, were a death sentence. They ate a simple diet, were locked in at night and if they were ever allowed out, had to wear men's togas to identify themselves as separate from the respectable citizens. The name *lupanare* reveals the Roman attitude to female sexuality. Literally translated as 'The Den of the She-Wolves', it becomes clear that to Roman men, women were either goddesses, housewives or whores. Hopefully, no such establishment existed in Eboracum, but as Roman fortresses and cities tended to follow an archetypal blueprint, it is highly likely that there was.

More evidence that suggests that Roman men based at Eboracum began to inter-marry with local Celtic women comes from the tombstone of Candida Barita, which was set up by her husband Marcus Aurinius Simnus. While his family name, Aurinius, dervies from Aurignan in the Huate Garonne department of south west France on the edge of the Pyrenees, his wife's *cogmonen*, Barita, is thought to be of Celtic British origin. Unfortunately, Candida was accompanied on her journey to the 'divine shades' by her two little daughters, Mantia and Tetrica, testament to the lack of medical knowledge and high infant mortality rate in the era.

Likewise, Sepronius Martinus set up a tombstone for his wife and daughter, both of whom died young. He had the stone mason inscribe:

'To the spirits of the departed of Julia Brica, aged 31 and of Sepronis Martina, aged 6, Sepronius Martinus had this set up. If only the ground could rise up.'

His devastation at the loss of his young family is evident in his desire to join them and it is believed that the *cognomen* Brica is of British Celtic origin also. Julia Brica's funerary monument is one of the few which depict the actual person and from it we can glean information about the clothes that Romano-British women wore.

Julia is dressed in a long under-tunic with a shorter knee-length tunic over the top, tied at the waist. A blanket-like mantle is wrapped around her shoulders to keep her warm in the British winters. This long rectangle of cloth bore the name *palla* and was multi-purpose as it could be draped across the shoulder like a shawl, pulled up over the head like a cloak or wound as a scarf around the shoulder and the neck. Due to the climate, British Roman women adopted a garment from Roman France called the Gallic coat, a wide loose tunic with sleeves. Most clothes were made of wool or linen, while on the continent wealthy women wore colourful silk imported from India and China. Poorer women made do with coarse brown or grey cloth, again fastened with a treasured brooch or pin. Their treasured possessions would have been of less valuable metals, such as bronze.

Leather sandals or shoes with wooden or leather soles would be worn outside, while at home they put on elegant slippers, some with wooden or cork soles to protect the feet from hot, wet floors in the bathhouse. Women who could not afford shoes went barefoot. Fashions were set in Rome by the ladies of the emperor's family and women in the cities copied their styles. Fashions did not change very much from one century to the next. While clothes were mostly simple in style, rich women showed off by wearing jewels. The Romans loved gold. Beautiful rings fitted with red and blue gemstones have been found in grave goods in York. As the empire grew richer, more and more people could afford gold rings. They were a status symbol, growing larger and larger and could bear the name of the owner. Gold earrings for pierced ears, pendant fittings and pendant chains have also been found. Several glass phials for perfume have been unearthed, which would have contained essential oils to make the bodies of both men and women smell sweet. The oils would have been rubbed into the skin, much like aromatherapy oils today.

After 27 BC blonde hair became fashionable amongst Roman women and to achieve the look they would either bleach their hair or wear a wig. Fortunately, women of Celtic origin were admired for their natural red-brown hair and henna was used to emulate their hair colour. All Romans were very body conscious. The grave of the ivory bangle lady contained a circular crystal mirror, testament to her wealth as glass mirrors were more expensive than metal. One female burial included a parasol and another a fan, which were clearly treasured possessions, although of not much practical use in wet and windy Britannia. Like jet, amber held magical powers for the superstitious Romans. Pliny wrote that it could be ignited by water and quenched by oil. Amber jewelry has also been found in York.

In the monument dedicated to Flavia Augustina by her husband Gaius Aeresius Saenus the parents and two children are wrapped in the folds of warm cloaks. Hair styles were quite uniform across the empire and Julia Brica and Julia Velva appear to have the prevailing style - a central parting with the hair waved and swept back, probably into a bun or a chignon. An actual surviving head of auburn hair from a grave in York appears to have this style. In contrast, a well-preserved pot in the shape of a head, which would have contained funeral ashes, is thought to be a representation of Julia Domna, the wife of Septimius Severus who resided in Eboracum with her husband between AD 208 to AD 211. Her hair is parted down the middle into a short bob just below her ears. Julia Brica's child wears clothes very similar to those of her mother and there does not appear to be much difference between the clothes of Roman children and adults.

While male Roman citizens with international origins married native British women in Eboracum, others arrived in Eboracum from far flung corners of the Roman Empire, most likely attracted to the garrison due to its career opportunities. The stone coffin of the wife of a *sevir* in the *colonia*, Julia Fortunata, was found in the late nineteenth century during remodeling of the railway station. She had travelled approximately two thousand miles over land and sea to Eboracum from Roman Sardinia. Her husband Vercundius Diogenes had come to tend to the spiritual needs of the population of Eboracum as a *servir augustal*, one of several men who were appointed as priests to the cult of emperor worship. What is interesting about their relationship is that we know that he was not from Sardinia, unlike his wife, but from Bourges in Northern France. An inscription, giving his place of origin has been found there, suggesting that he was an itinerant priest, moving from posting to posting as opportunities arose throughout the empire. Consequently, here we have evidence of a truly cosmopolitan couple from different corners of the Roman world, living together in Eboracum. With his official position they would have had a good lifestyle, corroborated by the quality stone coffins that they left behind.

Nevertheless, the story of Diogenes' coffin is a sad tale, testament to the historic lack of care that our ancestors seem to have shown to our precious ancient heritage. Diogenese's stone coffin was discovered approximately three hundred years before that of his wife in 1579, a quarter of a mile west of the York's city walls, near Scarborough Bridge, a completely different place to the location of Julia Fortunata's sarcophagus. For some reason Diogenes' coffin was taken to Elizabethan Hull where it was put to use as horse trough. After a century in its new resting place, all trace of it has disappeared and no-one knows of its whereabouts to this day.

In contrast, Julia's stone coffin was unearthed during the building of the new railway station in York in 1877. Diogenes had the stonecutter poignantly write as her epitaph,

'To the memory of Julia Fortunata from Sardinia. Dear wife to her husband, Verecundius Diogenes'.

Image: Marcus Cyron

While Diogenes' final resting place was not respected by the Elizabethans, his tomb sequestered and put to a different use, Julia's tomb was also exploited by others after her death. Upon opening the tomb and expecting to find the remains of a woman inside, archaeologists were surprised to find the skeleton of a tall man aged between 35 and 40, with an aquiline nose and a broad, masculine forehead.

He had lost one of his teeth before death, while another had been broken. The remaining ones were worn down, suggesting a hard life, subsisting on bread with remnants of millstone grit in it.

It seems likely that the mourners of the man with the broken teeth took Julia's gritstone coffin from the area around Scarborough Bridge, relocated it to the cemetery where the railway once was and re-used it for the remains of their dead male relative. One can only speculate as to what happened to Julia's remains. Unfortunately, even though they had lived together thousands of miles from their places of birth in the final frontier of the Roman Empire, Julia and Vercundius were physically separated in death.

Sardinia, Julia's birthplace, had been a Roman province since 232 BC. Under Roman occupation, the island was bled of its natural resources. The Romans took Sardinia's minerals, agricultural produce (especially grain) and taxed the inhabitants, without any benefit accruing to the people. Although the island was rewarded for supporting Julius Caesar in Rome's civil war of 49-45 BC, little was done over seven centuries to instil Roman values or develop the island, which was often entrusted to corrupt officials. The attitude of the Romans towards Sardinia was summed up in the fact that they used it as a place of exile for those whom they considered to be undesirable elements of the empire. Tiberius (r.AD 17-37) sent 4000 Jewish people and early Christian subversives to the island. Perhaps Julia Fortunata was grateful that Verecudius Diogenes could give her a better life in a new frontier town.

Although Septimus Lupianus' military career was progressing extremely well, nothing could protect him from the loss of his wife and son. As an *evocatus* he served in the Praetorian Guard, the personal bodyguard of the commander of the fort, for 16 years. A detachment of the Praetorian Guard would definitely have been in York when the huge entourage of the emperor Septimius Severus arrived in the early 3rd century, perhaps dating his life in Eboracum to this time.

Septimus Lupianus was then promoted to legionary centurion and again, may have received this honour while serving in Eboracum. Having reached the young age of 29 years, 2 months and 15 days, Septimius' wife Julia Victoriana died. He also lost his son, Constantius, at the tender age of four years, 11 months and 21 days. The accuracy with which he recorded their ages shows the high regard in which he held them.

Although the inscribed coffin of Julia Victoriana and her child was unearthed during work at the Castle Yard in 1956, it would not have originally been intended for burial. The discovery of other burials nearby and the wall fragments make it highly likely that the inscription was part of a tomb chamber that would have been funded through contributions to a collective burial club, designed to fund the building and upkeep of the tomb. Julia and Constantius' stone coffin had been re-used for the remains of a man. It is possible that Julia and Constantius died in the third century and the coffin was reused when the *centuriate* could no long protect the burials of its members, or had ceased to function. Or perhaps a natural disaster had befallen the tomb.

Marcus Antonius Stephanus also lost his wife and son at a very young age. An inscribed stone dedicated to Eglecta, aged 30, and their son Secundius Crescens, aged three, was discovered in 1931, built into the wall of All Saints church. It had been there since the 17th century and was somewhat weathered. Felicius Simplex, a centurion of the Sixth Legion Victrix must have been heartbroken when his 10-month-old baby, Simplicia Florentina died between AD 200 and 300. Her gritstone coffin was uncovered in 1838 on land owned by the railway near Holgate Bridge. The epitaph hints at the injustice that Simplex must have felt when he described her as 'an innocent soul'.

Like all parents, Roman parents suffered when their children died before them, even when they reached a mature age. A canister with the remains of Ulipia Felicissimna was found in 1875. On it was inscribed,

'To the spirits of the departed and of Ulpia Felicissima, who lived 23 years, 11 months, ...days; her parents Ulpius Felix and Andronica, set this up.'

Although women were financially hobbled by Roman inheritance laws, they did find the money to finance memorials to their loved ones themselves. Aurelia Censorina may have been part of the centurionate tomb burial club that was located near to Castle Yard coffin. The coffin that she set up for her young husband was found with the dedication,

'To her husband Aurelius Super, centurion of the Sixth Legion, 29 years, 4 months and 13 days.'

Inside the skeleton was of strong proportions and the skull was cracked, indicative of a fall or a heavy blow. His sudden and early death must have been devastating for Aurelia. Their names suggest that they were members of a family that may have acquired citizenship after AD 212 when Caracalla decreed that all free born people in the Roman Empire could become citizens. At the age of 7, Caracalla's father renamed him Marcus Aurelius Antonius Augustus and it was customary for people to show their gratitude to the emperor who gave them citizenship by taking his name.

Another female who found the means to commemorate a loved one was Vitellia Procula, who had a stone inscribed to the memory of her 13-year-old child. It was found after it had been reused in a medieval building in Clementhorpe. After being pulled out of the demolished rubble in 1865, it reads,

'To her child who lived 13 years, the mother, most dutifully set this up. Hail Mary'.

The final appeal to Mary appears Christian and it is believed that these two words were added later in an attempt to sanctify what would have been considered a heathen inscription in subsequent centuries.

In AD 312 Constantine, who had been declared emperor in Eboracum by the legionaries in AD 306, decreed the end of the persecution of Christians and one of the most interesting female burials from Eboracum shows evidence of belief in Christianity.

In 1901 the coffin and grave goods of an anonymous female burial were found at Sycamore Terrace near Scarborough Bridge. Inside the coffin a bone was found, inscribed with the words, 'Hail sister, may you live in God.' While this suggests belief in Christianity, the glass drinking vessels and jewelry were consistent with a pagan burial. Evidently, the transition from paganism to Christianity would have been a gradual process. The other grave goods including a blue glass perfume jar, a bracelet of blue glass also, two jet bangles, glass beads, silver and bronze lockets, two yellow glass earrings and a small, round crystal mirror, as well as an African ivory bangle show that she was from a wealthy family.

In 2010 her skeleton was re-examined, and the world was shocked to discover that she was of black African ancestry, suggesting that the society that she lived in was more diverse than the society of York today. Isotope evidence from the re-examination, funded by the Arts and Humanities Research Council, suggests that up to 20 percent of people were 'probably long distance migrants. Some were African or had African ancestors, including the woman dubbed "the ivory bangle lady"', according to Hella Eckhart, senior lecturer at the department of archaeology at Reading University. Analysis of her bones shows that she was brought up in a warmer climate. The shape of her skull suggests mixed ancestry, including black features.

We will never know if she was independently wealthy or the wife or daughter of a wealthy man, but it is clear from the richness of the grave goods that she was part of the elite of Eboracum society. Her premature death between the age of 18 and 23, with no obvious sign of disease or cause of death, would have been a shock to her loved ones. The inscription on the bone suggests that her brother may have taken the news particularly badly.

Hella Eckhardt summed up the significance of this discovery well,

The case of the "ivory bangle lady" contradicts assumptions that may derive from more recent historical experience, namely that immigrants are low status and male, and that African individuals are likely to have been slaves. Instead, it is clear that both women and children moved across the empire, often associated with the military'.

By the end of the fourth century, Roman Britain was in decline due to repeated foreign attacks on all the provinces of the empire and an unstable political system, fractured by incessant revolts and usurpations of emperors. Evidence from the remains of the fortress suggest that there were changes in the standard of maintenance of the buildings with some floors being overlaid with domestic refuse, such as animal bones and pottery. It is not entirely clear what is signified by these changes, but Patrick Ottaway argues that 'it does indicate that at this time the remaining garrison was not apparently observing the discipline of former years and may have lived with their families and other civilians in the fortress'. Therefore, by the time the garrison was about to leave, women were even more likely to have been allowed inside. By AD 410 the Roman garrison had pulled out of Britain to return to Rome to shore up the collapsing capital of the empire, under attack by foreign invaders. Roman rule in Britain ended and the native Britons were left to fend for themselves against hostile incursions from the Picts of Scotland and Germanic tribes from overseas. What happened to the women of Roman York? It is likely that some of them left with the men on their military campaigns, while others who considered themselves now to be of Romano-British origin, stayed to make the best of the situation that they now found themselves in, without the protection of Roman military forces.

Bibliography

1. RCHME Inventory Volumes, British History Online :1) Burial Evidence 2) Funerary Inscriptions 3) Jet 4) Civilian Settlements.
2. Ottaway, Patrick, Roman York, The History Press, 2011
3. Chrystal, Paul, The Romans in the North of England, Destinworld, 2019
4. Williams Brian, Ancient Roman Women, Internet Archive, 1943.
5. Knapp, Robert, Invisible Romans, Profile Books, 2011
6. Birely, Anthony, Life in Roman Britain, BT Batsford Ltd, London, 1964

CHAPTER THREE

Queen Ethelburga

Game of Thrones

PRINCESS ETHELBURGA OF Kent married King Edwin of Northumbria in the church at York near the site of current minster in AD 625. Their marriage was a political alliance designed to unite the powerful southern kingdom of Kent with the growing power of Northumberland. After the Romans had left Britain in AD 410, the native Celts were left abandoned. According to the eighth century chronicler, Bede, all the able-bodied sons of the Celts had been forced to march to Rome to assist the Roman army in the defence of the capital of the empire. With those who had ruled them for four hundred years gone, the native Britons called across the water to the Germanic tribes of the Angles, the Saxons and the Jutes, asking them to come to their aid to help protect them from attack from the wild tribe of the Picts in the north of the country.

The Germanic tribes arrived as mercenaries, but saw the richness of the land. In contrast to the rich pickings of Britannia, climatic change on mainland Europe was making life difficult for the warrior tribes. However, it was not long before the newcomers seized the land for themselves, driving the Celts to the extremities of the territory. By AD 613, the Anglo-Saxons now controlled England and the country was divided into seven kingdoms – Kent, Sussex, Essex, East Anglia, Wessex, Mercia and Northumbria, collectively known as the Heptarchy, each ruled over by a warrior overlord.

The time during which Princess Ethelburga lived was one of extreme violence and disorder. While King AEthelfrith was alive, his young kinsman, Edwin, was forced to live in exile as he was vulnerable to assassination by rival factions. The threat to Edwin's life from King AEthelfrith must have been constant, as Edwin moved to the protection of three warlords during his youth. Firstly, he was fostered by King Cadfan ap Iago of the kingdom of Gwynedd. Then by the 610s he moved to Mercia to be under the protection of King Cearl. During his time at the court of Cearl, he married his host's daughter, Cwenburg, the union being used to seal an alliance between the two men.

By around AD 616, Edwin moved once more to the protection of another king in East Anglia called Raedwald. An indication of how treacherous the times were was the fact that cunning AEthelfrith tried to persuade Raedwald to murder Edwin, but Raedwald was dissuaded by his own wife. Finally, when Raedwald defeated AEthelfrith in battle by the River Idle, he installed Edwin as the King of Northumbria. Raedwald then came to dominate the country with Edwin as his client king, ruling until his death a decade later. Edwin was already the King of Bernicia and Diera that made up Northumbria, but ever ambitious for more territory and influence, he immediately began to expand his own power base and expelled Ceretic, King of the realm of Elmet that lay between West Yorkshire and North Yorkshire.

Edwin was hungry for power and began to expand to the west. The Irish annals report that the king of the Uliad laid siege to Edwin's seat at Bamburgh in Bernicia in 623-4. Always on the lookout for new territory, Edwin also set his sights on the Isle of Man. Edwin's bellicose behaviour was not atypical for the time. Unsurprisingly, war was an integral part of life for a warrior king and neighbours were attacked almost every year in order to obtain tribute, submission and slaves. It is likely that through his annual wars that Edwin extended his kingdom from the Humber and the Mersey to the Southern Uplands and the Cheviots, emerging as a force to be reckoned with in the north of the country.

However, King Eadbald was still the ruler of the most powerful kingdom of the time. Edwin knew that the odds were stacked against him if he were to attack Kent. Instead he took a different approach to gain power and influence in the south. After Edwin's first wife died, he approached Eadbald asking for him for his sister, Ethelburga's, hand in marriage. Eadbald had no appetite for war with Edwin and agreed to the union on one condition- that after marrying Ethelburga, Edwin would convert to Christianity. The Kingdom of Kent had become Christian since Eadbald's mother, Bertha, had converted his father.

Today Ethelburga is known by her Latinised name, but during her lifetime she would have been known as AEthelburh, pronounced Athelburch, with the last syllable sounding like the Scottish word for 'loch'. Her name was a feminised version of that of her father, King AEthelberht of Kent.

To the Anglo-Saxons female relatives were valuable assets that could be used to forge links with other royal households through marriage. The practise was extensive and during the 7th century Kentish princesses were married off to three of the most powerful kings. Princess Ethelburga would have been brought up to expect to be used in this way to seal a political alliance and to convince her that being a mere pawn was acceptable, she would have been taught that it was her duty to her family and her nation.

As a member of two royal households, Ethelburga would have been used to the routine of the royal court, which involved moving regularly from one royal vill to the next, dispensing justice and ensuring that royal authority remained visible throughout the land. The court would live off food renders, a form of food tax levied on subjects. Edwin's realm included the royal sites of Yeavering in Bernicia and Campodunum in Elmet. He also controlled the former Roman cities of York and Carlisle, both of which appear to have become more important during the seventh century, although it is not known whether they were inhabited as urban centres during this period. Seeing that Edwin was becoming militarily preeminent in the north, Ealdbad dispatched his sister to create a blood link between the two royal households.

However, Ealdbald was serious about his condition that Edwin should stop worshipping his pagan Germanic gods and convert to Christianity. According to Bede, in his 'Ecclesiastical History of the English Nation', Eadbald told Edwin 'that it was not lawful to marry a Christian virgin to a pagan husband, lest the faith and the mysteries of the heavenly king should be profaned by her cohabiting with a king that was altogether a stranger to the worship of the true God'. Clearly, Ethelburga was even more valuable because she was a virgin bride.

Although Edwin did not swear to convert overtly, he 'promised not to act in opposition to the Christian faith' and would allow Ethelburga and her court the freedom to continue to worship however they chose and suggested that he might convert in time. Eadbald was keen to seal the deal with Edwin and was satisfied with this response so 'the virgin was promised, and sent to Edwin'. Ethelburga arrived in York with a Roman cleric, Paulinus, who had been sent to Kentish court to help it maintain its faith in daily worship and to avoid it being corrupted by the pagans.

Paulinus was a member of a missionary group sent to Britain by Pope Gregory I who had decided that he wanted to Christianise all the Anglo-Saxons. Paulinus landed on English shores as part of the pope's second missionary expedition. After Ethelburga's marriage to Edwin in the wooden church that once sat near the site of the current minster, Paulinus was consecrated as the first Bishop of York in 625 by Justus, the fourth Archbishop of Canterbury. Spurred on by his promotion, Paulinus was ambitious in his desire to convert Edwin and was 'wholly bent on reducing the nation' to Christianity.

The tradition of Christian worship in Ethelburga's family can be traced back to her mother, Bertha, who was the daughter of Caribert of Paris, a Frankish tribe. When Bertha was married to AEthelburht, the second king of Kent, she came from France with a bishop called Liudhard. Her marriage to King AEthelberht of Kent resulted in the conversion of Kent to Christianity and he went on to found the first cathedral at St Paul's.

It was convenient for the Frankish tribes to convert the Saxons of Kent to Christianity as it would ensure that they had more influence and authority in the country. Kent was the most powerful kingdom in the Heptrachy because of its geographical location by the side of the English Channel. Its proximity to France facilitated trade, commerce and cultural exchange with the mainland.

Not long after they were married, Edwin was in danger once more. He had offered protection to the kings of Wight, thereby thwarting the ambitions of Cwichlem of Wessex. In response Cwichelm sent an assassin to Edwin's court. Bede records the dramatic events. Cwichelm told Edwin that he wanted his messenger to deliver a message to him. They met at the River Derwent and the treacherous assassin carried a two-edged sword with the end dipped in poison, to make sure he didn't fail in his mission. Quickly, he drew the dagger from under his garment and lunged at the king. Seeing the danger his master was in, Lilla, a devoted servant threw himself before the assassin's blade and received the killer stroke himself. However, the dagger penetrated so deep that the king was wounded through the body of his loyal knight.

As Edwin survived the treacherous attack, Paulinus used the occasion to try to persuade Edwin to convert to Christianity, pointing out to him that he had been saved by the grace of God. Edwin listened to Paulinus' arguments, but was still not ready to abandon his old gods.

The following year Ethelburga gave birth to a daughter, who she named Eanfled. Again Paulinus tried to persuade Edwin that her safe delivery was down to God's providence. Hearing Paulinus' arguments, Edwin made a bargain with him. If God would grant him victory over King Cuichlem of the West Saxons, who had sent the assassin, he would convert to Christianity. As a pledge to maintain this promise, Edwin allowed Paulinus to baptise Eanfled, along with twelve other members of his family.

When he had recovered from his wound, Edwin's army attacked the West Saxons and either slew or subdued those who had conspired to murder him. However, despite his victory and his promise to Paulinus, he was still reluctant to embrace the faith. Although he no longer worshipped idols, he wanted some instruction from Paulinus before he made his final decision.

The church in Rome saw the importance of converting Edwin as this act would allow it to extend its influence in Britain beyond Kent. Pope Boniface sent a letter to Edwin in 625 exhorting him to embrace the faith. He then asked Queen Ethelburga to covert her husband in order to save his soul. The pope had already sent letters privately to Ethelburga and her mother to convince them to convince Edwin to convert. But still Edwin held out. Edwin then went on an extensive consultation exercise with his ministers, deliberating on the pros and cons of converting. Finally in 627 he agreed to be baptised.

After the ceremony in the Saxon church in York, Edwin ordered the construction of a more spectacular building in stone near the site of the original church. Bede records that:

'He was baptized at York, on the holy day of Easter, being the 12th of April, in the church of St Peter the Apostle, which he himself had built of timber, whilst he was catechizing and instruction in order to receive the baptism. In that city he appointed the see of the bishopric of his instructor and bishop, Paulinus. But as soon as he was baptized, he took care, by the direction of the same Paulinus, to build in the same place a larger and nobler church of stone, in the midst whereof that same oratory which he had first erected should be enclosed'.

This was the first Minster of York, later reconstructed in the 12th century using Gothic architecture. According to Bede, the result of Edwin's decision to convert was to bring peace to Britannia, so much that 'even if a woman with a recently born child wanted to walk across the whole island, from sea to sea, she could do so without anyone harming her'. Bede's description of peace is a stark insight into the frightening lawlessness of the time.

Upon Edwin's conversion, his sons Osfrid and Eadfrid by his first wife, were baptised. Next came his children by Ethelburga, who ultimately gave him three children – his daughter, Eanfled, and his two sons – Ethelhun and Wuscfrea. Edwin's baptism created a 'fervour for the faith' and Paulinus, while staying at Edwin and Ethelburga's country seat, spent the next thirty-six days baptising and catechizing.

From 627 onwards, Queen Ethelburga's husband was the most powerful king among the Anglo-Saxons, ruling Northumbria, much of eastern Mercia and the Isles of Man and Anglesey. His alliance with Kent, the subjugation of Mercia and his recent successes in battle added to his power and authority.

For approximately five years, Edwin's power went unchallenged until Penda of Mercia rose up against him in 632-633. Edwin faced Penda at the Battle of Hatfield Chase, a low-lying area near Doncaster. Bede records that Edwin was killed 'on 12th October in the year of our lord 633, being forty-seven years of age, and all his army was either slain or dispersed.' One of his sons by his first wife was also killed and his other son by her was captured and killed later. Edwin's body was allegedly hidden in Sherwood Forest and the village later became known as Edwinstowe, Edwin's resting place. His body was buried in Whitby Abbey and his head was taken to York where it was buried in the church of St Peter the Apostle, which he had begun. However, Edwin did not live to see his church completed, with Oswald, his successor completing the work instead.

After Edwin's death, chaos ensued in the country. 'A great slaughter was made in the church or nation of the Northumbrians'. Penda and the kingdom of the Mercians still worshipped the old Germanic gods and was 'a stranger to the name of Christ'. His ally Cadwalla, professed to be a Christian but was 'so barbarous in his disposition and behaviour, that he neither spared the female sex, nor the innocent age of children, but with savage cruelty put them to tormenting deaths, ravaging all their country for a long time, and resolving to cut off all the race of the English within the borders of Britain'.

In this climate of extreme violence and danger, Queen Ethelburga fled with her children back to her homeland in Kent. Bede records that Paulinus orchestrated their escape and they returned to Kent by sea, fearing ambush if travelling overland. Bede records:

> 'The affairs of the Northumbrians being in confusion by reason of this disaster, without any prospect of safety except in flight, Paulinus, taking with him Queen Ethelburga...returned into Kent by sea and was honourably received by Archbishop Honorius and King Eadbald. On his journey into Kent he was protected by Bassus, a valiant soldier of King Edwin.'

Nevertheless back in the court of her brother, Ethelburga still feared for the safety of her children. Their existence not only threatened Oswald's claim to power, but that of her brother also, who might become uneasy at their presence in his court. She then took the radical decision to send them to France to be placed under the protection of King Dagobert, who was most likely her kinsman on her mother's side.

Ethelburga travelled with her daughter and sons, as well as Iffi, Edwin's grandson by his first wife. With her children safe, Ethelburga lived for a time in a monastery in Brie, alongside one of her brother's daughters. Due to the fact that there were very few monasteries in the 'country of the Angles', many Christians went to the monasteries of the Franks and the Gauls. Eventually, Ethelburga became the abbess at the monastery of Brie. It is not known when Ethelburga decided to return to

England, but we do know that her two sons died in infancy in France and perhaps this was the stimulus for her return.

Back in the Kentish court her brother awarded her the territory of Lyminge, where she decided to build a church. Excavations in 2019 found that the first church on the site dates back to Ethelburga's time, approximately 633. The remains were made from crushed Roman bricks, which indicate that stonemasons may have been brought from France. A fragment of a column demonstrated that the stone for the ornamental features of the church was probably imported from France also. It is highly likely that the interior of the church was decorated with painted plaster. Painted white on the exterior, it would have stood out magnificently in the countryside where all other buildings would have been made of earth and timber with thatched roofs. It may even have had a lead roof due to the proximity of lead mines in the area.

Over time a monastic settlement grew up around Ethelburga's church with a series of buildings surrounding it. In 647, Ethelburga died in Lyminge, three years after Paulinus. A small room was uncovered on the north side of the apse of the current church, which may have been where Ethelburga was originally buried. The supposed burial place fits a description of her final resting place written in the eleventh century. Later her remains were removed to Canterbury where there is now a major shrine to her at Collegiate Church.

After Edwin's death his realm was divided and his successors reverted to paganism. The warring continued until eventually Northumbria was united once more. After his death, Edwin came to be venerated as a saint by some, although his cult was eventually overshadowed by the cult of his successor, Oswald, who was killed in 642. Both were perceived as Christian martyrs after having fought the pagan Mercians and the British.

Ethelburga's daughter, Eanfled, was used to continue the tradition of political marriage alliances, like her mother. In 642 she became the second wife of King Oswiu of Northumbria. If Oswiu's goal in marrying Eanflaed was the acceptance of his rule in Deira, the plan was unsuccessful and warring continued. After his death in 670 she retired to Whitby Abbey, which had been founded by one of her relatives, Hilda of Whitby. Upon Hilda's death, Eanfled became abbess jointly with her daughter. It is during this time that Edwin's remains were reburied at Whitby. After becoming abbess in around 680, she remained there until her death. Subsequently, the abbey became important in the establishment of Christianity in England.

After Ethelburga's death her community of nuns survived for nearly two centuries, probably abandoning Lyminge in the course of the ninth century. Monasteries near the coast were vulnerable to Viking raids and the nuns seem to have taken refuge in Canterbury where they were granted land in 804. By the tenth century the monastic community seems no longer to have been in existence, and the church at Lyminge passed into the possession of the Archbishops of Canterbury. First Dunstan in 965 and then Lanfran in the 1080s rebuilt the church. The fate of Ethelburga's relics is not known and may have been taken to Canterbury in the late eleventh century.

Ethelburga's life was one of contrasts. She would have been brought up to expect an arranged marriage that would be of benefit to her dynasty and she would have been told that this was an honour. Her own Frankish mother would have provided the example and schooled her in how to manage life as the wife of an ambitious warlord. Like all those who make war, her husband lived by the sword and died by the sword. Edwin ruled for seventeen years, but he was never secure on the throne, as shown by the early assassination attempt. His annual wars must have been a burden to Ethelburga who would fear for his life and that of the father of her children.

In 633 her worst nightmare was realized and she was forced to flee for her own life and that of her children. Still not safe in the court of her brother, she had to take radical action to protect their lives. Unfortunately, her efforts proved to be in vain for her sons never saw maturity. After a tumultuous life as consort to a bellicose king, the constant danger that Ethelburga and her family lived in must have taken its toll on her. It is understandable that after all the peril of her life with Edwin, Ethelburga decided upon the relative tranquillity of a monastic life, dedicated to the Christian God. She had been brought up in the Christian faith and had been used to spread its influence. Now she could pour her energy into promoting Christianity in a less pressured manner, as well as being able to continue her own personal worship.

Ethelburga's life mirrored that of her mother, while that of Ethelburga's daughter, Eanfled, mirrored that of her mother. In a world dominated by warring men, both Ethelburga and Eanfled sought sanctuary in abbeys, ultimately taking the lead roles of abbesses. It seems that this role would have afforded them some status and authority, a rare opportunity for a woman to wield influence and power in a man's world.

Before Eanfled became abbess of Whitby Abbey, the important Synod of Whitby took place in 644, a conference during which Eanfled's husband, King Oswiu of Northumbria, decreed that thereafter Easter would be calculated following the customs of Christian Rome, rather than the customs of Iona. Christian Rome became the preeminent religion in the country, and it was also decided that the Episcopal seat of the Bishop would transfer from Lindisfarne to York. Consequently, all British Christians to this day have inherited practices that Ethelburga and her family were key in forging.

Women of York

CHAPTER FOUR

The Naughty Nuns of the Priory of St Clements

THE PRIORY OF St Clements once stood in modern-day Clementhorpe, an area to the south-west of the city of York. It was founded in 1130 by the Archbishop of York, Turstin of Bayeaux, to serve the Parish of St Clement. A Benedictine convent, it housed between ten to fifteen nuns at any one time.

In medieval times it was the custom of those higher up in society to marry off their daughters, who were not expected to work, but to be kept by their husbands. Society viewed it unladylike for women to work and only those women who had to work did so. Marrying off daughters could be an expensive business for fathers, given that prospective husbands expected their new wife to bring a dowry with them. Families with more daughters than financial means, often resorted to sending the remaining ones to nunneries.

One benefit for a girl living in a nunnery could be education, as this was one of the few places a woman could learn to read and write. However, the daily regime of a nunnery could be quite austere and tedious for many young women. Nuns were expected to commit to a life of poverty, chastity and obedience. They would spend much of their time praying for the souls of those who had donated money to the priory. While some women would have elected to enter a priory as they could then avoid the demands of marriage and the dangers of childbirth, others would choose to enter monastic life due to sincere religious belief. However, some women simply could not endure the life in a convent and chose to exercise their right to freedom. Several nuns of the Priory of St Clements are known to have rebelled against the culture and discipline of the house.

The first recorded trouble in the Priory of St Clements dates back to forty-two years after it was founded. In 1192 the all-powerful Archbishop at the time, Geoffrey Plantagenet, decided to give the priory to the Abbey of Godstow. The nuns did not like his decision and appealed to Rome to overturn his choice. It is even believed that the prioress, Alice, travelled all the way to Rome to plead their case. Clearly, unhappy with their behaviour, the archbishop retaliated by excommunicating the nuns. However, their strategy of appealing to the pope worked and he overturned the decision of Geoffrey Plantagenet and allowed them to keep their independent status. This is the first indication of the strong-mindedness of the nuns.

For over a century, things were peaceful at the priory until 1301 when it was recorded that one night 'certain men came to the priory gate leading a saddled horse'. They were greeted one of the nuns named Cecily. Quickly, she discarded her nun's habit and put on a lay person's dress. Mounting one of the horses, she was whisked off by the riders, ending up fifty-five miles north in Darlington. There, Gregory de Thornton, most likely her lover, was waiting for her. We know that she lived with him for three years or more and then all trace of her disappears from the record. It is possible that she would have been recalled to the convent by the archbishop, but he could not enforce her return.

The early fourteenth century was a particularly eventful time in the history of the priory. In 1310 Joan de Saxton is recorded as serving penance for misbehaviour. Even though the archbishop of the time showed her clemency and reduced her punishment to a less severe one, she was not allowed to leave the cloister, but had to 'keep to the convent at all times'. She was also barred from taking any position of responsibility within the institution. A virtual prisoner within the walls of the convent, she was allowed to occasionally visit the orchard and the garden for recreation or 'solace', but then only in the company of other nuns. Visits from friends were allowed twice a year, but these had to be held in the presence of the prioress or other discreet nuns. Something had happened between Joan and someone called Lady de Walleys because she was 'to have nothing to do with the Lady de Walleys, and if the Lady de Walleys was then in their house, she was to be sent away before Pentecost'. Some have speculated that there was a lesbian relationship between the two, as it is then recorded that 'the archbishop further forbade the nuns to have girls over twelve years of age as boarders, and they were only to keep washerwomen and other necessary servants in the house'. Clearly, there is some concern that some of the nuns may be a corrupting influence on younger girls.

That same year as the incident with Joan de Saxton, the archbishop gave permission for Isabella of Studley Roger, near Ripon to enter te convent. Little did he know that twenty-one years later she was going to cause a whole heap of trouble.

Isabella is recorded in 1331 as having been directed to return to St Clements after having been sent away to Yedingham to undergo a penance imposed upon her. She had been found guilty of rejecting her religion (apostacy) and of *super lapsu carnis*, which when translated from Latin means a 'huge lapse into sin of the flesh' or 'carnal desire'. If that wasn't enough, she was also accused of 'other' mysterious 'excesses'. The archbishop warned her that if she was disobedient to the prioress or quarrelsome with her sisters, or if she indulged in blasphemy, she would be transferred to another house and remain there permanently. Clearly, the restrictions of convent life did not appeal to Isabella in the slightest, but it is not known if she took heed of the dire warning and settled down into a more cooperative life.

Six years later there was political strife at the priory. The prioress Custance Basy had either died or resigned and this caused 'discord to prevail' whereby two rival factions developed in support of her prospective replacements. One side supported the election of Beatrice of Brandesby and the other elected Anges de Methelay. The dean and chapter of York Minster arbitrated the final decision and appointed Anges de Methelay, who was prioress for eight years until she resigned in protest at the fact that the archbishop had issued a commission to inquire into the defects of the convent.

It wasn't until 2019 when archivists began digitising the records kept by William Melton, Archbishop of York between 1317 to 1340 that the scandal of the nun, Joan of Leeds came to light. Like Isabella de Studley, it seems that Joan was so desperate to escape the confines of the convent that she hatched a deviously elaborate plan. First of all, she created a dummy in her own image and likeness. She then went on to pretend to be seriously ill. It is not clear whether she either duped or enlisted some of the other nuns to bury her body in a mock funeral. After having faked her own death, she was discovered thirty miles away in Beverley, leading a life of 'indecency'.

In 1310 Archbishop Melton wrote to the dean of Beverley about the 'scandalous' rumour and told him to 'warn Joan of Leeds ...that she should return to her house'. He had probably complied with his duty in issuing this demand and possibly might have hoped that such a troublemaker did not return.

Melton was unimpressed with Joan's behaviour to say the least and wrote that 'she perverted her path of life arrogantly to the way of carnal lust and away from poverty and obedience. Having broken her vows and discarded the religious habit, she now wanders at large to the notorious peril to her soul and to the scandal of all her order'. We do not know how the story ended for Joan. If she returned to a religious house, she would have had to perform a very severe penance. She was recorded as living with a man in Beverley and may have continued to do so.

The convent caused Archbishop Melton quite a bit of trouble. On January 25th 1317 he decided to visit the 'house' and must have found the culture and customs to be a little too relaxed for his liking. He subsequently sent the new prioress, Agnes de Methelay, a list of injunctions relating to how the rule should be observed. He was not happy when he discovered that the nuns had been sending fourteen loaves of bread to the Friars Minor of York and the Friars Preachers of York every alternate week. The nuns were instructed to stop supplying the loaves as long as the convent was in debt. Once the books were balanced, they could only supply the loaves with the archbishop's consent.

He also banned the nuns form giving the annual clothes allowance of any dead nun to the friars. He prohibited any secular women within the house from chatting with the nuns as he feared this could lead to 'evil suspicion'. No one of any age whatsoever, male or female, was allowed to sleep in the dormitory of the nuns! He must have been worried about their chastity because the nuns were warned not to allow the frequent access of secular men and women to the house again, 'lest evil or scandal should arise'.

We know that by 1467 there was a permanent position of an anchorite attached to St Clement's Church, which also served the nuns. An anchorite is someone who withdraws from secular society to lead an intensely prayer-orientated, ascetic religious-focused life. Alice Derby must have been happy to take on such a strict and isolated religious regime.

As we have seen the priory could fall into debt and it seems to have been financed in an ad hoc manner. In 1391 Pope Boniface IX encouraged penitents to give alms for the preservation of the priory of St Clement without the walls of York and in 1470, Elizabeth Medlay, a resident of the priory left instructions in her will that her body be buried in St Clement. She bequeathed each nun 12 shillings with 16 shillings for the prioress. She must have been particularly fond of the head of the convent because she also her left her her best coat.

On 13th June 1536 the priory fell victim to Henry VIII's Dissolution of the Monasteries and was the first religious house to be suppressed in York. Just two months later the Priory of St Clements was dissolved, and the eight nuns and nine servants were forced to leave the premises. The commissioner, Leonard Beckwith, took an inventory of the small number of items of value owned by the priory. The three bells were worth seventeen shillings, a chalice was more valuable at forty-four shillings, one silver cup was just under seventeen shillings and some reliquary glasses in argento were valued at five shillings. Beckwith himself did well out of his work as commissioner for Henry VIII and was described by W. Wilberforce Morrell as 'one of those enterprising individuals who elevated their social position and built up their houses on the ruins of the monastery'. In 1541 the manor of Selby was transferred to Beckwith and he became High Sheriff of Yorkshire in 1550. Subsequently, he was knighted by Henry's son, King Edward VI.

King Edward VI seems to have been reluctant to pay the pensions of the nuns who were forced to leave their home. He commissioned an inquiry into which of the nuns were still alive and took an inventory of the pensions that were paid to them. His list shows that at the time of the Dissolution there were fifteen nuns, not including the prioress, Isabel Ward, who were entitled to pensions. The fifty-six-year-old prioress received the highest pension of all the women, collecting £6 13s and 4d a year. This was for eighteen years of service between 1518 and 1536.

Of the fifteen nuns, two had died and another had not been 'herde of'. The youngest ex-nun was Elene Bayne who was thirty years old and received a pension of 34s 4d. Anges Archer was thirty-nine years old and had not been paid her pension of 40s for one whole year. Two others had not received payments for one whole year – sixty-year-old Jane Watson (40s) and forty-six year old Dorothy Maw (40s). One wonders how they coped without this income that was due to them. Four of the ex-nuns were sixty years old and received payment ranging from 40s up to 60s, the calculation of their payment probably dependent on length of service to the convent. Interestingly, six of the ex-nuns were called Agnes!

Of the fate of the ex-nuns, we know the most about the ex-prioress, Isabel Warde. As a Benedictine convent, the Priory of St Clements had always had close links with Holy Trinity Church in Micklegate, which was the home of a Benedictine monasterial complex before the Dissolution of the Monasteries. Jacobs Well, a beautifully preserved medieval building dating from 1474, lies within the boundaries of the ex-monastic complex on Priory Street, and was originally the parish room for the Priory Church of Holy Trinity.

Fortunately for Isabel Warde, in 1547 she was able to buy Jacob's Well for herself and her sister. She may have been helped by the fact that her brother was a monk in Holy Trinity. In 1566, three years before her death in 1569, she made a Deed of Gift to the parishioners of Holy Trinity Church to provide a charity for the parish. A romantic agreement was made between Isabel and her trustees. She proposed that she be allowed to live in the house for the rest of her natural life upon the annual payment of one red rose, given on Midsummer Day. In return, on her death, the house would revert to the trustees.

After the dissolution of the Priory of St Clements, the building fell into gradual decline. The stone was taken and re-used in the city walls. All that stands today is the remains of two adjoining walls and a plaque to commemorate its existence. Fortunately, some records remain to challenge stereotypes of convent life and show us that women loved their freedom, no matter what age they lived in.

CHAPTER FIVE

Margaret Clitherow
The Martyr of York

THE MOST COMPREHENSIVE record of the life and death of Margaret Clitherow was written by Father John Mush, one of the priests who she was executed for harbouring in March 1586. Although Mush was captured in October of the same year, and condemned to die, he escaped with two other priests. In 1619 he published 'A True Report of the Life and Martyrdom of Mrs Margaret Clitherow', so that her shocking and terrible fate would be recorded for posterity.

Margaret Clitherow, née Middleton was born at a time when England was a maelstrom of political and religious turmoil. In 1534 Henry VIII decided that he wanted to obtain an annulment of his marriage to Catherine of Aragon. As the pope would not accede to his request for a decree of nullity, Henry passed the First Act of Supremacy which declared that he and his successors were now head of the Church in England, effectively replacing the authority of the pope. Henry wanted to enjoy 'all the honours, dignities, pre-eminences, jurisdictions, privileges, authorities, immunities, profits and commodities to the said dignity'. With this legislation, thus began what has come to be known as the English Reformation and what has been described as the greatest act of vandalism that the country has ever seen – the Dissolution of the Monasteries, during which process Henry proceeded to confiscate all the land and wealth of all the religious houses in his realm.

Although there was opposition to Henry's desire to destroy the power of the Catholic church, he decisively quashed The Pilgrimage of Grace in 1536, executing the leaders of the protest in a move that was designed to quell all opposition to his designs. Just under ten years later, Henry began to dissolve all the Catholic religious houses in the country, beginning with the least powerful chantries, religious guilds and hospitals and subsequently moving onto the abbeys, convents, priories and monasteries. Between 1535 and 1669 forty so-called martyrs of England and Wales were executed for treason and other related offences due to their opposition to his actions.

In 1547 Henry VIII died and his Catholic daughter, Mary, succeeded. She tried to restore to the Church the property that had been confiscated by her father, but was largely thwarted by parliament during her five-year reign. Nevertheless, she had over 289 religious dissenters burnt at the stake, which led to her becoming known as 'Bloody Mary' by her Protestant opponents. It was into this dangerous time of political and religious chaos that Margaret Clitherow was born in York in 1556, the fourth year of the reign of Queen Mary.

When Queen Mary died, Margaret Clitherow was two years old. Queen Elizabeth I, Mary's successor, was quick to pass the Second Act of Supremacy, which declared her and all her successors as the Supreme Governor of the church, a title that the British monarch still holds to this day. Elizabeth I instituted the Oath of Supremacy, which required anyone taking public office or church office to swear allegiance to the monarch as head of the church and state. Anyone refusing to comply could be charged with treason. When Margaret's father took the oath so that he could become Sheriff of York, he was so ill with gout that he had to lie in his bed.

Margaret was possibly born in her father's house in Davygate, the daughter of a successful wax chandler. In 1530 Thomas Middleton was allowed to become a freeman of the City of York by the Company of the Merchant Adventurers, which meant that he was entitled to trade in the city. By 1552 he had gained the position of chamberlain on the town council and between 1564 and 1565, he was the sheriff of the city. Nevertheless, his influence and status in York could do nothing to save Margaret from the terrible fate that awaited her. Besides, by the time that Margaret was brutally and horrifically murdered, her father had been dead for nineteen years.

Margaret was eleven years old when her father died leaving her the house in Davygate, to be received after the death of her mother and 'one silver goblet and half a dozen silver spoons'. It seems that Thomas was a civic minded and generous man as his will provided money for the poor of York on the condition that 'they prayed for the repose of his soul'. He also bequeathed a further crown to each of his three servants, on condition that they do the same.

A mere four months later, Margaret's mother, Jane, married her second husband, Henry May, who eventually became Lord Mayor of York, long remembered for his great passion for all things ceremonial. Margaret was brought up a Protestant in a privileged middle-class household with some civic status and influence. Nevertheless, as a woman her education was limited to being taught how to run a household and she was unable to read and write. Nevertheless, it seems that she had a natural intelligence, despite her limited education. Her contemporaries remembered her as 'sharp and ready with a readiness of speech'.

In 1571, at the tender age of fifteen, she became the second wife of John Clitherow, a prosperous wholesale and retail butcher, old enough to be her father, and who was also on his way to becoming a person of influence in the city. At the time of his marriage, he was a bridgemaster, a member of the committee responsible for the upkeep of the bridge over the Ouse. They lived above his butcher's shop in the Shambles and a year later he was sworn in as a special constable, whose job it was to assist in the hunting down of Catholic suspects. Two years later he became Chamberlain of York, an office that entitled him to the rank of gentleman. Like her father, John Clitherow would have had to swear an oath of allegiance to Elizabeth I, and would therefore have had to publicly declare himself to be Protestant.

The same year that she married, Margaret converted to Catholicism. It is not clear how it happened, but her husband had several staunch Catholics amongst his near relatives, including his brother who may have been imprisoned for his faith in York Castle and who later became a priest. It may have been the case that Margaret visited him and other priests in York Castle prison and was persuaded to the Catholic faith by one of them. Many Catholics in York were to be found among the trading communities, such as butchers, bakers, tailors, chandlers, saddlers and tillers. Therefore, she could easily have come into contact with those who followed the outlawed religion.

John Clitherow was indifferent to religious belief himself, as well as towards his wife's choice of faith. While Margaret was concerned with the loss of souls and the trouble in God's church, religion was unimportant to her husband. Nevertheless, he repeatedly paid the many fines that Margaret received for failing to attend Protestant church services. He also tolerated her work for priests.

Margaret's position as the Catholic wife of a Protestant husband was not an uncommon one. A complex pattern of relationships existed among some families, which helped the old faith to be maintained and even to spread. Margaret and John proceeded to begin a family and she bore him three children. Meanwhile, Margaret gained a reputation as a strict mother and mistress to her servants. She is reported to have had a pleasing appearance, to speak in a low, gentle voice and to enjoy a simple diet of rye bread, milk, pottage and butter. Others regarded her as witty, sociable, popular with her neighbours and competent in business. She is reputed to have helped regularly in her husband's butcher's shop.

By 1872, it was becoming increasingly dangerous to be of the Catholic faith in York. The Earl of Huntingdon came to the city as President of the Council of the North with the ambition of eliminating the last vestiges of Catholicism from the city. Undeterred by the danger, in 1576 some priests from Cardinal Allen's Seminary in Douai reached England, whereupon Margaret gave them shelter.

In 1577 she became a marked woman and was sent to prison for the first time for two years for failing to attend church services. On the second occasion she was released because she was expecting her third child. While in prison she may have had time to improve her literacy skills. In 1580 Jesuits arrived in England and persecution became even more ferocious. Fines for non-attendance at church increased and a sentence of six months was imposed for hearing Mass.

Four years later a shocking even occurred when Dorothy Vavasour, the wife of wealthy Thomas Vavasour was imprisoned in the New Counter lock-up on Ouse Bridge. Dorothy had made her York townhouse the principal centre of Mass in York. On the Feast of the Assumption, her house was raided. Mrs Vavasour spent the remainder of her life in the insanitary kidcote lock-up, located below Ouse Bridge. The lock-up was known to flood when the level of the river rose, and it is unsurprising that Dorothy did not survive the ordeal of being incarcerated there. As a result of Dorothy's death, greater responsibility for the safety of priests fell on Margaret. She prepared a second mass room in the city to take the overflow from the rooms that she had prepared on the Shambles. She also began a small school to teach the Catholic faith.

In 1582 five priests were captured in York. Each was dragged in turn from York Castle prison over Ouse Bridge, along Micklegate, out through the bar and down to the Knavesmire, where they were executed. Secretly, Margaret would sometimes go barefoot at night to the gallows, meditate there, then steal back home. She is reported to have said that 'there is a war and a trial of God's Church. If God's priests dare venture themselves to my house, I will never refuse them'. One year later she was back in prison, this time for eighteen months.

When the Jesuits Act of 1584 was passed, Catholic priests were given just forty days to swear an oath of allegiance to Elizabeth I, or to leave the country. Anyone who knew of their presence and failed to inform the authorities would be fined, imprisoned or executed. Undeterred, Margaret hid two priests - one in the Shambles and one in a property further away.

In 1885 Margaret sent her son, Henry, to Reims to study at the English College where he was to train for the priesthood. Her husband was summoned before the authorities to explain why his eldest son had gone abroad.

As a notorious shelterer of priests Margaret was soon in trouble again when someone denounced her activities. On March 10th 1586 her home was raided. In a panic, a Flemish boy who was residing with the Clitherows, took the authorities to some vestments and other objects used in the Catholic Mass. Margaret and her family were arrested and placed in various prisons and lock-ups around the city. Although her daughter, Anne, was only twelve years old, she was interrogated by the authorities and refused to give any information that incriminated her mother.

While imprisoned in York Castle, Margaret was interrogated at length by both the civic and ecclesiastical authorities, but she would not give in to their demands that she renounce her faith. On March 14th she was charged with treason for having harboured Father John Mush and Father Francis Ingleby, and for having attended Mass. The charge against her was that she had harboured and maintained Jesuits and seminary priests, traitors to the queen's Majesty and her laws, that she had heard Mass and 'such like', the last phrase being a possible reference to sending her son to a seminary in Douai.

She was arraigned before Judge John Clinch and Judge Frances Rhodes, as well as other four members of the Council of the North at the York assizes. The trial took place at the Guildhall, where once she may once have attended official banquets as the wife of a prominent member of the council. The room was crowded with spectators. In answer to the charge brought against her, she calmly replied that she never harboured enemies of the queen. Following the indictment, Clinch asked her how she wished to be tried and she replied, 'By God and the country. Having made no offence, I need no trial'.

Judge Clinch pressed her to plead, but she only answered, 'If you say that I have offended and must be tried, I will be tried by none but God and your own consciences'. At this point the vestments that had been found in her house in the Shambles were produced. 'Two lewd fellows' put on the robes and paraded around the courtroom for all to see. The judges began to taunt her by asking her how she liked them. Refusing to lose her self-control, her answer was, 'I like them well if they are on the backs of those who know how to use them for God's honour as they were made.'

Judge Clinch made yet another effort to induce her to plead while his fellow law lord, Judge Rhodes put pressure on her by making sexual slurs about the nature of her relationships with the priests that she harboured. He stated publicly, 'it is not for religion that thou harbourest priests, but for harlotries.' On 15ᵗʰ March she was again brought to court and further attempts were made to make her alter her determination. But she only used the occasion to make her case clearer. 'Indeed I think you have no witness against me.' She pointed out, 'but only children which with and an apple and a rod you make to say what you will'.

The Judges pressurised her to no avail and she continued to refuse to enter a plea. She knew that if she pleaded 'not guilty', then her children could have been made to testify against her. As a loving mother, she wanted to spare them the ordeal of unintentionally condemning their own mother. Furthermore, she knew that as they were the only witnesses against her, they would share the guilt of her death. She also wished to protect the Flemish boy who was a guest in her house and who had been forced to give up the vestments and the altar plate under the threat of receiving a beating. She remained defiant when she stated, 'Having made no offence, I will need no trial. If you say I have offended, I will be tried by none but by God and your own conscience'.

However, with this momentous and brave decision, a terrible fate was wrought down on her. The automatic punishment for not entering a plea was death by 'peine forte et dure', a French term meaning to be pressed to death. After calling her a 'naughty, wilful woman', Judge Clinch proceeded to describe to her the gruesome method of execution that she was to suffer in the coming days:

'You shall return to the place from whence you came, and in the lower part of the prison be stripped naked, laid down on your back to the ground, and so much weight be laid upon you as you are able to bear, and thus you shall continue three days without meat or drink, except a little barley bread and puddle water; and the third day you shall have a sharp stone put under your back, and your hands and feet shall be tied to posts that, more weight being laid upon you, you may be pressed to death.'

Her calm responses must have infuriated those who wished to force her to renounce her faith for she simply replied. 'God be thanked, I am not worthy of so good a death as this'. While awaiting the terrible day of her execution, Margaret prepared a shift in the hope that she might be spared the humiliation of being stripped naked in front of the various men who would supervise her ordeal. Margaret's husband, John, was not able to bear the sentence as bravely as his poor wife. When he heard of the ruling, 'he fared like a man out of his wits and wept so violently that blood gushed out of his nose in great quantity'. He is reported to have said, 'let them take all I have and save my wife, for she is the best wife in all England and the best Catholic also.'

She spent the next ten days in the filthy and unsanitary lock-up on Ouse Bridge. When news of her sentence spread in the city, her name was on everyone's lips. Still, during her final imprisonment, she was repeatedly urged to save her own life. When it was discovered that she may be pregnant, the judges again tried to persuade her to relent. However, she refused to confirm or deny her condition, knowing all the while that being pregnant could have saved her life. She simply replied. 'I die not desperately nor procure mine own death, for not being found guilty of such crimes as were laid against me, and yet condemned, I could but rejoice – my cause also being God's quarrel. I die for love of Lord Jesus'.

During her imprisonment clergymen went to visit her, as well as her stepfather, the then Mayor of York. The authorities knew that her execution would be controversial and began a smear campaign against her to counteract the negative press they were receiving due to their decision to hound this innocent woman to death. It was put about that she had been unfaithful to her husband, that she had sinned with priests and had entertained them in a luxurious style, while she let her own children go hungry. But it was impossible for the council to be rid of her without making her a martyr. No-one and nothing could persuade her from her steadfast determination to 'live and die in the same faith'.

On the eve of her execution, at midnight she put on the long linen robe that she had fashioned for herself while in prison. She was, understandably, greatly disturbed by the threat to strip her naked. She knelt in long prayer and then went to rest. When she rose she made practical arrangements for after her death. She sent her hat to her husband in a 'sign of her loving duty to him as the head of the family'. She then had her shoes and stockings sent to her twelve-year-old daughter, Anne, a symbolic gesture 'signifying that she should serve God and follow her steps'.

At last the momentous day arrived. On 25th March 1586, at 8am the sheriffs took her from the kidcote to the Toll Booth on Ouse Bridge, a few yards from the prison. She was forced to walk over the bridge barefoot. There was no respite before death. Still the judges harangued her, telling her to admit that she died for treason, despite her protestation of loyalty to the queen. She contradicted them to the last. 'No, no, Mr Sheriff, I die for the love of my Lord Jesu'.

Partially covered by the shift that she had prepared, she was forced to lie down on the hard, cold stone floor. The two sergeants who had been entrusted with her execution did not have the courage to carry out their sentence. Instead, they hired four beggars to carry out the terrible deeds. First her arms were stretched wide apart, in the shape of a cross and tied to poles with cords. Then they placed a handkerchief over her face and a sharp stone, the size of a man's fist directly under her spine in the middle of her back. The motley crew then put a door directly on top of her. Next huge rocks weighed the door down on top of her fragile body. As the weight increased agonisingly, Margaret cried out in excruciating pain, 'Jesu! Jesu! Jesu! Have mercy on me' and these were the last words that she ever spoke.

For fifteen long and terrible minutes she endured unimaginable suffering. By 9.15am her chest had given way and was crushed, causing her ribs to burst out from underneath her skin. As if that was not enough, her body was then left for a further six hours as a public admonition of the indignity of her fate.

In one final attempt to humiliate and disrespect her, later that same day her lifeless corpse was flung beside a dunghill in the city. For six weeks she lay in this ignominious place until her friends were able to rescue her body. Before burying her body with honour, her hand was taken and mummified. This religious relic is now kept safe in the Bar Convent.

Despite what had happened to their mother, her stepson, William, and her own son, Henry, both became priests. Her husband John Clitherow went on to re-marry but was still plagued with worry. His daughter, Anne, did continue in her mother's footsteps and practised the Catholic faith and was persecuted for her behaviour. Her father tried to use his influence to have her freed from prison on at least one occasion. He must have been relieved when ultimately, she went to a far safer place when she became a nun at St Ursula's in Louvain.

In 1929 Margaret Clitherow's piety was officially recognised when she was beatified by Pope Pius XI. On October 25th 1970, Pope Paul VI made her one of the Four Martyrs of England and Wales in St Peter's Basilica in Rome before a crowd of 50,000 people. Currently, schools all over the country – in Manchester, Middlebrough and London, as well as in Ohio, USA are named in her honour. At present the Catholic church maintains a peaceful shrine in her honour in the Shambles, near where she once lived with her husband. Today we are all welcome to visit the little room in the Shambles, where we can sit and contemplate what it is to have the courage to sacrifice one's life for one's beliefs.

Women of York

CHAPTER SIX

Jennet Preston

Executed for Witchcraft

ON MONDAY 27TH July 1612, Jennet Preston stood alone at the prisoner's bar of York court room, accused of witchcraft and on trial for her life. Incredibly, this was the second time in a mere fifteen weeks that she had had to answer to the charge of murder by witchcraft. Looking down on her from their lofty seats behind the bench sat the same Judge Bromley who had freed her in on 6th April. Would he be merciful a second time?

Unfortunately for Jennet, today the imposing and serious Judge Bromley was accompanied by Judge Altham, a man seasoned in sending women to the gallows for witchcraft. Five years earlier he had condemned an alleged witch to death at the Chelmsford Assize. In the same year as Jennet's trial, Judge Altham was making a name for himself in the judiciary. He had been involved in a high-profile case which had caused none other than King James I himself to intervene. The King had written to ensure Bartholomew Legate was burned at the stake for heresy in Smithfield amid a vast crowd of people and Judge Altham believed that he had received royal approval for his lack of mercy. If Jennet was hoping for pity from either of the men who sat in judgement upon her, she was sorely mistaken.

Ranged before her in the cold, open courtroom were the several witnesses against her, along with her accuser, Thomas Lister junior. William Preston, her husband of twenty-six years and loyal supporter throughout her trials and tribulations, was there to bear witness to his wife's ordeal, perhaps with some other friends and family. Nevertheless, her loved ones would have been cold comfort to Jennet. Trials in early modern England were chaotic affairs. The historian Cockburn writes that they were:

'public spectacles, noisy, boisterous, almost carnivalesque, with the crush of spectators, prisoners, jurymen, prosecuters and court officials. Trials would often therefore take the form of altercations between, prisoner, prosecutor and witness, with ongoing interjections from the judge". (Cockburn, page 110-111)

Amidst this pandemonium, having just been taken from York Castle prison, Jennet must have thought that she was losing her mind because for Jennet, history was quite literally repeating itself. This time her accuser was the exact same man who had pointed the finger of blame the first time. In April of 1612, Thomas Lister Junior, gentleman, and heir to the Lister estates in Gisburn, had accused her of killing Dogson's son by witchcraft. The evidence had not been enough to convince the jury and Jennet had walked free, able to return to her family and her home. She had narrowly escaped death by hanging. So, what had happened to cause her to face such a calamitous situation for the second time in just over three months? It was a matter of life or death again and the simple answer was that she had offended well-connected men, who held the power of life or death over her.

Jennet Balderston's marriage to William Henry Preston is recorded in Gisburn parish register on May 10th, 1587. (Lumby). Being one of the "common folk" it is likely that Jennet was around eighteen years of age on her wedding day and that her husband was around six years her senior. At that time the village of Gisburn was in the county of Yorkshire, lying seven miles to the north of Pendle Hill in Lancashire. Consequently, both her trials took place in York.

The Listers, a prominent local family, lived at Westby Hall. The precise nature of Jennet's relationship with the Lister family is unclear, but the fact that she had one is without doubt. Perhaps she was a serving woman in some capacity. That she was initially held in some regard by the family is hinted at in the main source of information that we have about her, a pamphlet called *The Arraignement and Triall of Jennet Preston* by the clerk of the court, Thomas Potts.

Published in November 2013, Potts' pamphlet alludes to a good, if unequal, relationship between Jennet and Thomas Lister Junior at first, "even in the beginning of his greatest favours extended to her". He later mentions that she once had "so great mercie extended to her". However, things soon turned sour because she began "to worke this mischief, according to the course of all Witches". Potts, among many other more damning insults, refers to "her execrable Ingratitude" towards the Thomas Lister junior. What could have gone so badly wrong that Jennet was accused of causing death by witchcraft for a second time, by the same man? And why was Thomas Lister junior so desperate to destroy her?

Having been unable to make the allegation of killing Dodgson's son stick, this time Thomas Lister junior went even further back in time, accusing her of killing his own father, Thomas Lister senior, five and half years previously in February 1607. The charge that he brought against her was that,

> 'shee felloniously had practised, used, and exercised diverse wicked and devillish Arts, called Witchcrafts, Inchauntments, Charmes and Sorceries in and upon one Thomas Lister of Westby in Craven, in the Countie of York Esquire, and by force of the same Witchcraft fellonioiusly the said Lister had killed'.

Thomas junior must have known that 'there was no better means to deal with one's enemy than by an allegation of witchcraft'. However, he wasn't taking any chances this second time and so he enlisted all the help that he could get. His uncle Leonard Lister was involved in bringing the prosecution and none other than his father-in-law was the prosecutor in the case.

In February 1607, Thomas Lister junior had married Jane Heyber, whose father Mr Heyber, was energetically pursuing Jennet judicially in the court room. As Potts admits, Heyber was 'one of his Majesties Justices of Peace in the same County having taken great paines in the proceedings against her; and being best instructed of many of the particular points of Evidence against her'.

Today this would be viewed as an obvious conflict of interest - the Crown prosecutor was the uncle of the accuser. Nevertheless, this kind of legal inconsistency would have been seen as a petty quibble in an age when defendants were not allowed defence council, were not allowed to know the evidence against them before the proceedings began or who the witnesses against them were. If you found yourself in court in early modern England, you were not allowed to bring witnesses yourself and had practically no chance of preparing a defence. Although Potts states that Jennet was 'admitted' to her 'lawful challenge' against the charges, the system had hobbled her from preparing a defence. There is no record of her having spoken one word at her trial and any deposition that she may have made prior to it is not recorded. She performs no action in the court room, except be present.

While the judicial system was rigged against the defendant, the burden of proof needed to be found guilty of witchcraft was laughable. In actual fact the burden of proof was zero. Even the biased Potts admits that bar was extremely low, 'And against these people you may not expect such direct evidence, since all their workes are the workes of darknesse, no witnesses are present to accuse them, therefore I pray God direct your consciences'. Because witchcraft was supernatural, how could supernatural evidence be presented in court? Verbal testimony and hearsay were enough to get you killed. The odds stacked against Jennet were extremely high. And this second time she wouldn't survive.

Nevertheless, the allegation of killing Dodgon's son had failed to convict Jennet, so Thomas Lister junior searched his mind for other ways to get rid of her. According to Lumby in 'The Lancashire Witch Craze', 'Lister wished to appear disinterested while destroying Jennet.' But that hadn't worked and although reluctant to use the death of his father in order to avoid scandal, this time Jennet wasn't going to get away, even if it meant a personal sacrifice for Lister to his family's reputation.

Events surrounding his father's death five years previously were embarrassing and painful for him to remember. He was concerned about the reputation and standing of his family's name and didn't want details of his father's life dragged through the mud. However, it must have dawned on him that there were details of his father's death that could be manipulated and twisted to make it look like Jennet had killed him through *malefacia*, that is witchcraft intended to cause harm to animals or humans.

While several witnesses were brought to testify against her, including Thomas Lister junior himself, the only one who is named in Pott's pamphlet is Anne Robinson. She claimed that when Lister senior was on his death bed 'lying in great extremity' he had 'cried out unto them that stood about him; that Jennet Preston was in the house'. According to Robinson, Lister senior had told them to 'looke where shee is, take hold of her.' Becoming increasingly anxious, he shouted out 'for Gods sake shut the doores, and take her, she cannot escape away. Looke about for her, and lay hold of her, for shee is in the house'. Robinson concluded that Thomas Lister senior, on his deathbed, was crying out for Jennet to all and sundry, 'so cryed very often in his great paines to them that came to visit him during sicknesse.'

Anne Robinson's hearsay was evidence of Jennet's *malefacia*. The suggestion was that Jennet had caused his sickness by bewitchment. It was also the belief at the time that if a dying person named their murderer on their deathbed, that was evidence of murder. As Malcolm Gaskill has stated, 'Crucially the last words of any person *in extremis* had strong evidentiary status in law on the assumption that those about to be judged by God were unlikely to lie'. (Gaskill, 1998)

Both Anne Robinson and Thomas Lister junior concurred on the next piece of damning evidence, stating that also when Lister senior was on his death bed, 'he cryed out in great extremitie; Jennet Preston lyes heavie upon me, Prestons wife lyes heavie upon me; helpe me, helpe me:' and that he died 'crying out against her'. This would have been seen as a sign that he had a 'night mare' caused by witchcraft and it was another nail in Jennet's coffin.

But why would Anne Robinson testify against Jennet? They may have had equal status at one time in the Lister household, both serving-women. They may even have been friends at one point. Was there some enmity between Anne and Jennet? Was Anne jealous of how highly regarded Jennet had been in by the Lister family? Thomas Lister junior testified to the exact same evidence. It is likely that he persuaded Anne to concur with him and back his testimony up. Anne could have easily been persuaded by the most powerful and wealthy man in Gisburn. Maybe he had offered her a promotion to head housekeeper of Wesby Hall? Interestingly, according to Lumby, one Anne Robinson was named in Lister's will as receiving some property. Was this payment for testifying against Jennet and so helping him to secure her conviction?

Evidence from witnesses was mounting up against Jennet. Nevertheless, Thomas junior was taking no chances at this second trial. He threw in a few more allegations for good measure, claiming that Jennet had not merely killed his father, but she also damaged his property and his livestock as he had 'received great losse in his goods and cattell by her meanes'. *Malefacia* also applied to animals and property. Although Lister was evidently desperate to destroy Jennet, new laws made it even easier for him. James 1's new Witchcraft Act of 1604 made intent to kill by witchcraft a capital offence. Lister didn't even need to prove that Jennet had killed his father, merely considered it. Jennet was done for and the fear that she must have experienced must have been unimaginable.

Aside from these anciliary charges, the prosecution focused on the allegation that Jennet had killed Thomas Lister senior and produced a third piece of even more damning evidence against her. Anne and Thomas junior concurred that the corpse of Thomas Lister senior had bled in Jennet's presence. Potts records that she was taken to 'Mr Lister after hee was dead and laid out to be wound up in his sheet'. When she was 'comming to touch the dead corpse, it bled fresh bloud presently, in the presence of all that were there present.' Imagine the gasps of shock and horror in the courtroom at this sensational piece of evidence. The judges would bang their gavels insistently, trying to wrestle control of the proceedings. The implication was serious: Jennet had failed a trial by ordeal.

Gaskill describes trial by ordeal as a 'controlled miracle' between God and human beings. The accused was set a test or trial and if they passed the test, God had intervened, and they were innocent. If they failed, it was God's way of showing that they were guilty. A famous trial by ordeal often associated with witchcraft was swimming. The accused witch was immersed in water, such as a river. If she floated it was a sign God had decided that the water had refused to receive her and she had shaken off the sacred water of baptism. Therefore, she was a witch. If she drowned, she was not a witch. Either way it was a lose lose situation.

Another trial by ordeal and a widely held belief in early modern England was that a corpse would bleed in the presence or at the touch of the murderer. As a consequence, this became one of several ways of testing whether someone was guilty of a crime. The idea had been disseminated by none other than King James I of England and VI of Scotland, who advocated this method of detecting criminals in his 1597 book on witchcraft, 'Daemonologie'. In it King James I wrote,

"For as in a secret murther, if the deade carcasse be at any time thereafter handled by the murtherer, it wil gush out of bloud, as if the blud were crying to heaven for revenge of the murtherer, God having appoynted that secret super-naturall singe, for tryall of that secrete unnaturall crime..."

To the twelve 'gentlemen of the Jurie of life and death', if Thomas Lister senior's body bled in Jennet's presence, then she was his murderer. Potts describes it as 'the wonderfull signes and tokens of God, to satisfie the Jurie to finde her guiltie of this bloudie murther...' Jennet's case was not going well to say the least. Potts admits that this allegation hardly ever failed to convict someone. The presentation of this evidence, 'hath ever beene held a great argument to induce a Jurie to hold him guiltie that shall be accused of Murther, and hath seldome, or never, fayled in the Tryall'.

Thomas Lister junior had hit upon gold with this one and Jennet must have shrunk in horror on hearing this testimony. Did any of her friends or family shout out that it wasn't true? Today we know that corpses don't bleed in the presence of other people and so we know that this was a fabrication designed to frame Jennet and send her to her death. But could there be a grain of truth in the allegations that gave Thomas Lister junior the framework with which to accuse Jennet? Was it possible that there was a much simpler, more innocent explanation for all these allegations? Were events, situations, comments and remarks being twisted and altered by the accusers to fit their own nefarious objectives?

Lumby suggests that there was a more rational, yet sinister reason why Thomas Lister junior wanted Jennet Preston dead: that she had been having an affair with his father. So, when Lister senior cried out for Jennet on his deathbed, he wasn't crying out to accuse her, but for her to come to comfort him because they were lovers. Lumby's theory is plausible because Thomas Lister senior and Jennet were about the same age.

The parish registers from Gisburn tell us that Thomas Lister died in Bracewell, west of Gisburn on 8 February 1607. He fell ill at the marriage of his son, Thomas, to Jane Heyber in Bracewell earlier that month. In the midst of the wedding, tragedy struck. A few days after his son's wedding, Thomas Lister senior became seriously ill and died. His unexpected death would have been traumatic for the sixteen-year-old Thomas Lister junior, who was practically a child on his wedding day.

What if Thomas Lister junior resented Jennet because she had humiliated the family? Instead of crying out for Thomas' mother, Jane, on his deathbed, his father had called out for a serving woman who he had been conducting a long-standing extra-marital affair with? Perhaps Thomas Lister junior was not only grieving and humiliated, he was furious that the last name on his father's dying lips was a woman who he saw as a replacing him and his mother in his father's affections. Perhaps there were also more practical considerations. Thomas Lister junior would not wish Jennet to inherit any of her lover's estate.

After the death of Thomas senior, Jennet no longer had his protection and was consequently extremely vulnerable. Perhaps Jennet's and Lister's relationship was an open secret and Jennet was used to having access to Lister's house and wanting for nothing. After his death she might have continued to expect some charity. However, the resentment of Thomas' mother and her son gradually led to the door being closed against her. When his mother died a year later, this only enraged Thomas junior more, along with his uncle Leonard. According to Lumby, knowing of his father's affection for Jennet, Lister junior was filled with guilt at his failure to provide for her. In order to assuage his guilt, he accused her of witchcraft, so he wasn't reminded of his failure to provide for her any more.

We will never know for sure Thomas Lister junior's motivation for his persecution of Jennet, yet there were others at the time who thought that he was carrying out a 'malicious prosecution'. The author of the 1613 pamphlet, Thomas Potts, admits as much in his introduction. Reading between the lines, Jennet's husband, William and her friends and relations must have begun to publicly question the guilty verdict. Potts accuses them of devising 'so scandalous a slander out of the malice of your hearts, as that shee was maliciously prosecuted by Master Lister and others; Her life unjustly taken away by practise.'

It has also been suggested that Potts was commissioned by the Lister family to write the pamphlet in order to limit the damage to the family's reputation that her execution had caused. It seems that the Lister family was afraid that Jennet's friends' and family's refusal to accept the verdict might convince others that Jennet had been judicially murdered, so they commissioned Pott's to write a 'short discourse' in order to 'oppose your idle conceipts able to seduce others'. Potts acknowledges that William Preston and associates had been trying 'to cleare her', although he argues that she was 'justly condemned and executed for her offence'.

Potts is by no means an unbiased chronicler of the arraignment and trial of Jennet Preston. As a clerk of the court, he was ambitious and used his report to curry favour with the judges who had the power to promote him. It can be argued that his pamphlet was not just designed to justify the decision to execute her, but to blacken her name even further after her death in order to defend the judges who were facing a backlash from her friends and family.

Potts is hardly subtle in his attempt to further smear Jennet. He uses a variety insults to describe her from 'dangerous and malicious' to 'wicked and bloud-thirstie Witch' and refers to her 'Devillish and wicked practices'. It is quite shocking to the modern ear when he writes of the dead woman that she was 'unfit to live'. He disparages her even further when he states that he can 'afford her no better place than in the end of this Booke'. He insinuates that she was of so little value that her story only merited being tacked onto the end of the pamphlet about miscarriage of justice that was the trial of the Lancashire witches of Pendle Hill.

One cannot imagine the suffering of her husband who had stood by her through two trials, was campaigning to clear her name and was grieving at the judicial murder of his wife of nearly three decades. The slanderous smears against his wife, hurriedly published in a best-selling, sensationalist pamphlet, can have done nothing but add to his torment and pain. In print Thomas Potts addresses William Preston directly with abject scorn,

> 'You that were husband to this Jennet Preston; her friends and kinsfolkes, who have not beene sparing to devise so scandalous a slander out of the malice of your hearts…'

The irony of Potts accusing the Preston family of slander and malice should not be lost on anyone. It is easy to imagine that William Preston must have been going out of his mind with grief and anger. And what if Jennet had been having an affair with Thomas Lister senior? It is a plausible possibility. Lister senior and Jennet were approximately the same age, about thirty-eight at the time of Lister's death and their families had a history together. A forebear of the Listers, another Thomas Lister who died in 1542 made bequests that favoured Jennet's family. His will reads: 'Nicholas Balderston 40/-' and to 'Agnes Balderston I guye strike', suggesting that the families had been firm friends for generations. Thomas Lister senior and Jennet Preston grew up in Gisburn together and their families were connected. If they had been having an affair, it can only be concluded that William Preston must have loved Jennet no matter what.

If William Preston loved Jennet so much that he was prepared to stand by her for nearly thirty years, through two trials and despite the fact that she was having a long-standing affair with the local squire, what was it that made Thomas Lister junior hate her so much that he was prepared to put her through two trials that would ultimately lead to her death? What had Jennet done to cause him to feel so much antipathy and animosity towards her that he wanted her dead? Potts does not mention any motivation on the part of Jennet as to why she purportedly turned against the Listers and likewise there is no motivation as to why Lister maliciously prosecuted Jennet. We can only speculate.

Phillip C. Almond in his book "The Lancashire Witches: A Chronicle of Sorcery and Death on Pendle Hill" argues that it was because Jennet 'was a local cunning woman…Thomas Lister junior had had an unusually bad run of misfortunes. His cattle had mysteriously been dying. He had heard that the child of Dodgson had died unexpectedly, and rumours of witches in Pendle were rife. He looked back at his own recent history. His mother had died at a young age, and his father of a mystery illness within days of his own wedding. With such a series of personal misfortunes, at home and abroad, present and past, it would not be surprising for him to suspect that he, and his family, were the victims of witchcraft. He therefore looked to the local witch as the perpetrator'.

Almond argues that in the feverish climate of witchcraft investigations and allegations taking place in Yorkshire and Lancashire at the time, Thomas Lister junior was swept up in the belief that Jennet had really done all the things that he had accused her of. This is far too simplistic a reading of events, pointing to Lister's innocent culpability - he was just a victim of the superstitious belief in witchcraft that was taking hold in his society and culture of the day. His monumental efforts in bringing her to court twice, of arranging several witnesses, testifying himself, asking his father-in-law to be the prosecutor cannot be explained away with the argument that she was the local a cunning woman and he must rid his village of this scourge. His energetic and determined involvement in the prosecution suggests that he was being driven by something other than what he perceived as justice in the light of contemporary thought patterns about witchcraft. Nevertheless, Almond could be right in one instance. Maybe there was some truth to the suggestion that Jennet was a cunning woman and as such, maybe he was afraid of her.

We know for a fact that Jennet Preston was an associate of the Device family of the Pendle Hill witch trials fame and her story became fatefully and inextricably intertwined with theirs. Four days after she was acquitted of the murder by witchcraft of Dodgon's son at her first trial in April 1612, she rode her pony the seven miles or so to Pendle Forest and met with around twenty others at what has now come to be known as the notorious Good Friday meeting at Malkin Tower.

By 10th April 1612, the matriarch of Malkin Tower, the eighty-year-old blind and lame Demdike (Elizabeth Southwern) was in custody at Lancaster gaol, along with her granddaughter, Alizon Device. Also incarcerated and awaiting trial was the head of the other rival cunning family in the area, eighty-year-old Chattox (Anne Whittle) and her daughter Anne Redfearne.

Jennet's presence at this meeting was used in evidence against her at her second trial. Potts records that she 'went to the great Assembly of the Witches at Malking Tower upon Good Friday last: to pray aid and help for the murder of Master Lister, in respect he had prosecuted against her ...' To the prosecuting magistrate, Roger Nowell, Jennet had attended a witches' sabbat and was part of a coven of witches operating in the Pendle Forest area.

When Nowell interrogated James Device, Demdike's grandson, James practically signed Jennet's death warrant when he told the justice of the peace that Jennet had been present at the meeting to ask for 'aide for the murther of M. Thomas Lister'. James' deposition to Roger Nowell was read out at Jennet's trial and in it he admitted that he was not able to identify Jennet by name at the time. On Roger Nowell's instigation, the constable of Pendle Forest took him to Gishurn to identify Jennet. James' deposition reads:

'this Examinate hath beene brought to the wife of one Preston in Gisburne Parish aforesaid by Henry Hargreives of Gold-shey to see whether she was the woman that came amongst the said Witches, on the said last Good-Friday, to crave aide and assistance for the killing of said Master Lister: and having had full view of her; hee this Examinate confesseth, That she was the selfe-same woman which came amongst said witches of the said last Good-Friday, for their aide for the killing of the said Master Lister; and that brought the Spirit with her, in the shape of a White Foale, as aforesaid'.

There were approximately twenty people present at the Malkin Tower meeting and James didn't know the names of all of them. Ambitious magistrate, Roger Nowell, went after the ones who he was able to identify and find. Jennet was one of the unfortunate ones who Nowell was able to identify. Had Gisburn been in Lancashire and not Yorkshire, Jennet would have stood at the prisoner's bar with all those accused of witchcraft in the Pendle witchcraft trial on 20th August 1612. Instead because of her address, she fell under the jurisdiction of the York Assize courts. Still Roger Nowell wasn't going to let this minor detail prevent him from securing another conviction and proving his thoroughness in wiping out witchcraft in Lancashire. When Nowell wrote up James's Device's evidence, he made sure that not only Thomas Lister junior was mentioned repeatedly as the object of Jennet's nefarious plot to kill him, he also dropped in that Thomas Lister junior's uncle, Leonard, was also the object of Jennet's murderous plotting. Nowell wrote:

> 'then al the said Witches gave their consents to joyne altogether to hancke [put a spell on] Master Leonard Lister, when he should come to dwell at Sowgill, and so put him to death'.

Therefore, according to James' deposition, written up by Roger Nowell, Jennet had gone to the meeting to at Malkin Tower to enlist the support of her fellow witches to kill Thomas Lister junior and Leonard Lister. It is incredible that James Device could not remember Jennet's name but could remember the names of her intended victims. Despite the fact that several sources state that James was a teenager with special needs, it is simply too convenient that Jennet had allegedly plotted to kill both Lister men. James made his statement on 5th May and word would have reached the Listers from Nowell that they were on Jennet's supposed 'hit list'.

Nowell was determined to secure as many convictions as he could. He wrote Leonard Lister's name into the deposition, knowing that he was a magistrate and had the power to bring Jennet to trial. (Thomas Lister junior later became a magistrate, but was too young at the time of Jennet's trial). Roger Nowell was providing the impetus to the Lister family to bring charges against Jennet because she lived slightly out of his jurisdiction. He would have to rely on them to secure the conviction for him. It could do no harm to make them think that they were in danger from a coven of witches. Nowell was behind the scenes, writing depositions to suit his own needs, manipulating witnesses and evidence in his obsession with stamping out witchcraft in the north and making himself a hero before James 1, who had an intense personal interest in witchcraft.

About sixty years old in 1612, Roger Nowell had succeeded his father to an estate in Read, under nine miles from Pendle Hill. He came from a Protestant family and his uncle, Alexander Nowell, was high up in the church and personally assisted Elizabeth 1 in her enquiries into the religious beliefs of the nation. In 1570 Pope Pius V had excommunicated Elizabeth from the Catholic church and stated that her subjects were no longer bound to obey her. In return Elizabeth banned Catholicism from the country. However, that was easier said than done in the north of England where old habits die hard. From the depositions of the Device and Chattox families it is clear that these cunning folks practised a kind of hybrid religion that mixed outlawed Catholic liturgy with image magic and spells. Nowell got the grandmother, Chattox, to tell him one of her spells which read:

'Three Biters has thou bitten,
The Hart, ill Eye, ill Tonge:
Three bitter shall by thy Boote,
Father, Sonne and Holy Ghost
a Gods name.
Five Pater Nosters, five Avies
and Creede,
In worship of five wounds
of our Lord'

Even though the Dissolution of the Monasteries had begun seventy-six years previously, it had been impossible to stamp out Catholicism in Lancashire and Yorkshire, not only amongst the elites, but the common folk as well. Roger Nowell's persecution of the witches of Pendle was a judicial prosecution to wipe out religious beliefs that he disagreed with. Nowell was a dangerous witch-hunter, more so than the infamous and renegade Matthew Hopkins, because he held legitimate authority and power. Nowell was ambitious and was trying to make a name for himself in judicial circles by proving his Protestant piety by ruthlessly and relentlessly persecuting those who practised the old religion of witchcraft.

Could it be that Jennet's motives in attending the Malkin Tower gathering were more innocent than those recorded by Potts? Had she gone to show support and solidarity with the Device family because some of their number had been accused of witchcraft and she had just been acquitted of witchcraft? Was she feeling vulnerable after her trial and needed some support from people who were of her kind - cunning folk?

The 'cunning' or 'wise' folk were practitioners of beneficent magic. They used herbal and magical medicine to heal the sick and the bewitched, find buried treasure, identify thieves, tell fortunes, induce love, and undo malevolent magic. If among the Protestant elite, the boundary between cunning folk and witches, white and black magic was blurred in principle, it was blurred in practice among the middling and lower classes. According to Almond, 'cunning folk could cross the boundary between good and evil, and when they did so, their powers were to be feared'.

When interrogated by the justice of the peace, Roger Nowell, both Chattox and Demdike admitted to being able to use cunning powers. Demdike's family scratched a living in the middle of Pendle Forest in a ramshackle cottage called Malkin Tower. They resorted to begging or stealing to get by. What was Jennet doing associating with people like this? Later they would be accused of gathering to plot to blow up Lancaster Castle in a daring heist to free the prisoners in what was later likened to the equivalent of the Gunpowder Plot. Jennet's presence at this meeting made sure that at her second trial there would be no acquittal. This time Thomas Lister junior would be successful, and she would lose her life.

It was the evidence of James Device, Demdike's wayward grandson that placed Jennet Preston in Malkin Tower on the fateful date of the fateful meeting. Having been apprehended by the ambitious Roger Nowell, James Device helped Nowell to piece together the guest list at the meeting and the reason for the gathering. At first James said the meeting was to initiate his sister Alizon into cunning practice. This might have been the initial purpose of the Good Friday meeting, but Alizon was now in gaol, so whatever had been planned could not take place. James then related that there had been talk of blowing up Lancaster Gaol to free the prisoners. While this must have been a flight of fancy on the part of those there, nevertheless it was taken deadly seriously by the authorities. Finally, he said that a woman from Gisburn had been there for 'the killing of Master Listby of Westby'.

There is one fact that we can be sure of: Jennet was present at the Malkin Tower meeting. However, from the statements of both Elizabeth Device the owner of the cottage and her son, James, no satanic rituals or dancing with the devil took place, which must have been disappointing to Roger Nowell. The guests gathered at 12pm and ate some meat including a lamb roasted on a spit that James had stolen for the occasion. So, what was Jennet doing there four days after being acquitted of the murder of Dodgson's child? Probably she was traumatised. James stated that she wanted Thomas Lister junior killed because he 'bore malice towards her'. She probably sensed that although she had been freed, she was in danger. Perhaps she was understandably angry at having been locked up in York Castle and then put on trial for a murder that she didn't commit. Maybe she was protesting loudly at the injustice of it all and made some flippant remarks about wanting the Listers dead. Why not? After all they clearly wanted her dead. On the other hand, maybe she had gone there out of charity to the Device family. Two members of their family, Old Demdike and Alizon, were languishing in the witches' well dungeon at Lancaster Castle. Jennet had just been through a trial for witchcraft herself. Maybe she could help them to understand what was about to happen to Elizabeth Device's mother and daughter. Could Jennet give them any information to help them?

There was a lot of wild talk that day. James reported that there had been conversation about blowing up Lancaster gaol in order to free the prisoners. It was highly unlikely that they would have the means or the wherewithal to carry out this suggestion. It was hardly a conspiracy on the scale of the Gunpowder Plot, but in these nervous times any mention of an assault on the Crown would help to justify Roger Nowell's ambitious prosecution of the cunning folk of Pendle.

The fact that Jennet was an associate of the Device family suggests that she may have had some knowledge of cunning crafts and might have been regarded as a wise woman herself in Gisburn. Perhaps Thomas Lister junior did fear her, as well as hate and resent her. These negative emotions towards her were enough to impel him to try to annihilate her twice. Roger Nowell had seen to it that the second time, Thomas would have the support of his more powerful uncle, Leonard Lister. Along with Mr Heyber, Thomas' father-in-law as prosecutor, Jennet was well and truly judicially corralled.

The ability of Roger Nowell and the other prosecutors to twist innocent details into devilish behaviour can be seen in James Device's statement about Jennet and the other guests' mode of transport to the Malkin Tower meeting.

They 'were gotten on horse-backe like unto Foales, some of one colour, some of another, and Preston's wife was the last; and when she got on horse-backe, they all presently vanished out of this Examinants sight'. The implication is clear. After having innocently arrived by pony, she didn't just disappear from James' sight, but she 'vanished', a supernatural mode of transport. From the depositions that Nowell took, it is clear that he used any means necessary to get the witnesses to tell him what he wanted to hear from encouraging to cajoling to threatening. He would have used leading questions and twisted and filtered what they said to suit his own obsessive ends. Although torture was not permissible as evidence in English courts, several sources suggest that he might have had Chattox tortured. He was absolutely fascinated by the tedious fall outs between the impoverished neighbours of Pendle Forest, who scratched a living from begging and magic. He was determined to exterminate their way of life from amongst his midst and he nearly succeeded.

In those days trials were swift affairs. Crown pleas 'were conducted at top speed, a full day's business beginning, even in winter, at seven o'clock in the morning and continuing, by candlelight, as late as eleven at night'. According to Cockburn, 'trials were short and sharp, taking as little as fifteen to twenty minutes for those who pleaded not guilty'.

Jennet was fortunate in one respect for the "Gentlemen of the Jurie of Life and Death had spent the most part of the day, in consideration of the evidence against her, they returned into the Court and delivered their Verdict of Life and Death'. To spend so long deliberating her fate, suggests that they were not completely convinced by the evidence. Nevertheless, she was found guilty of the murder of Thomas Lister senior by witchcraft.

It is not known if she was paraded through the streets of York in a cart and taken to the Knavesmire, the place of execution outside the city walls. The exact date of her execution is not known, it may have even been the very same day as her conviction. Although Potts criticises her for going to the gallows, 'impenitent and void of all feare and grace', his perpetual criticism hints that she was able to maintain dignity in front of a crowd of witnesses both hostile and loving at the same time.

In Jennet's day, the York authorities were still using the long drop, as opposed to the short drop that broke the victim's neck more quickly, shortening the time it took to die. Jennet was offered no respite and would have taken approximately fifteen minutes to die. One cannot imagine the emotions she was feeling or the thoughts going through her head, nor those of her husband, witness to the macabre spectacle. Although Thomas Potts was commissioned to write his pamphlet to refute allegations of corruption against the authorities and the Lister family, it is this very pamphlet that today provides us with the incontrovertible evidence that she was the victim of a murderous judicial conspiracy carried out by men in power to fulfil their own ambitions and desires for revenge. If Jennet was guilty of anything, it was of having an affair with a married man. However, this is not a crime punishable by death. Ironically, Potts' pamphlet was designed to put a stop to the doubts about the veracity of the crimes that she was accused of. Instead, it has come down to us four hundred years later as proof that, along with the estimated 500 people executed for practising witchcraft, she was none other than a victim of a gross miscarriage of justice and a victim of judicial murder. Hopefully, all these years later, her soul is finally at peace.

CHAPTER SEVEN

Mary Tuke and Mary Anne Craven

The Queens of Confectionary

IN 1725 MARY Tuke was a thirty-year-old single woman when she took the decision to open her own grocery shop in Walmgate, in the heart of the city of York. Her father, William, had passed away when she was nine years old and her mother, Rebecca, had died two years earlier. She was now the head of the family. Of the seven children that William and Rebecca had produced, three had died in infancy. Consequently, it is likely that Mary had three younger siblings to look after, one of whom was named Samuel. In a bold move, she decided to set up a grocer's shop, alongside a diverse range of traders such as butchers, bakers, brewers, coopers, tailors, shoemaker, comb makers and pipe makers. Between the medieval gables and the incipient terraces of Georgian townhouses, Mary began to trade. Specialising in tea, coffee and cocoa, her shop would have carried the everyday commodities of a grocer's stock in trade. While Walmgate was never regarded as one of the smarter streets in town, when Tuke's opened it was respectable enough. However, the street would unfortunately later degenerate into a slum that was eventually cleared by the Corporation.

In 1725, having set up shop on Walmgate in what is likely to have been a medieval gabled house, Mary would have been neighbours with the fourteenth-century timber-framed Bowes Morrell House. The churches of St Margaret's and St Deny's, were the only remaining two in the Walmgate area of what had originally been six. She must have been aware of the dubious reputation of the unscrupulous tradesmen in neighbouring Fossgate, also known as Trickster's Lane. On Walmgate, surrounded by innkeepers, rag merchants, woollen warehouses, and other retailers typical of the period, Mary Tuke was exceptional in that she was the sole proprietress of her business.

Had Mary been a married woman, her choices would have been much more limited. It was not until 1882 that married women were allowed to keep the property that they owned and not have to forfeit it to their husbands upon marriage. During Mary's lifetime English law labelled the wife 'feme covert', or hidden woman, emphasizing her subordination to her husband. The married woman was put under the 'protection and influence of her husband, her baron, or lord'. Legally, upon marriage, the husband and wife became one person and the property of the wife was surrendered to him. Her own legal identity ceased to exist. Any personal property acquired by the wife during the marriage, unless specified that it was for her own separate use, went automatically to her husband. If a woman writer had copyright before marriage, the copyright would pass to the husband after marriage. Furthermore, a married woman was unable to draft a will or dispose of any property without her husband's consent.

Women were often limited in what they could inherit. Males were more likely to receive real property (land), while females with brothers were sometimes limited to inheriting personal property, which included clothing, jewellery, household furniture, food, and all moveable goods. In an instance when no will was found, the English law of primogeniture automatically gave the eldest son the right to all real property, and the daughter only inherited real property in the absence of a male heir.

In contrast to wives, women who never married or who were widowed maintained control over their property and inheritance. An unmarried adult female was considered to be a "feme sole". Once married, the only way that women could reclaim their property was through widowhood. The dissolution of a marriage, whether initiated by the husband or wife, usually left the divorced females impoverished, as the law offered them no rights to marital property.

Therefore, it was a dangerous time for women to marry and we do not know whether these considerations impacted on Mary's decision not to marry at this time. Perhaps she was too busy or had not found anyone suitable. Or perhaps she did not wish to forfeit all that she had strived for to a potential husband. By marrying she would have gained a husband, but at what cost? No longer an independent woman, she would have to forfeit her work, her business, her financial and her physical independence.

Aside from the financial deficit that a woman would accrue upon marriage, there was another huge disincentive for women to marry - childbirth. In the eighteenth century the statistic for infant mortality was fifty percent. In other words, half of all the children under the age of one died. Childbirth was a highly dangerous process. Any myriad of complications and infections could take the mother's life both during and after the birth. One in ten women could expect to die in childbirth. On average a woman would become pregnant five or six times during her married life. Consequently, if ten percent of labours proved fatal, a woman had a 41 to 47 percent of dying during her reproductive life. Mary would have been aware of the dangers. Her father's first wife, Sarah Merry, had died in 1692, less than a month after the death of their second child. Their first child had died in 1690, aged just two days. Her own mother lost three of her seven children. Did Mary choose to remain single to preserve her life and her financial independence? This must have been a consideration for practical-minded women during these times.

When Mary launched her grocer's shop, she would not have been the sole female trader in a city dominated by men. However, female business activity was traditionally limited to three main areas of trade - clothing, food and drink. In the realm of clothes, women were engaged in dressmaking, millinery (hat-making), haberdashery, hosiery and linen drapery. In manufacture, there would have been women chandlers (candle-makers). In the food industry there were victuallers (people licensed to sell alcohol and other foodstuffs) and coffee house keepers tending to the growing fashion for men to meet in this type of premise. Women were effectively confined to entrepreneurial roles that equated to servicing the domestic sphere of life. Oftentimes they would use their own homes as their business premises. They may have even piled up their goods for sale in one of the rooms of their house, perhaps even the space where the family lived and slept. Plate-glass shop windows to attract customers did not become commonplace until the late nineteenth century. To entice customers into their shops, women may simply have had to rely on a few products in their domestic windows to indicate the nature of their shop.

While Mary chose not to marry, this did not mean that she was free from problems with men. Mary was continuously hampered in her path to building a thriving business by the male-dominated Merchant Adventurer's Company. In 1357 a number of important men came together to form a religious fraternity and to build the Merchant Adventurer's Hall. By 1430 most members were mercers (dealers in textiles), and alongside the fraternity they set up a trading association or guild. They used the Merchant Adventurer's Hall, Fossgate, to transact their business affairs, to meet socially, to look after the poor and to pray to God. Despite their charitable works, they kept a stranglehold on trade in the city. In 1581 Queen Elizabeth granted them a monopoly over most goods imported into the city. Membership was by inheritance or nomination only. To be able to trade in the City of York, merchants had to be both Freemen of the City and a Member of the Company. As a woman, Mary was not allowed to become a member. There was no way that she could obtain the necessary license to trade.

Nevertheless, cannily, Mary used her inheritance to gain the status of Freeman by naming her father as a deceased member. The inscription on the Freeman's Roll of the City of York states, "Maria Tuke, spinster Fil Willelmi Tuke, blacksmith". However, unfortunately, this was not enough alone to allow Mary to trade. She still failed to meet the company membership criteria and consequently ended up trading without the necessary license.

The Merchant Adventurers took Mary to court, whereupon she was ordered to dispose of the goods in her shop in a mere six months and cease trading. Although she must have been devastated at the loss of everything that she had worked for, as well as her potential future livelihood, Mary would not acquiese to the order. Defiantly, she continued to trade while battling the company's attempts to put her out of business. It is difficult to imagine the stress and anxiety that Mary must have undergone in trying to keep her business afloat, against the collective might of the Merchant Adventurer's Company. Nevertheless, although she was unmarried, Mary was not entirely alone and this might have given her the strength and fortitude to continue her fight for survival.

Mary was by religion a Quaker, a member of the Society of Friends, and the movement had a long-standing history in the York. The founder of the Society of Friends, George Fox, had visited York in 1651. After preaching in the Minster, he was unceremoniously thrown down the steps outside. While religious intolerance was still rife during Mary's lifetime, one of the tenets of Quakerism could have helped her with her own struggles. The movement advocated equality between the genders, teaching that all were children of God and members of a universal fellowship. This was a radical notion in the Georgian era.

By 1650 the Quaker, Elizabeth Hooton, became the first woman to begin preaching in public. Within the society, women writing and speaking on a par with men had been the practice for a number of years and by 1666 Margaret Fell defended it in *Women's Speaking Justified, Proved and Allowed by the Scriptures*. For the Quakers, a woman's independence within the family and community was accepted and completely unrelated to her marital status. Deference to a husband was not necessary, as a wife was allowed to share equally in 'all the business of society.' As a member of this more open-minded community, perhaps Mary received the moral support that she needed to continue to battle against the unfair, restrictive practices of the Merchant Adventurers.

A further boon of being a member of the Quaker community was the positive reputation as trustworthy businesspeople that they were building for themselves. In parallel with their quest for religious and social justice, they began to be viewed as honest and reliable. Bartering was the norm in this day and age, but the Quakers were among the first to set a fixed price for their goods. It was a matter of conscience to the Quakers that no foodstuff should ever be adulterated. It was not unheard of for unscrupulous manufacturers to add poisonous red lead as colouring to sweets. Sometimes brick dust and wax were mixed into chocolate. Discerning customers might have noticed that sand had been added to coffee or that starch powder was added to cream. Consequently, customers appreciated the Quakers' ethical approach to business, which in turn gave them a competitive edge over their rivals.

It is within this context then that Mary continued to fight against the decrees of the powerful Merchant Adventurers, refusing to be put out of business for the mere fact of being a woman. For almost five long years Mary was fined and threatened with imprisonment. Finally, in the face of Mary's remarkable tenacity, the Merchant Adventurers relented. She was allowed to continue to trade on the condition that she pay an annual fine of 10 shillings. In 1730 one shilling had the purchasing power of approximately £6.51, so her fine would have amounted to an annual payment of approximately £60.50, almost £7000 today. A further condition was that she buy all her merchandise locally. It is likely that Mary would have jumped at the offer. The relief that the long, traumatic battle was over must have been immense, despite the financial penalty.

Then in 1732 the Merchant Adventurers relented even further and granted her permission to trade for the rest of her life, after making a one-off payment of £10, approximately £1,161 today. What drove the Merchant Adventurers to change their minds? Had their consciences begun to prick them? Or were they becoming aware of the bad publicity that putting an honest woman out of business was generating? Perhaps they realised that they were fighting a losing battle and that their hobbling of the economy had to end. Fortunately, Mary was financially resilient enough to meet what must have seemed like a windfall tax upon her business. Fortunately, she worked hard enough to generate the funds to buy them off.

Not only did the company's strict adherence to its sexist, exclusionary rule hamper and impede Mary Tuke, it also stifled the economy of the whole city. While other northern towns like Leeds and Bradford were being swept up in the Industrial Revolution, York languished as an industrial backwater, a parochial market town, servicing its own basic needs. Only until the city fathers decided in the same century to make York a tourist and entertainment playground for the élite, was the economy given the oxygen it needed to breathe.

While Quakerism could have been a crutch for Mary, it could also have been another problem for her to deal with. She lived in an age of intense religious intolerance and persecution. Her own grandfather, William, was imprisoned on two occasions for his refusal to renounce his faith. Being detained in the Sheriff's Prison, a kidcote under the chapel that used to stand on old Ouse Bridge, must have tested his faith or made him even more determined to exercise his free will. While he survived imprisonment, his property was confiscated because of his religious beliefs. It is with this psychological heritage and lack of financial inheritance that Mary continued to fight for her rights.

Despite being strapped for cash due to the Merchant Adventurers' penalty clauses, Mary probably tried to improve the appearance of her shop. Gas-lighting was not patented until 1799, so a tallow candle would still have sputtered on her counter. However, she may have invested in some interior fittings to allow for the separation and storage of her products. Fortunately, by the time Mary had set up shop, the high import duties on cocoa beans had been reduced. Nevertheless, along with tea and coffee, these were luxury goods that all but the very rich would have been able to afford. Were some of Mary's customers the servants of the élite who were beginning to make York their playground, alongside the ordinary folk who would want more affordable grocery products?

By 1746, Mary was 51 years old. Her small grocery shop must have prospered as she was able to take on her nephew, William Tuke, as her apprentice. From her nephew's Apprentice Indenture, we also learn that by this time she had also married. William was indentured to 'Mary Frankland of York, grocer, 1746'. Unfortunately, however, by this time her husband Henry Frankland had died.

Although when women married, they automatically forfeited their property to their husband, Mary seems to have retained control of the business, even providing a living for Henry through her enterprise. It is thanks again to the fastidiousness of the Merchant Adventurers in their desire to control business in York that we know of his involvement in her company.

By 1735, the Mary and her husband were in trouble again. In the court session for 1st July, the Merchant Adventurers archives list Henry Frankland as 'following the trade of grocer without having served an apprenticeship in that business'. Fortunately, Mary's hard work and business acumen made it so that she had enough liquidity to be able to pay the Merchant Adventurers off once more. The couple were able to pay the sum required for his admission to the 'Freedom of the Fellowship', allowing him to become a fully fledged member, without him having to serve said apprenticeship. Ever the pragmatists, Mary and Henry must have accepted that it you couldn't beat the Merchant Adventurers, you had better join them.

However, by 1740 Henry had died leaving Mary a childless widow, aged forty-four and sole owner of Tuke's Grocers once again. With her apprentice and nephew, William, she moved her business premises to a more prominent location on the corner of Coppergate and Castlegate. Then Mary died in 1752 at the age of fifty-seven, leaving all her property to William Tuke.

After some initial hesitation, William decided to continue in the family business, which branched out from retailing into manufacture. The same year that William came into his inheritance, he became a Freeman Grocer and member of the monopolising Merchant Adventurers who had fought so hard to exclude his aunt from access to prosperity. Perhaps she would have been happy that he did not have to face the fines and legal challenges that she had been tormented by.

In 1785 William's son and Mary's great-nephew, Henry (1755-1814), abandoned his medical degree and joined his father in the family business. Together they took the enterprise to new heights. While William had been successful with 'Tuke's Superior Rock Cocoa', in unison they introduced "Tuke's British Cocoa Coffee", 'Tuke's Rich Cocoa', 'Tuke's Plain Chocolate' and 'Tuke's Milk Chocolate', the latter for mixing with milk to make a cocoa drink, the forerunner of hot chocolate.

Mary's nephew, William, was not merely a successful businessman, building on his aunt's legacy, but also a philanthropist. It was a combination of Quaker spiritual beliefs and personal experience that encouraged him and his son, Henry, to establish The Retreat in York, an asylum for the mentally ill where humane treatments for psychiatric disorders were pioneered.

In 1790 a Quaker woman from Leeds called Hannah Mills was admitted to York County Lunatic Asylum, suffering from 'melancholy'. One month later she was dead. Although several York Quakers had tried to visit her, no-one had been allowed access on the grounds that she was undergoing 'private treatment'. After a visit was finally allowed, it was reported that those receiving care were treated 'worse than animals'. William's grandson, Samuel Tuke, spearheaded a campaign to expose the terrible conditions of the York Asylum.

At the Retreat, William Tuke took charge of a project to do away with the debilitating purges, the painful blistering, the freezing cold baths and the chaining of patients to walls. Instead, he advocated a benevolent and comfortable environment in which patients were allowed time for reflection. In 1796 The Retreat opened with a therapeutic programme designed to restore self-esteem and self-control, with minimal use of restraint. Straightjackets were a last resort. Security measures were made more discreet with door locks encased in leather and bars on windows were incorporated into frames. Patients were encouraged to enjoy the pleasant gardens and an early form of occupational therapy was introduced. The values of the institution were personalised attention, kindness, moderation, order and trust. A religious component was included in the form of prayer. Although initially derided, by the time William's son Henry and grandson Samuel took over the running of the Retreat, it was eventually acknowledged as a model for the effective treatment of those suffering psychological disorders.

In turn Samuel's son, James Hack Tuke assisted in the management of the Retreat. His other son, Daniel Hack Tuke became a leading physician dedicated to the study of mental illness and in 1858 published, 'A Manual of Psychological Medicine'. Nevertheless, William Tuke didn't stop with the foundation of The Retreat, but also helped to found Ackworth School in Pontefract for Quaker boys and girls in 1779. In 1818 he proposed Bootham School and helped with founding the Trinity Lane Quaker Girls' School, the forerunner of the Mount School.

Meanwhile Mary's great-nephew Henry Tuke and his son, Samuel, continued to steer Mary Tuke's business until 1862 when they sold it to one of the godfathers of the chocolate industry, Henry Isaac Rowntree. After purchasing the cocoa division of Tuke & Co, Henry Isaac Rowntree rebranded 'Tuke's Superior Rock Cocoa' as 'Rowntree's Prize Medal Rock Cocoa' and Tuke and Co evolved into the Rowntree family business and their legacy. The Rowntrees and the Tukes were both Quakers, both families knew each other well. Did the Tukes' philanthropism inspire the Rowntrees?

And what of Mary Tuke? She has been called the 'mother of York's chocolate industry'. But she was much more than that. She was a woman who was put in extremis by the death of her loved ones, with no other option but to take control of the situation to fend for herself and her brother. She took a financial risk to become an independent trader and then had to battle for survival against a powerful guild of men whose restrictive practices are now the subject of company case history. As a woman she was the underdog and she battled and she fought and she succeeded, refusing to give up or be cowed, bullied or financially ruined. In the face of attempts to ruin her, not only did she succeed, she prospered. At the helm of her business as sole proprietor for twenty-one years, she was able to pass on to her nephew a business that enabled him and his son to undertake philanthropic work which changed modern perceptions of the treatment of mental ill health. In turn, the Tukes may have influenced the Rowntree family, whose legacy the people of York enjoy to this day in the parks they have left for public use, among many other bequests.

Undoubtedly, her Quaker ethics and the Quaker community she belonged to would have given her the support and strength to continue. Thomas Clarkson (1760-1846), a Quaker who was highly influential in the abolition of slavery, recognised the empowering effect that Quakerism had on the female character when he wrote around thirty years after Mary's death that it gave:

> 'a new cast of character. It produces in them, a considerable knowledge of human nature. It produces in them thought, and foresight, and judgment... It elevates in them a sense of their own dignity and importance...'

Perhaps Mary was able to draw on these same qualities in her fight to succeed. Practical in the face of the fines and taxes levied by the Merchant Adventurer's, she possessed a relentless spirit for survival in a hostile male-dominated world, leaving an entrepreneurial and philanthropic legacy that is still being built on to this day.

Mary Ann Craven

Fifty-eight years after the death of Mary Tuke, in 1810, Mary Ann Craven was born the daughter of Joseph Hick, a confectioner in York in partnership with Richard Kilner. In 1803 their partnership was dissolved, and Mary Ann's father continued to trade on his own at 47 Coney Street. Today Terry's and Rowntrees have become household names, but by 1850 a third confectionary business was to have a significant impact on the development of York. The Cravens manufactured quality sugar products and at one time were the world's largest boiled sweet manufacturer.

In 1851 Mary Ann Hick married Thomas Craven who had his own shop at 31 Pavement where he sold confectionary, teas and coffees. His business prospered so much that he was able to buy the premises at Pavement outright and take on a further site at 10 Castlegate. He had a workforce of sixty-three men and sixty boys. The family finances were boosted when Mary Ann's father died leaving his estate to be divided between his three children.

Then disaster struck and Mary Ann's husband died in 1862, leaving the thirty-three-year-old to manage the upbringing of three children and the running of two confectionary businesses. Understandably, her initial reaction was to sell both concerns. However, as the sale dragged on due to the negligence of her solicitor, Mary Ann continued to face financial burdens. To solve her financial woes, she took the decision to merge both business in an attempt to survive. She then began trading under the name of MA Craven and Son.

Reputed to be a lady of short stature, Mary Ann would sit on a highchair so that she could supervise production. Her factory was in Coppergate where the Jorvik Viking Centre stands today and was known as the Ebor Confectionary Works, also known as the French Almond Works, specialising in sugared almonds, pastiles, gums, mints, boiled sweets, toffees and nougat.

Dotted around the city were four shops stocking her confections. Her flagship shop on the Shambles was called Mary Ann Sweet Shop and proud of her manufacturing process, it included a confectionary museum on the first floor. Her business philosophy was that only the best was good enough. As a matter of conscience she would never allow any foodstuffs to be adulterated. In 1881 her son Thomas joined the business. When Mary Ann died in 1902 her family commissioned a beautiful stained-glass window in All Saints, Pavement, just across the road from where her factory had once been.

Like Mary Tuke, Mary Ann Craven was forced to pick up the reigns of a family business due to personal adversity. Not only did both women succeed in their own lifetimes but left a lasting legacy for their families to build on. The fame of York as the chocolate city has its origins in the manufacture of confectionary, with the businesses of both Terry and Rowntree originating in this field. The Rowntrees learnt from the Tukes and Joseph Terry Senior adapted his pharmaceutical knowledge to create sugared sweets and lozenges. Terry's later evolved into chocolatiers under the direction of Joseph Terry Junior. With the advent of the railway in York in 1839 and the use of the River Ouse for the importation of raw materials from overseas, York became home to Terry's and Rowntrees, the undisputed 'Kings of Chocolate'. It is a little-known fact that there were also two 'Queens of Confectionary'.

CHAPTER EIGHT

Elizabeth Montagu and Sarah Scott

Contrasting Lives

IN JUNE 2019 York Civic Trust unveiled a
blue plaque outside the Treasurer's House
dedicated to the 'founder member of
the Bluestocking movement, writer and
patron of the arts', Elizabeth Montagu.
Born in 1718 at Gray's Court, which was
once contiguous with the Treasurer's
House, Elizabeth was the daughter of
Matthew Robinson of Yorkshire and
Elizabeth Drake of Cambridge. Two
years later Elizabeth's sister, Sarah, was
born and baptised at Holy Trinity church,
Goodramgate, completing the family of
nine Robinson children.

The likeness between Elizabeth and
Sarah was such that Sarah was nicknamed
'the pea'. Known affectionately for her
boundless energy, Elizabeth was given
the moniker 'Fidget', while Sarah was dubbed 'Bridget' due to their resemblance.
Although the Robinson family was middle class and intellectual, the girls' parents
were somewhat aloof. Matthew Robinson enjoyed the pleasures of the city more
than the country and was sometimes to be found discussing important matters of
the day with Laurence Sterne, the celebrated writer and later relative by marriage,
in Sunton's coffee shop in Coney Street. Fortunately, for the sisters their step-
grandfather, the eminent Cambridge don, Conyers Middleton, took an interest
in them and they spent a lot of time with him and his wife Sarah Morris, the
girls' grandmother.

Elizabeth and Sarah's parents owned Gray's Court until they moved to Mount Morris in Kent in 1736. Growing up the sisters received a comparatively good education at home, learning Latin, French, Italian, as well as studying literature, while their six brothers were put through school. Both were avid fans of published letters and read the collections of the poet Alexander Pope and the writer Jonathon Swift. The girls were close and Elizabeth once complimented Sarah, believing her to be 'superior in certain respects, particularly intellectual and literary interests'.

Throughout their lives they corresponded with one another, as well as friends and acquaintances, although they did become estranged for a time. After Elizabeth's death, her heir and nephew, Matthew Montagu, published a collection of her letters, which help to convey a vivid picture of her personality. Unfortunately, Sarah instructed the executor of her will to destroy all her correspondence. While some of Sarah's letters survive, it is more difficult to piece together her equally as interesting, though less famous life.

In 'Companions Without Vows', Betty Rizzo states that the sisters were devoted to each other when growing up, but that it can't have been easy for Sarah, always in the shadow of her dazzling older sister. After her death, Matthew Montagu, Elizabeth's adopted son described her as a beauty who was:

'most admired in the peculiar animation and expression of her blue eyes, with high arched dark eyebrows, and in the contrast of her brilliant complexion with her dark brown hair'.

While staying with their grandparents in Cambridge, it is likely that Elizabeth Montagu made the acquaintance of the richest woman in Britain at the time, a relationship that was to radically change her life. The family seat of Lady Margaret Harley (1715-1785) was at Wimpole Hall, Cambridgeshire. Margaret grew up surrounded by the books, paintings and the sculpture that her ancestors had collected. Highly influenced by her sophisticated and refined surroundings, Lady Margaret was ambitious to become the owner of the greatest collection of antiquities and natural history in the country. After she married the Duke of Portland, she wanted her natural history collection to contain and describe every living thing. The jewel in the crown of her collection was the famous Portland Vase, a two-thousand-year-old, exquisite dark-blue glass Roman vase with delicate white cameo reliefs, purchased in 1784.

Growing up the sisters' mother was already an invalid. With the cost of putting six brothers through school, it is unlikely that the family had the money to launch the girls into society through a season in London. It is possible that Elizabeth decided to make her own arrangements. In the 1740s Elizabeth would spend months at Bulstrode, the Duchess' country seat, becoming her intimate confidante and companion. Through her connection to the Duchess, Elizabeth was given an entrée into the highest echelon of British society. At the Duchess' parties she met a dazzling array of the great and the good. In 1740 she met George, Lord Lyttleton at a party given by Lady North, who became her good friend. However, they could not marry because as a lord he needed a bride with a larger dowry than the £1000 a year that had been apportioned to Elizabeth Montagu.

Elizabeth Montagu and Sarah Scott

Although Elizabeth wrote to Lady Harley in 1738 that she had no desire for men or marriage, she nevertheless tied the knot with Edward Montagu, the grandson of the 1st Earl of Sandwich in 1742, after being introduced to the eligible bachelor by her aristocratic friend. With this marriage, Elizabeth was promoted from the gentry to the aristocracy, sharing with her husband the profits from his numerous coal mines and the rents from his sundry estates in Northumberland. She was a mere twenty-two years old and he was fifty. Although she described him in one of her letters as 'the best of husbands', it does not appear to have been a very passionate marriage. One of her fellow bluestockings, Mrs Chaperone, described her as an 'ignoramus in love'. It is hard not to come to the conclusion that it was a marriage of convenience for Elizabeth, which would allow her to achieve all her social and economic ambitions.

In a letter to the Duchess of Portland she describes her wedding ceremony in a particularly unemotional way, 'I behaved magnanimously; not one cowardly tear, I assure you, did I shed at the solemn altar, my mind was in no mirthful mood indeed. I have a great hope of happiness; the world, as you say, speaks well of Mr. Montagu, and I have many obligations to him which must gain my particular esteem; but such a change of life must furnish one with a thousand anxious thoughts'.

She then ended her letter rather obsequiously, 'Adieu, my dear Lady Duchess, whatever I am, I must still be with gratitude, affection and fidelity, yours'. With his estate valued at £7000 on his death in 1775, Elizabeth had every reason to be grateful to the Duchess for the introduction. As well as an ancient manor house in Northumberland, his main seat was Sandleford in Berkshire. Elected MP for Allerthorpe in 1745, he and Elizabeth would divide their time between his country seats, as well as their townhouses in London and Bath.

In return, Edward Montagu probably thought that by marrying Elizabeth he would have a companion in old age, especially in consideration of the asset that she had been to the Duchess of Portland. He possibly did not realise, however, that he would also ultimately gain a business manager for his financial interests.

Elizabeth often flattered the Duchess in her letters. In March 1742 she signed off, 'I am with the greatest gratitude, and affection, and love, your Grace's most obliged and faithful servant'. However, as time progressed and the friendship deepened, her letters become less obsequious, although oftentimes littered with long-winded references to classical literature, in which she attempts to show off her learning and education. However, living in the country and writing letters did not satisfy Elizabeth, who loved to socialize. The same year that she married, she wrote to Mrs Donnellan Mount Morris, using the flowery language that she often used, that the countryside bored her:

> 'I want to know how the world goes on: we stand still here. Dullness in the solemn garb of wisdom, wraps us in its gentle wing.'

The prospect of spending the winter away from London was one that Elizabeth found hard to countenance. She admitted that she:

> "cannot abide the country in winter. I love peace with pleasure; but I have such a tendency to dulness, that I am afraid of mere tranquility. I love to be a spectator

of the rapid world while my little machine is at rest; the actions and passions of others keep me awake, without so far disturbing the constant mood of my calm thoughts, as to make me uneasy."

She continues by asking for news of the political situation and seems anxious to know what is going on in London. Her letters are eager for society and political gossip, interspersed with some long-winded moral pronouncements and overblown literary allusions. Already she is cultivating the 'femme savant' persona that she would develop to its full after the death of her husband. She presents herself as someone who knows her own mind and wishes to show off her classical education. More importantly, she already displays a desire for attention and company that would later become a need that was to dominate the latter part of her life.

Elizabeth craved London life so much that she was even prepared to travel the uncomfortable and dangerously long journey from her country seat while pregnant with her first and only child. She wrote that she had taken a 'sober journey of ten tedious days [so that] I may get to town.' In 1743, at the age of twenty-five, Elizabeth gave birth to her beloved son, John, who she doted on, writing to the Duchess:

'My little boy will cost me a sigh at parting; it is a pleasure to me to see him gathering strength every day, and I hope making a provision of health for years to come'. Later she told the Duchess of her feelings of 'paternal felicity'.

However, her happiness was short-lived as her son died suddenly and unexpectedly after a convulsion from cutting his teeth. Of her loss she wrote to the Duchess of Portland on September 16th 1744:

'I know it is my duty to be resigned and to submit; many far more deserving than I am have been as fortunate. I hope time will bring me comfort, I will assist it with my best endeavours; it is in afflictions like mine that reason ought to exert itself, else one should fall beneath the stroke. I apply myself to reading as much as I can, and I find it does me service. Poor Mr Montagu shews me an example of patience and fortitude, and endeavours to comfort me, though undoubtedly he feels as much sorrow as I can do, for he loved his child as much as ever parent could do. My sister has been of great service to me; and on this, as on all other occasions, a most tender friend".

Although she expressed a desire to have more children hoping that 'the same Providence that snatched this dear blessing from me may give me others; if not I will endeavour to be content if I may not be happy', the Montagus never produced any more children. It is likely that in an attempt to distract herself from her grief she began to host the conversation parties in her London townhouse that were to become the most famous literary salon in the history of England.

In stark contrast, the year before Elizabeth's marriage, her sister Sarah contracted smallpox, a horrific disease that could leave victims terribly scarred and disfigured. Her illness was long and severe and Elizabeth, who was terrified of the disease, left home and did not see Sarah for long periods. The trauma of this illness was life-changing for Sarah. Once recovered, no one ever suggested that the sisters looked like peas in a pod again, or complimented her beauty. Even after Sarah's recovery, Elizabeth did not linger at home in Kent, but went to stay in London with the Duchess of Portland.

At just twenty-one, Sarah experienced a sense of emptiness and loneliness that could only be satisfied by the presence of her sister. However, Barbara Rizzo in her book 'Companions without Vows' argues that 'although Elizabeth Montagu would always feel a special attachment to her sister, her ambition and her vastly enlarged opportunities ensured that Sarah would never again be her only or even her first object.' In turn, Sarah's disillusionment with her sister would eventually become 'radical'.

It was at this time that writing became Sarah's solace. Unlike her sister who craved company and society, Sarah decided to pour her energy into this solitary pursuit. She wrote to Elizabeth in 1741 that 'the love of writing you see, enters into me as soon as you go out of the house; while you are with me I have all I desire, content is then my companion; but when you are gone I can't help writing hopes you will send me some return for the affection and spirits that are gone with you, all of me that is portable you carry with you.'

Sarah's need for the companionship of her sister is plaintive. Unfortunately, it wasn't forthcoming. After living at home to nurse her dying mother in 1746, with the death of her mother, Sarah became homeless. Her father, Matthew Robinson, moved to London to live in lodgings with his housekeeper/lover and dedicated the rest of his life to his own entertainment and pleasure. In contrast, Sarah spent the next period visiting a round of friends trying to ensure that she had a roof over her head. First she visited Bath with Mrs Cotes, a family friend and doctor's wife. Under her protection she 'danced at balls, played shuttlecock with assorted men and women and learnt to be agreeable like Elizabeth'.

It is at this time that she made the fateful acquaintance of George Lewis Soctt, the son of friends in Canterbury. Gradually becoming closer over time, Scott escorted Sarah and Mrs Cotes to visit the Montagus at Sandleford in October 1743. Sarah was rather ambivalent about her new beau from the very start. She wrote 'I am persuaded he will never go farther and indeed I believe it would be very inconvenient if he shou'd for I find he is very dependent upon his Mamma'. Unimpressed with his lack of independence and ambition from the start, little did she know that it would be her financial portion that would finance his lifestyle for the rest of his life. If only she had heeded her inner voice.

Sarah then went to visit Elizabeth and Edward in Bath where they had a townhouse at 16 Royal Crescent. Although Elizabeth was keen to have a female companion after the death of her son, shown by the fact that she took Dorothea Gregory into her household, the fifteen year-old orphan daughter of distant relations, Sarah refused her sister's protection. It was a brave decision as she could have lived in some comfort and luxury. However, Sarah knew that the price that she would have to pay would be the complete loss of her autonomy. Inevitably, under Elizabeth's roof and financial control, she would come to dominate Sarah, just as she tried to dominate Dorothea Gregory later.

Dorothea's father agreed that she should go live with Elizabeth Montagu and she was duly separated from her sister. Over time Dorothea became Elizabeth's executive, arranging her domestic affairs and intermediating with her servants, trades people and tiresome relations. According to Rizzo, Dorothea, 'listened to Elizabeth, agreed with her, soothed her, brightened her day and was on call at all hours to serve in any capacity at any time of the day'. When Dorothea refused to marry Elizabeth's nephew and heir, Matthew, preferring to marry for love, Elizabeth 'never really recovered and never forgot or forgave'. Elizabeth then practically cut Dorothea off, even though she had been part of her household since she was a teenager. Rizzo explains:

> 'Because she [Montagu] never offered Gregory any help with her new set, her response to Gregory's rejection and help reveal Montagu's essential nature – resolute, resourceful, utterly determined and vindictive'.

Knowing Elizabeth as she did, Sarah was prepared to sacrifice potential protection, luxury and comfort for her own freedom. Sarah must have suspected the Faustian pact that she would have to make to have a place in Elizabeth's household and took an entirely different, albeit much more insecure path. Perhaps Sarah disapproved of her sister's life choices, believing that marrying a rich older man was not a compromise that she could make.

Life was tough for Sarah at this point in time. In 1747 she stayed with her cousin Lydia Botham in Albury. Five weeks later she was under the roof of her favourite brother, Morris, who was a lawyer in Tunbridge. She had a brief spell with her father, then she accepted the offer of the sister of George Scott. The fact that she was struggling comes from a letter that she sent her sister in September of that year in which she asks her to 'beseech her maid' to find some of her warmer clothing because she didn't know where her woolens were. She was managing on an allowance from her father that was so small and she was constantly worried whether he would settle her accounts and whether he would be 'pleased' or not. According to Rizzo, 'her father's unwillingness to disburse to her would plague her until his death in 1778 and perhaps afterward'.

Fortunately, while in Bath, Sarah befriended Lady Barbara Montague, a woman whose friendship would change her life. Also affectionately known as Lady Bab, Lady Barbara Montagu was the daughter of the 1st Earl of Halifax and no relation to Elizabeth Montagu. Upon her father's death, each of his six daughters were apportioned the sum of £5000. Her money was placed in an annuity by her brother that paid her the comparatively small annual income of around £100. Lady Bab had a heart condition that gave her severe palpitations and made it so that she could not live with her siblings, who had fashionable and hectic lifestyles.

Consequently, the two women decided to pool their resources and set up home together in Bath among a community of women who found themselves in similar circumstances. Sarah moved into Lady Barbara's rented house in Trim Street in August 1748. They lived frugally and Lady Bab introduced Sarah to the charitable work that she carried out. Interested in education, she made flashcards with easily digestible information on a variety of topics to educate working class children. With the proceeds of the sale she helped a poor neighbour. Lady Bab tried to raise funds for working class women by encouraging them to use their skills to knit mittens, which she then sold to her circle of friends. Lady Bab's charitable works inspired Sarah who began to teach Sunday school classes for children. The pair became so close that it is believed that Sarah wanted Lady Bab to go live with her when she married George Scott in 1751.

Sarah had been betrothed to George Lewis Scott for a number of years when she married him on 15th June 1751. He was a mathematician who was appointed to serve as tutor to the future King George III. By April of the following year things had gone so terribly wrong that Sarah's father and brother went to their house in London to remove her from it. The exact details of the marriage breakdown were never revealed. According to family letters the marriage was never consummated and there were rumours of incompatibility, abuse, an illicit affair and even the nondisclosure of a previous marriage on the part of Scott. Others suggested that Sarah's insistence that Lady Babara live with them was also a stumbling block. In order to protect his career and her reputation, the details of the collapse of the marriage were kept quiet. Nevertheless, Scott benefitted from the breakdown more than Sarah.

The separation agreement was not favorable to Sarah. Scott insisted on keeping half of her £1000 dowry and returned the other half to her father, Matthew Robinson, who pocketed the money. Scott finally agreed to pay her an allowance of £100 a year, probably as her family had been influential in his appointment as tutor in the royal household. Nevertheless, the payments did not arrive regularly and in 1753 she complained that the first installment had not been paid. As she was no longer with her husband, she became her father's legal ward and he decided to punish her for the failure of the marriage by giving her no money whatsoever. Furthermore, he forbade Elizabeth or Sarah's brother, Matthew, from doing anything to relieve Sarah's poverty. Now completely dependent on her father and husband's continued prosperity and goodwill, Scott probably had an income of well under £200 a year and was in real need of Lady Barbara's help. Fortunately, Lady Bab stood by her and they set up home together again in Bath.

It is thought that the rift between Elizabeth and Sarah could have begun at this time because Sarah had refused to confide in Elizabeth her feelings about Scott and her marriage. It seemed that Elizabeth resented not being the sole focus of Scott's intimacies. Complaining to the Duchess of Portland, Elizabeth was advised that Sarah 'might want to obey her in all other respects, but could not control her affections'.

By this time of Sarah's tumultuous personal life, Elizabeth had gained a reputation for herself as a patron of writers in the salons that she held in her London homes, firstly Hill House and then Montagu House in Portman Square. In her book 'Reconsidering the Bluestockings', Nicole Pole explains that the first salons began in the courts of the Italian Renaissance. Beatrice D'Este surrounded herself with a group of artists and men of letters who were invited to her home for philosophical discussions. Even Leonardo Da Vinci visited her salons. The ideals of the salon then passed over to France where the Marquise of Rambouillet, who was half Italian and knew the traditions of the nobility, presided over a renowned salon in the Hotel de Rambouillet. Pole explains that one defining feature of the salon is the central role it gives to the female hostess:

'The one unfailing characteristic of the salon, in all ages and in all countries, is the dominant position which it gives to woman. It is woman who creates the peculiar atmosphere and the peculiar influence of salons; it is she, with her instinct for society and for literature, who is most likely to succeed in the attempt to fuse two ideals of life apparently opposed, the social and the literary'.

The Marquise de Rambouillet became the archetype for all later hostesses. For a salon to be successful, there were several common characteristics. The house in which the company gathered must have something of royal splendor. The conversation should retain an aristocratic tone, without being subject to the strict formality of the aristocracy. Wit, intellect and personality, rather than noble birth were the entry criteria into the group. The chief entertainment was the conversation of both a literary and philosophical nature. Discussion could be stimulated by reading original poems, essays, sermons and plays. Deep friendships also developed between the French salonniers and their guests. Madame Necker and Edward Gibbon developed mutual respect for each other, as did Madame de Deffand and Horace Walpole.

However, a salon was more than just a literary club. Its aim was to exert a creative influence in the literary world. It was directly concerned with improving the condition of authors and was blatant in its attempt to mould public opinion. It was a system of patronage. Authors were offered protection and publicity. Gifts of money could be given, unofficial pensions granted, printers' bills could be paid. Some salonniers even gave their authors homes, such as Mrs Vesey to Samuel Johnson.

Pole notes that the salon reached its zenith during a period when publishing was in transition. The system of patronage was dying out and reading was becoming more democratic. By the dawn of the eighteenth century the salon died away because it was newspapers that created opinion and dispensed fame. New authors began to feel disgust at the salon because it had come between them and their public. Later authors wanted to be independent and meet their readers on equal terms. Samuel Johnson came to hate patrons calling them 'a wretch who supports with insolence and is paid in flattery'.

No doubt Elizabeth Montagu reveled in being the hostess and centre of attention at her salons. She learnt from the French salonniers and in 1750 Madame du Bocage visited her in London and took breakfast at her house in Hill Street, where the two ladies paid elaborate court to each other. Elizabeth gifted Madame Du Bocage an edition of Milton and in return Madame Du Bocage wrote a poem in French praising her hostess. While Madam Necker was in England she visited Elizabeth and 'was pleased with her amiability, and, again, like every one, amused at the stiffness of her conversation'.

It is not known exactly how the group of women who Elizabeth Montagu invited to her home to discuss literature and philosophy came to be known as the bluestockings. The group came to be regarded 'an informal women's social and educational movement, emphasizing self-development and mutual cooperation', although there is little evidence of charitable work outside the circle itself, unlike Sarah Scott and Lady Barbara's efforts.

By 1760 Elizabeth's salons had become famous and celebrated. She organized literary breakfasts with Gilbert West, a minor poet included in Samuel Johnsons'

'Lives of the Most Eminent English Poets.' Also present was Lord George Lyttleton, friend, statesman, author and patron of the arts. Among the men who accepted her invitations were writers Samuel Johnson and Horace Walpole, artist Joshua Reynolds, philosopher Edmund Burke, theatre manager David Garrick. Characteristic of her salons was the prohibition on card playing and strong drink. Elizabeth's dislike for alcohol is evident when she wrote:

'I am very happy that drinking is not within our walls we have not had one person disordered by liquor since we came down; though most of the poor ladies in the neighborhood have had more hogs in their dining room than ever they had in their hogsty'.

While in her home in Hill Street her guests were able to enjoy her exquisite taste in décor in her Chinese room or her Athenian room, or even her feather room. Renowned artist Angelica Kauffmann was commissioned to decorate some of her chambers. Of the men who visited Elizabeth Montagu, Rizzo explains that 'it seems to have been the habit to attend her fashionable parties, flatter her face and then mock her insatiable appetite for flattery behind her back'.

Consequently, the term 'bluestocking' came to be applied more to the women who gathered at Elizabeth's homes, although she did financially support some men. She developed longer relationships with some of the women, perhaps because they were more in need of her patronage than the men, who had more opportunity to earn an independent living.

Among these women were the teacher and philanthropist Hannah More who wrote poems, narratives, tragic dramas, essays and critiques of conduct. She was chosen to represent the group in print, as Mrs Montagu represented them in the salon. She wrote the poems 'Bas Bleu' and 'Sensibility' directly in honour of the group. When Mrs More made £600 from her play 'Percy' the bluestockings were triumphant. However, as time progressed, Mrs More began to draw away from the group, becoming increasingly religious, she began to view her association with them as wicked. In 1794 she wrote in her diary, 'Dined with friends at Mrs M's…What does thou here, Elijah? Felt too much pleased at the pleasure expressed by so many accomplished friends on seeing me again. Keep me from contagion!' Clearly, Mrs Montagu's salons did not suit everyone.

Hester Chapone was a writer of books of conduct for women. Elizabeth read the letters that Mrs Chapone had sent to her favourite niece advising her on religion and was so impressed that she advised her to publish them. She helped by proofreading them and correcting them with her 'elegant pen'. The book became a success, with even the Princess Royal being given a copy. Mrs Chapone considered that her success was due to the patronage of Mrs Montagu.

There were some eccentric visitors to her salon, such as Messenger Monsey who was the physician in charge of the Royal Hospital Chelsea. He became more infamous for his bad manners than his writing. The talented writer and bluestocking, Fanny Burney, called him a 'strange gross man'.

In 1766 Elizabeth met a poet called James Beattie whose cause she took up with unparalleled gusto. He was a young professor of philosophy in Aberdeen, shy, nervous and self-conscious, totally lacking self-confidence. He was prone to constantly altering and correcting his work or even destroying it. After reading the first part of his poem 'Minstel' in 1771, she set to work to make a name for him in the world of letters. She sent a copy of his poem to Lord Chatham, recommended it to the attention of Lord Percy and praised it to Lord Lyttleton. She offered advice on marketing and wrote to a bookseller who she knew advising him to recommend the work to 'all people of taste'. Her mind teemed with projects to help him advance. She even contacted the Archbishop of York to try to get him a job at the University of Edinburgh. Finally, he was introduced to the king who granted him a pension of two hundred pounds and a degree of Doctor of Law from Oxford. Beattie was so grateful to Elizabeth that he named his son Montagu in her honour. His story is testament to the influence that she could wield.

The most intellectual of the bluestockings was Elizabeth Carter who was well-versed in the classics. Mrs Montagu's letters are full of classical allusions and she styled herself as a 'femme savant', a wise and erudite woman. However, Pole believes that a lot of her knowledge of the classics was derived second-hand from Mrs Carter, who translated the works of Epictetus from Greek in 1758. Mrs Carter distanced herself from social rivalries, preferring not to follow an ostentatious life. Although she was of a different social class to Mrs Montagu, they were firm friends. Towards the end of her life, Mrs Montagu paid her a pension of £100 a year from her own money. Elizabeth Carter is seen as contributing intellectual gravitas to the bluestockings and Mrs Montagu was a loyal and supportive friend to her throughout their acquaintance.

Sarah Fielding, the sister of Henry Fielding, who had had great success with his comic novel 'Tom Jones', was also a member of the bluestockings. A mutual friend of both sisters, Sarah Fielding was also invited to become a member of the female community that Sarah Scott and Lady Bab set up together in Bath.

While Mrs Montagu's literary gatherings became famous, after Sarah's failed marriage she and Lady Bab went to Batheaton in 1754, where they pooled their resources once more and set up a community for single women. The philosophy of the community was based upon the utopian ideals that Sarah would go on to write about in her most successful novel, 'Milenium Hall' (1762).

By the time Sarah and Lady Barbara set up the female community, Sarah was already a published author. The year before she married George Scott, she had published 'The History of Cornelia,' the portrait of an ideal and pious young woman, probably semi-autobiographical. Due to her financial dependence on others, Sarah began to use her intellectual talents and began to pursue professional literary translation to help with her expenses. Fluent in French, in 1754 she translated 'An Agreeable Likeness' into English. However, this did not satisfy her creative imagination and in the same year she published 'A Journey through every Stage of Life' , which was a series of tales told by a young servant girl to her mistress, a princess who had been exiled by her mother, inspired by the Arabian Nights.

Sarah's writing was not mere romance. She was interested in politics and history and in 1761 she wrote a political history of Gustav I of Sweden, emphasizing the concept of the 'patriot king' or the selfless ruler acting for the greater good of the country. Sarah was eager to promote her ideas on how to create a better society than the one that she was living in. However, she was realistic and practical and decided to put her talents to use on more commercial subjects. Capitalising on the nations' fascination with Queen Charlotte, the wife of George III, she wrote 'The History of Mecklenburgh'.

Her most successful novel with the catchy title of, 'A Description of Milenium Hall and the Country Adjacent' was a utopian vision of a community of women who pool their resources and devote their lives to artistic pursuits that drew on her own experiences. The ideas of the community were based on education, Christian values and philanthropy. One of the characters had been badly scarred by smallpox, but continued to lead an interesting life and be a valuable person. It was her one great success and by 1788 it had run to four editions. Even her father found 'wit in it', to the astonishment of his daughter.

By this time, Sarah and Elizabeth had developed diametrically opposite ideologies on how women should live their lives. It is evident that Lady Brumpton in 'Milenium Hall' is a satire of Sarah's more famous sister:

> "She was by nature generous and humane, her temper perfectly good; her understanding admirable. She had been educated with great care, was very accomplished, had read a great deal, and with excellent taste; she had great quickness of parts, and a very uncommon share of with. Her beauty first gained her much admiration; but when she was better known, the charms of her understanding seemed to eclipse those of her person. Her conversation was generally courted, her wit and learning were the perpetual subjects of panegyric in verse and prose, which unhappily served to increase her only failing, vanity. She sought to be admired for various merits. To recommend her person she studied dress, and went to a considerable expense in ornaments. To shew her taste, she distinguished herself by the elegance of her house, furniture, and equipage. To prove her fondness for literature, she collected a considerable library; and to shew that all her esteem was not engrossed by the learned dead, she caressed all living genuis's… She aimed at making her house a little academy'.

Unsurprisingly, relations cooled between the sisters and they developed a more formal relationship. Meanwhile in Sarah's female community, Lady Barbara, concerned about the growing problem of prostitution among destitute women, paid for the 1759 publishing of 'The Histories of Some of the Penitents in the Magdalen House, as Supposed to Be Related by Themselves'.

Then in 1763 Lady Barbara's pension increased to £300 and Sarah did not feel the need to write for a while. However, disaster struck a mere two years later when Lady Barbara died. The loss that Sarah felt can be sensed in the letter that she wrote to Elizabeth:

> 'My Dear Sister will wish to know how I am after the great and irreparable loss she will hear I have sustained. And I would not commit to any other hand the office of telling her that I am better than I could hope after such a grievous shock….Mrs Cutts was with me and is so every day'.

Lady Barbara left the remaining £2900 of her portion to be divided amongst her friends. After all the annuities and bequests had been paid, Sarah Scott was left with the remainder of the money that would eventually pay her £60 a year.

Lady Barbara's character is revealed by her cousin when he wrote to Horace Walpole that:

'She was the one I always loved and passed all my youth with in daily gaiety and joy, for she had all the wit and humours of the family, generous, and beneficent; her constitution so delicate that her life has been a sufferance for many years'.

Two years later, with encouragement from her sister, Sarah began writing again and published a sequel to 'Milenium Hall' called 'The History of Sir George Ellison', another utopian novel. The following year Sarah decided to take the courageous step of attempting to put her abstract ideals into practice by creating a real Milenium Hall in Buckinghamshire. She envisaged a communal household that would include a school and other charitable institutions for the impoverished community and invited fellow writer Sarah Fielding to go and live with her. She offered to pay the expenses of her friend, but unfortunately Fielding was dying and could not go. Other members included Mrs Cutts, Mrs Arnol and her cousin Grace Robinson Freind. It was on the estate owned by Grace Robinson Freind at Hitcham in Buckinghamshire that the location the experiment was to take place. Each member was asked to invest £50 each in the project. In encouragement and support, Elizabeth Montagu donated livestock, land and staff.

Unfortunately, the experiment failed due to financial difficulties, ill health and quarrels. A key factor seems to have been Grace Robinson Freind's decision to invite someone else into the community without consulting the rest of the group. Plagued by the headaches that she suffered throughout her life, Sarah went to Chelsea to seek medical attention.

Alone, Sarah returned to writing, publishing 'The Life of Theodore Agrippa D'Aubinge' in an attempt to cash in on the emerging interest in a man who had fought mob rule and absolute monarchy. Clearly, Sarah was ambitious in her choice of subjects, it is hard not to think that she wanted to use her writing to disseminate her ideas on the nature of government and how society could be improved. Sarah was also a Protestant and as the lives of both sister progressed, they became more devout in their Christian faith. That same year Sarah published her final novel, 'The Test of Fillial Duty', a novel written in letter form addressing the rights of a daughter to choose her husband. Like many writers, she drew on her own personal experience and wanted to show the disadvantages that women suffered due to their inferior status to men.

In contrast, Elizabeth Montagu had been persuaded to put pen to paper herself. In 1760 encouraged by George Lyttleton she contributed three sections to a work called 'Dialogues of the Dead', at first published anonymously. The concept of the book was a series of conversations between the living and the illustrious dead, intended to be a satire on eighteenth century vanity and manners. Pole believes that the dialogue between Mercury and a Modern Fine Lady is the best one, although 'somewhat pretentious', while the dialogue between Hercules and Cadmus is the worst because it is 'full of platitudes'.

Unperturbed by the lukewarm reception to the 'Dialogues of the Dead', Elizabeth Montagu ventured into the world of literary criticism with 'An Essay on the Writings and Genius of Shakespear', in which she proclaimed Shakespeare was not only the greatest writer in the English language, but of any nation in the world. She attacked Samuel Johnson's 'Preface to Shakespeare' from 1765 as not having praised Shakespeare's plays enough. At first the work was published anonymously, but when her name appeared on the title page, unsurprisingly, she and Samuel Johnson became estranged.

Nine years later she championed Shakespeare again in her essay with the modest title of 'An Essay on the Writings and Genius of Shakespear, Compared with the Greek and French Dramatic Poets, with some Remarks upon Misrepresentations of Mons. de Voltaire'. With this work she established a reputation for herself as a critic and not just patron and salonnier. However, among the chorus of praise for the book, there was one voice of discord. Dr Johnson is reported to have said that 'there is not one sentence of true criticism in her book'. His verdict was kind in comparison to Mr Lounsbury who called it 'in many ways one of the most exasperating books' because of her misconceptions and her incapacity to comprehend Shakespeare's true intentions and techniques'.

In 1775 Elizabeth's husband, Edward Montagu died after a lengthy illness. Even though their father was still alive, Elizabeth ignored his prohibition and began to pay her sister a pension of £200 a year, which obviously enabled Sarah to lead a more comfortable lifestyle. By this time Elizabeth was fifty-five years old and Sarah was forty-eight.

Perhaps to take her mind off her grief, Elizabeth Montagu travelled to Paris where she socialized with French salonniers. She was presented to all the 'beaux esprits', as she described them. In contrast, some of her acquaintances were not as complimentary about her. In 1776 she met Madame du Deffand who she found to be gay and lively. In return when Deffand wrote to Horace Walpole she described Elizaebth as 'without doubt boring, but nevertheless a good woman'.

When Elizabeth went to Paris, some of her protégées were hoping that she would return having learnt how to create more of a relaxed atmosphere at her gatherings. Unfortunately, Elizabeth reveled in the elaborate and complicated and many described her manners as grand, not easy. Gradually her assemblies became larger and therefore less intimate and more overpowering. Several of her bluestocking circle complained about her lack of softness and simplicity. Fanny Burney was somewhat overwhelmed by her grand manner from the beginning. Some of her guests simply did not like her. Lady Louisa Stuart recorded that 'there was a deplorable lack…of that art of kneading the mass well together'.

Ironically, her supposed friend, Lord Lyttelton who had encouraged her to contribute to his 'Dialogues of the Dead' wrote of her that:

'no one can take more pains than Mrs M to be surrounded with men of wit; she bribes, she pensions, she flatters, gives excellent dinners, is herself a very sensible woman, and of very pleasing manners; not young indeed, but that is out of the question - and in spite of all these encouragements, which one would think, might make wits spring out of the ground, the conversations of her house

are too often critical and pedantic - something between the dullness and the
pertness of learning. They are perfectly chaste, and generally instructive; but a
cool and quiet observer would sometimes laugh to see how difficult a matter it
is for la belle Président to give colour and life to her literary circles'.

Horace Walpole dismissed her as 'a piece of learned nonsense' and used her for her money. He wrote in 1768 that 'our best sun is Newcastle coal'. Some of her set began to gravitate to the less ostentatious salon of Hester Thrale, who became the champion and confidante of Dr Johnson. Dr Johnson saw Elizabeth Montagu and the bluestockings as trying to set themselves up as patrons of literature, but were really over-privileged meddlars whose wealth and social position had given them their position in the literary world. He believed that as she had no genius herself, she used her salons to put herself in a position of authority. Inevitably, her salon was a reflection of her own character, which was stiff and formal.

Nevertheless, through her exertions, Mrs Montagu did achieve considerable influence and was a loyal friend and champion to those who reciprocated her favour, like Elizabeth Carter. She used her substantial wealth to support struggling writers and paid pensions to some of her circle who were less fortunate than herself. She brought comedies to the attention of theatre manager, Garrick and suggested subjects to Hannah More and Mrs Carter. However, 'when because of flattery she mistook her interest in literature for the critical authority of a scholar, she incurred the wrath and scorn of the likes of Johnson and Walpole'.

The vitality of Elizabeth's salons naturally waned. Writer and politician Nathaniel Wraxall summed them up when he wrote that 'the old little parties are not to be had in the usual style of comfort. Everything is great and vast and late and magnificent and dull'. Ironically, it was Elizabeth who abhorred dullness and had set up her salon as its antidote. Now it was she who was accused of being a bore.

In 1778 Sarah and Elizabeth's father died. Sarah received a little more money and she published no more works in her life time, suggesting that not only did she love writing, but used it as a means of economic support.

Elizabeth Montagu appears to have had boundless energy and ambition throughout her life. As well as playing the hostess, she oversaw the construction of Montagu House in Portman Square for nearly ten years until its eventual completion in 1781. After she succeeded to her husband's empire in 1775, she spent a lot of time at Denton Hall in Newcastle overseeing her coal mines and was recorded as an astute businesswoman who always tried to get the best price for her coal. According to Rizzo she would manage her workers by looking after them adequately and then lavish spectacular annual treats on them to show off her greatness. By 1783 'she oversaw five hundred miners toiling in her pits in Yorkshire, sixty reapers in her cornfields, and a brick, tile and tar manufactory'. However, Montagu did not see the connection between the coal that she produced and the child chimney sweeps in the major industrial cities:

'The chimney sweeps of London were in a way the product of her coal mines,
the emblems of her prosperity, and she gave no thought to alleviating their

miseries except that in her later years she gave them a feast every May Day consisting of roast beef and plum pudding on the lawn of her Portman Square mansion'. (Rizzo)

She tried to help her tenants, but was aware that 'our pitmen are afraid of being turned off and that fear keeps an order and regularity amongst them that is very uncommon.' While she enjoyed the collier's singing, she found that their spoken dialect was 'dreadful to the auditors' nerves'. Betty Rizzo is unequivocal in her preference for Sarah Scott over Elizabeth Montagu:

'Unlike her sister Sarah Scott, Montagu saw nothing wrong with the system with which she clambered to a position unprecedented for a woman'.

Upon her husband's death she was left sole heir to his estate. It was customary at the time to leave the wife a life interest in the priceless furniture of an aristocrat, but in Montagu's case he left his wife everything, except for £3000 to his nephew, Matthew. Just before his death, Sarah wrote to Elizabeth hinting that he might write her out his will. Elizabeth was confident that this was highly unlikely:

'You are very kind in what you hint at; there is no danger of that while his understanding keeps clear; if he should grow partly childish he might be wavering in this point, but his opinion and his good will are much too fixed for him ever to alter them'.

It seems that she had spent a long time cultivating his good opinion of her. She then goes on to describe how her husband regarded her during their marriage

'Indeed his esteem for me and his humour seem to be well matched: they have been fighting these 20 years, the esteem never subdued the humour, nor the humour the esteem'.

She seems to be suggesting that her husband begrudgingly admired her. He had been ill for a long time and became irritable and irascible in consequence. Her marriage is likely to have been a long and testing one for her.

It was quite an achievement on Elizabeth's part to be the main beneficiary of Edward's will. It seems that she put up with his irascible nature and rather than trying to rule him, manipulated him. Her letters hint at this. If she suggested a trip somewhere that he objected to, she admitted that she would 'never love to labour a point till ye time comes near, I said no more of it'. Then when the time of the trip approached, she would subtly reintroduce the topic and he would agree.

With her boundless energy, as late as 1780 Elizabeth extended Sandleford Priory and had Capability Brown design the garden and alter the park. In that same year she died at Montagu House in London on 25th August, at the age of sixty-two, leaving her estate to her nephew.

Elizabeth Montagu was a controversial figure during her own lifetime. Shortly after her death the family land bailiff and steward, James Woodhouse, wrote a poem in her honour, alleging that she surrounded herself with writers 'for they could best bestow delightful dow'rs, by flattering speech, or fam'd poetic pow'rs'.

To sum up the contribution of Montagu's literary salons, Pole writes that:

'They never became true disseminators of ideas, they were never devotees of new and daring philosophies and radical transitions, unlike their Parisian counterparts. They were always on side of law and order and conservative tradition. They stood for the classism of English literature'.

Although born in York, Elizabeth Montagu had a tenuous connection to the place. On October 10th 1744 she wrote a letter to Mrs Donnellan:

'I am now writing to you from the very place from whence I began my journey in life. You will think that I may feel some uneasiness on the reflection of returning to this place, after so many years wandering through the world, with so little improvement and addition of merit, which is all that time leaves behind it. ...From hence we came to York, where we have just being viewing the cathedral; of all Gothic buildings I ever saw, the most noble, taken together, or considered in parts. Gothic architecture, like Gothic government, seems to make strength and power of resistance its chief pride; this noble cathedral looks as if it might defy the consuming power of all-devouring Time. We are to visit the fine assembly room before we leave York, which I hear, is built in the manner of an Egyptian hall, or banqueting room. Dr Shaw would tell us in what place Cleopatra would have chosen to sit..."

We do not know if Sarah Scott ever returned to the city of her birth. She died after a long illness in Norwich in 1795 at the age of seventy-five. By the nineteenth century her works were largely forgotten and one was even attributed to another writer called Oliver Goldsmith, perhaps an indirect compliment as it was considered good enough to have been written by a man. However, the following century saw a renewed interest in her work, particularly from a feminist perspective. The fact that she instructed that her letters be burnt upon her death has, without doubt, helped to send her name and work into obscurity. It is only through her connection to her more famous, more illustrious and wealthier sister that we even hear about her today.

Although they began life just two years apart and looked like two peas in pod, Elizabeth Montagu and Sarah Scott lived very different lives based on their ideological beliefs. Elizabeth Montagu embraced the opportunity to become a capitalist entrepreneur. Sarah Scott lived as a utopian social reformer wanting to end financial powerlessness for everyone. Towards the end of Montagu's life we have a picture of her as an aging Miss Havisham, trapped in a time warp of her own making. One of the visitors to her salon, Wraxall, complained that she tastelessly ornamented her emaciated person with diamond necklaces and bows. He wrote, 'I used to think these glittering appendages of opulence sometimes helped to dazzle disputants.'

The failure of Sarah's family to provide her with an independent income meant that she had to forge a life for herself, which she did through genuine friendship and her talent for writing. She had avant-garde ideas about the role of women, society and the nature of power. Rizzo believes that she was expected to 'adopt the usual half-shadowy life of the indigent single gentlewoman. Not at all. She was to flower into a self-sufficient personage, as powerful, in her own way, as her sister Montagu, as effectual and considerably more altruistic'.

Rizzo believes that all Montagu's benefactions were planned so that she could get back more than she gave. She 'publicized them so as to get full credit, and rarely – unless it was to maintain their dominance –gave their dependents what they themselves wanted or needed, or what could lead them to independence'.

In contrast, Sarah Scott did lead an altruistic life, sharing what little she had with others. She wrote novels to present ideas of how to create a better society, not just for women, but for men also. And not least she had the courage to try to live out the utopian ideals that she advocated. She was an example of a woman who had a true and real friendship with another woman, who helped, supported and encouraged one another to live in a world of few opportunities for women. Perhaps it is time that a blue plaque be erected to Sarah Scott also outside the Treasurer's House in York.

Women of York

CHAPTER NINE

Women of the Bar Convent

IN 1633 GALILEO was thrown into prison by the Roman Inquisition for daring to declare that the earth orbited the sun. One year earlier, Mary Ward, had been summoned from modern-day Belgium to Rome to answer the charge of heresy levelled at her due to the institution which she had set up and named the Congregation of Jesus in 1609. After walking the 1,500 miles over the Alps with some of her followers, Mary Ward did not know what fate awaited her at the hands of Pope Urban XIII.

Born in Mulwith near Ripon on 23rd January 1585, Mary had grown up in a staunchly Catholic family during a time of great conflict and persecution for those who practised this faith. Two of her uncles, John and Christopher Wright, had been involved in the Gunpowder Plot to assassinate Protestant James I of England and VI of Scotland. As a young girl she spent much of her life on the run, separated from her family for her own safety, growing up with relatives. The distances that she travelled between the family homes, often during the bitter Yorkshire winters, prepared her for the many journeys that she made through Europe, including several crossings of the Alps in winter and on foot.

In 1595 her home was burnt down in an anti-Catholic riot. She and her siblings were rescued by their father. That same year she moved to the house of Sir Ralph Babthorpe of Osgodby in Selby but did not stay there long. At the age of fifteen she felt the calling of the religious life and went to northern France where she entered the monastery of the Poor Clares in Saint-Omer. The Poor Clares observed a strictly orthodox Franciscan way of life which included prayer and penury. Showing an early capacity for leadership, in 1606, at the age of twenty-one she founded a monastery of Poor Clares at nearby Gravelines. However, in defiance of the rigid strictures laid down by that order, she proposed a more active ministry, involved with society, rather than the contemplative life. Her vision for her order was ground-breaking for the time.

After three years she came to realise that a life of prayer and obscurity, enclosed in a convent, did not appeal to her and decided to return to London. A group of like-mined companions, in whom she had inspired loyalty and devotion, followed her. Under her guidance, the group engaged in charitable works in the community, disregarding the restrictive laws against Catholics at the time. However, later that year, she came to believe that God was calling her again to some form of religious life that was 'more to his glory.' With this in mind she returned to Belgium with her disciples and founded her first religious house in St Omer.

The religious community that she established was radical. Together the women opened a school for girls, based on the model created by the Society of Jesus (the Jesuits), which had been created to educate boys. At the time, the work of religious women was confined to what could be carried out inside the walls of a monastery, such as teaching boarding school students or nursing the sick in adjoining hospitals. Mary Ward ripped up the rule book. Her female followers were no longer to be enclosed, there was no obligation to have a choir or to hear daily offices (religious services). Instead they were allowed to carry money and did not have to wear a religious habit. Finally, they were free from the jurisdiction of the local bishop.

However, she modelled her community on the Society of Jesus, which was deeply distrusted. Combined with the fact that there were divisions within the Roman Catholic church, her convent inspired mistrust. Opposition to her work began to grow. Although the Jesuit theologians Francisco Suarex and Leanoardus Lessius praised the way of life of the new institution, in their opinion, it required the sanction of the pope. The problem was that Pope Pius V had declared that solemn vows and strict enclosure within the walls of a convent were essential to all communities of religious women.

All the while that Mary Ward was arousing suspicion and distrust within the hierarchy of the Catholic church, the popularity of her message and the rules of her orders were growing. With her followers, she opened more convents in Bavaria, Austria and Italy. In 1629 one James Wadsworth, who among his many adventures claimed to have been sold into slavery to the Moors of Africa, wrote that there were two hundred 'Jesuitesses' in colleges in St Omer, Liège and Cologne and that despite the disapproval of the pope, Mary Ward was trying to establish new houses in Rome and Vienna. He added that the nuns were expected to visit England imminently. Despite what did appear to be outright rebellion, Mary did apply to the pope for approbation that same year.

Mary's followers were highly educated women who were dedicated to preserving Roman Catholicism through learning and working as teachers. Many of them had studied classical languages and new sciences. Ward taught her religious sisters not to wear habits and trained them to work with the poor and persecuted, as well as founding and teaching in Catholic schools. She also encouraged them to perform in plays, a move considered scandalous at a time contemporary with Shakespeare, when all female roles were played by boys. It led to her nuns being derided as 'chattering hussies' and caused shock all over Europe where actresses were viewed with the same contempt at showgirls and prostitutes.

After applying for approval to Pope Urban VIII, Ward was forced to travel to Rome to plead her cause in person before a congregation of Cardinals on two separate occasions, each time walking the arduous journey over the Alps. Her application was denied on both occasions. Then in 1631 she was officially summoned by Urban VIII and she made the long and perilous journey over the Alps to Rome one more time.

While meeting the pope in person, she is reported to have said, 'Holy Father, I neither am nor ever have been a heretic'. Although no trial took place, on this occasion not only was she met with disapproval, but was thrown into prison. This was her punishment for leading an order of devotees for two decades, which lived in defiance of the Vatican's strict rules that confined nuns to their cloisters. By then she had a following of three hundred women. From prison in 1631 she wrote, 'it is good pleasing the Friend of friends, and labouring in eternal works, and above all to be entirely and forever at our Master's disposal'.

Upon her release from prison, she was forbidden to leave Rome or to live in a community. Seeing that there was no way that she could continue to fight against forces mightier than herself, she decreed that her order be suppressed, in compliance with the pope's papal bull. Even though Ward had been requested to open schools and houses all over Europe, often by those in positions of power in society, still the papal approval eluded her.

By 1637 she was allowed to visit Spa and England due to her ailing health. Even after suppression, she refounded her order on a less ambitious scale, placing less emphasis on the independence of the nuns. After some years in London, she went with her household north and established a convent at Heworth near York. Three years later she died at Heworth on January 30th 1645 during the siege of York in the English Civil War.

It was feared that her body may be desecrated if she was interred near the city centre, so it was decided that she would be buried in Osbaldwick church yard the following month. The 'vicar was honest enough to be bribed' to allow the funeral to take place. Both Catholics and Protestants alike attended her funeral in tribute to her educational and charitable works.

Although she had died, Mary Ward continued to inspire devotion and women continued to follow her teachings and her example. In the following century, English nuns persuaded the pope to lift the suppression of the order, but the head of the church would only do so on the condition that Ward was not recognised as the foundress of the order.

In the 1670s one of Ward's companions, Frances Bedingfield (1616-1704), established a school in York, after establishing another in London. She was also plagued with trouble. In 1679 there was anti-Catholic fury at what became known as the Popish Plot. A troublemaker called Titus Oates claimed that there was an extensive Catholic conspiracy to assassinate King Charles II. Although Oate's intricate web of accusations fell apart during his trial, leading to his conviction for perjury, nevertheless, twenty-two men were executed.

With the help of Sir Thomas Gascoigne's donation of £450, in 1686 Frances Bedingfield and her small group of nuns bought a modest seventeenth century house just outside the city walls at Micklegate Bar, where she established the Bar Convent. Housing just ten nuns, it educated between thirty and forty girls, who often later became nuns themselves. Firstly, the set up a boarding school for Catholic girls and then a free day school in 1699. Besides running the school, the nuns ministered to the spiritual needs of the local Catholic population and dispensed medicines, as well as providing nursing care for poor Catholics. They also had contacts with the local business community and would lend money out at interest, although the declining number of professions in the later eighteenth century meant that the convent ran into financial difficulties. Due to political problems on the Continent, the Bar Convent more or less lost contact with its sister houses overseas.

Unfortunately, Catholic persecution persisted and the nuns became known secretly as the 'Ladies at the Bar'. The sisters concealed their identity by wearing modest slate-coloured gowns to avoid arousing suspicion. The nuns were referred to as 'Mrs' and never 'Sister'. Frances Bedingfield used the pseudonym 'Mrs Long'. However, they were hiding in plain sight. In 1694 Bedingfield was locked up for the second time in the notoriously squalid and dangerous kidcote underneath Ouse Bridge for her religious beliefs, along with her great-niece, Dorothy Pastor Bedingfield. In the same year the convent was attacked and badly damaged by an angry anti-Catholic mob. In 1704, Frances Bedingfield resigned as Superior in favour of her niece and returned to Munich, where she had attended school.

By 1727 Elizabeth Stansfield paid off all the community's debts with her personal fortune. For twenty years between 1766 and 1788 Ann Aspinall worked with the architect Thomas Atkinson to remodel the convent buildings. The original house was demolished and replaced with the current Georgian House. The first Mass was held in Mother Apsinall's new chapel with its magnificent neoclassical dome, hidden from the outside world by a trick pitched roof. Situated at the centre of the building, the chapel is undetectable from the street. Its unadorned windows fail to betray its true nature. With eight exits in case of a raid, plus a priest hole, the nuns were ever cognisant of the risks that their faith put them in.

While there was political upheaval in France due to the revolutions and the Napoleonic wars, the convent gave aid to refugees and émigré priests. In the same century the building was extended to provide a new community wing and kitchens. In 1853 some of the sisters went to teach at St George's School in Walmgate, which had been newly opened to serve the Irish immigrant community fleeing the potato famine.

In 1885 the school was transferred to the Diocese of Middleborough after being run by the community for 299 years. It then became a comprehensive school taking the name All Saints Catholic School. In the 1900s there was a growing movement among Mary Ward's followers to have her restored as the founder. A French member of the order, Sister Magdalen Gremion, asked Pope Pius X to restore Ward as foundress. Immediately, he denounced Ward as a heretic, but later capitulated, concluding that there was no case against her. In 1909 Ward was finally recognised as the foundress of both the Institute of the Blessed Virgin Mary (also known as the Loreto sisters) and the Congregation of Jesus.

During World War One, Belgian nuns and refugee children were given a home at the convent and the Concert Hall was converted into a hospital for wounded soldiers. During World War Two the convent was bombed during the Baedeker raids on York that targeted buildings of cultural and historical significance. On Wednesday 29th April 1942 five nuns were killed when a delayed action bomb ripped through the building. Six of the nuns-in-residence were firewatchers and stayed above ground when the raid started. Everyone else, including the pupils, went down to the air raid shelters.

When the dust settled, the firewatchers were still missing. Searching for their sisters, someone could hear Mother Mary Agnes. Furiously, the rescuers searched the rubble. Little did they know that below the dust and debris Mother Mary Agnes lay beside an unexploded bomb. As the rescue team rushed for a ladder, the bomb exploded, killing Mother Anges and all but one of the rescue party. During the raid on York which lasted for two hours, eighty-six people died including fourteen children. Another ninety-eight were seriously injured. Of the 9,500 homes that were damaged, 2000 people were made homeless. In the night of carnage, the Guildhall and St Martin Le Grand Church were also badly damaged.

In 2002 the convent was finally allowed to take the name 'Congregation of Jesus', which was the name that Mary Ward had intended for her order, as well as the constitutions of the Jesuits. By 1921 the day school and the boarding school were merged together to become the Bar Convent Grammar School. Recognised by the Board of Education in 1923, it received grant status in 1929. In 1932 Pope Pius XI opened Mary Ward's case for sainthood and later praised her as 'an incomparable woman'. The first step on her journey to sainthood was to pronounce her 'Venerable'. Then the Vatican Congregation for the Causes of Saints reviewed the decision by scrutinising a 5,500-position paper on Ward's life. There has been no movement on the decision regarding canonisation since this time.

Today two high schools and one elementary school in Toronto have taken Mary Ward's name. There are also several schools in Germany and Australia. The Bar Convent is still home to Mary Ward's religious order and lives in a Grade 1 listed building that is open to the public as a museum, shop, café, guest house and meeting rooms. The chapel, which is open to all who wish to worship, is where the hand of the Catholic martyr, Margaret Clitherow can be seen, and her terrible fate meditated upon.

Mary Ward was not just a religious pioneer who knew how to lead, teach and inspire others. She had the courage to live out her convictions in a very dangerous time for anyone who veered away from orthodoxy. She was also a feminist who saw the potential of other women and their need for education. She once said 'there is no such difference between men and women that women in time to come will do much'. Her prophetic words are emblematic, not only of her own struggle, but of the long struggle of women all over the world for equal rights with men.

Women of York

CHAPTER TEN

Anne Fairfax

Sole Survivor

WHEN ANNE FAIRFAX was born in 1724, she was the second daughter of Charles Gregory Fairfax, 9th Viscount Fairfax of Emley (1770-1772) and his second wife, Mary Fairfax. By this time Charles Gregory had only been in England for five years, as he had hastily returned from Germany after his father, William, had received the unexpected news that he had inherited the title of 8th Viscount of Emley. The premature death of his uncle meant that William now controlled the estate of the Fairfax of York, which comprised the ancient family seat of Gilling Castle, along with numerous landholdings in North Yorkshire, including Walton, Scawton, West Heslerton, Acaster and Coulton.

With his sudden, and what must have been welcome entry into the aristocracy, Anne's father, Charles Gregory did not take long to establish connections with one of the other most important families in the county, the Constables of Burton Constable. A mere one year after his return to the land of his birth, Charles Gregory married Elizabeth Constable, the widow of the 4th Viscount Dunbar. It had been two years since her first husband had died and Elizabeth was probably pleasantly surprised to receive the proposal of a handsome young man much nearer her own age. Besides being forty-one years her senior, her first husband had also been a notorious philanderer.

Although Charles Gregory was next in line to inherit the title of Viscount of Emley, it did not mean that he was cash rich. In fact, the family business was in trouble. Through his marriage to Elizabeth, Charles was introduced to Francis Chlomely of Brandsby, who helped turn the fortunes of the estate around with better management than his predecessor. Several financial trusts were set up that took over the Fairfax estates, making Charles Gregory a life tenant that allowed him to draw an income from them. A huge sale of timber from the estates took place, which raised £2000, the equivalent of £232,000 today, allowing all the debts to be paid off.

Despite the need for fiscal caution, both Fairfax and his new wife could be reckless with money. According to Gerry Webb, author of 'Fairfax of York' and curator of Fairfax House for many years, 'Elizabeth was dangerously addicted to dabbling in the South Sea Bubble'. This was a joint-stock company founded in

1711 to supply African slaves to the islands in the South Seas and South America. Initially, the value of the shares in the company rose exponentially, then collapsed suddenly, bringing economic ruin to thousands of investors. Elizabeth was reputed to have a quick temper and was offended when her cousin, Cuthbert Constable, would not acquiesce to her request to lend her a further £1000 to invest in her favourite risky venture.

Charles Gregory also enjoyed the high life in London and often exasperated his new estate manager, Francis Cholmeley, with his 'reckless ventures'. Unfortunately, within a year Charles Gregory's young marriage was over. On a trip to Bath to sample the waters in 1721, Elizabeth contracted smallpox. She suffered for over a week, dying after an agonising ten days. Charles Gregory must have been eager to start a family because approximately one year after Elizabeth's death, he remarried. His second wife was his cousin, Mary Fairfax, who was the sister of the 6th Viscount Fairfax who had died in 1715.

Mary became pregnant quickly and the year after their marriage in 1723 their first daughter, Mary, was born. The following year came Anne. Exhaustingly, for the next five years Mary Fairfax was pregnant every single year, although heartbreakingly, her next three children did not survive infancy. After a two-year gap she was pregnant once more and proceeded to give birth to another four children over the course of the next eight years.

Unfortunately, only one child from her second round of pregnancies survived. By 1850 only the fourteen-year-old Elizabeth and the twenty-six year old Anne were alive. In Mary's portrait by Philip Mercier she wears a gorgeous grey silk gown with a marine blue shawl. Her skin is the pale shade of a typical English rose. Her soft auburn hair curls frame her delicate features and her mouth is pursed. Her large blue eyes, that mirror the colour of her shawl, have a hint of sadness about them.

According to Webb, of the children, 'Only Mary, Anne and the second Elizabeth lived long enough to receive any formal education. We know that Mary was educated at the Bar Convent School in York, as her name appears on the school records for 1735. Hugh Aveling in his 'The Catholic Recusancy of the Yorkshire Fairfaxes' states that Anne was also educated at this school from at least between 1733 and 1736 and possibly also at a convent in France. There is also the record of some mishap while Anne was at the Bar Convent because her poor father was presented with a bill for a broken window.

Devastatingly, when Anne was just twelve years old, her older sister Mary died of smallpox at the age of thirteen. This must have been a crushing blow to Anne who had seen all her other young siblings die too. It must have made her question the nature of the world and it would have been difficult for her not to come to the conclusion that it was a very cruel place.

It is likely that Anne and her mother would have been comforted by Anne's formidable grandmother, Lady Hungate, who is known to have lodged at the Bar Convent during the year that Mary died. We cannot be certain how long Anne spent at the Bar Convent school or how satisfied with her education her father was. In the archives Webb discovered a bill for December 1747, submitted by one John Coultish 'for learning the young ladies writing'. Evidently, Anne's education was interrupted by the repeated illnesses in her family. At the time of Coultish's bill, Anne would have been twenty-three years old and her only surviving sibling, Elizabeth, thirteen. Anne's papers held at Northallerton County Archives office do show a rather shaky and unconfident hand. Anne's father, Charles Gregory, was an educated man with an extensive library and the ability to speak fluent French. He must have arranged some catch-up classes for his daughters.

In 1742 Phillip Mercier, the French portrait painter made his way to York after being banished from the court of George II in mysterious and perhaps scandalous circumstances. Lord Fairfax seized the opportunity to have such an eminent artist paint his family. He commissioned three portraits – one of his wife, one of his two remaining daughters, Anne and Elizabeth and another of Anne alone.

In the portrait of the two siblings, the sisters are dressed in their finest gowns of sumptuous pale pink and lemony-gold satin. The eighteen-year-old Anne looks playful, sitting at a desk toying with a hamster that is fascinated by a ball of wool. Next to her Elizabeth, aged eight, holds the wool and looks directly at the viewer while Anne stares absent-mindedly into the distance. They are pretty with soft, delicate skin and rosy cheeks. The backdrop is an ornamental garden with a fountain. Clearly, Lord Fairfax was already thinking about the marriage market for his daughters, advertising their eligibility alongside his wealth. Their delicate features resemble their beautiful mother, Mary.

By 1741 the young family had been devastated by the tragic loss of so many children when a further disaster was to strike. Just two years after her most recent loss, Anne's mother was also struck down by smallpox, the disease that had carried away all her children before her.

Smallpox has been described as one of the deadliest pandemics in the history of the human race. Its reign of terror is believed to have endured for twelve thousand years. Infection occurs through a virus that causes ugly rashes on the face, hands, forearms and torso, which eventually turn into sore blisters. The patient suffers fevers, chills, body aches and malaise. In some cases there may even be vomiting. If an infected individual recovers, they can be left scarred and disfigured for life. After being ravaged by the disease, a survivor could also find themselves permanently blinded.

During the eighteenth century there were repeated waves of smallpox epidemics that touched all classes of individuals. No one was safe, including royalty. Although there were some desperate experiments, there was no treatment or cure until 1796 when Edward Jenner was credited with successfully developing the first ever inoculation against any infectious disease. He developed the smallpox vaccine from his work with a similar strain of the disease found in cows. Due to his pioneering work we have come to call all inoculations 'vaccines', the Latin root of which is 'vacca', meaning cow.

With so much illness, suffering, death and grief in her short life, it is no wonder that Anne Fairfax became 'emotionally disturbed' as Webb has described her. Then as if her suffering wasn't enough, another disaster struck Anne and Charles Gregory. In 1753, at the age of seventeen, Anne's only surviving sibling, Elizabeth, was taken by smallpox also.

Thus by the time she was thirty years old, Anne had witnessed all her siblings suffer and die, along with her beloved mother. It is unimaginable the grief and confusion that she must have suffered. Naturally, Anne was to become the last remaining comfort to her father. In turn, he would grow protective of her, while she became heavily reliant upon him. As the smallpox virus could be spread by contact with infected bodily fluid or airborne through coughing and sneezing, it is a wonder that Anne and her father survived at all, as it would have been extremely difficult to isolate from so many infected members of the family.

It is not known whether Anne or her father suffered what has come to be known as survivor's syndrome, a mental condition that occurs when a person believes that they have done something wrong by surviving a traumatic or tragic event. Now considered to be within the gamut of post traumatic stress disorder, it is easy to envisage both Anne and her father suffering mentally as a consequence of the pain that they had witnessed and the bereavements that followed. Fortunately for Anne, her father had been devoted to her mother and was a loving father. Webb relates that:

> 'Nothing gave him greater pleasure than being surrounded by his children and hearing from those to whom he was related. He could inspire affection in others too. Lady Westmoreland thought that "he is so good a man I wish him what he likes best". More children is what she had in mind'.

However, having lost both his wives to the ravaging disease, Lord Fairfax never remarried. Instead, Anne grew up at her family's ancestral seat at Gilling Castle. In 1771 the agriculturalist, Arthur Young, made a tour of the north of England and described Gilling thus:

> 'The castle stands very high, and has a noble and diversified prospect, but a confined one... Lord Fairfax has a command of an whole vale, contemplating the plantations of Mr Worsley at Hovingham, the old castle at Slingsby and terminates in view of the wolds about Malton. Directly under the hill lies the beautiful village of Oswaldkirk... He has changed a park which would not fatten his deer, into beautiful closes of pasture and meadow...you ride through cultivated grounds and a fine lawn by a gentle ascent, with flourishing plantations on each side of you, to an elegant pavilion or summer dining room, erected by John Carr, Esq; now Lord Mayor of York...In this castle are two rooms worth notice, viz. a very good parlour, in modern taste, and a remarkable antique dining-room, of a compleat size and good proportion; both the floor and sides wainscoted with fine oak, and the windows with painted glass, the arms of all the gentlemen in the weapon-take.'

The final reference is to the Elizabethan Great Chamber which was created by Sir William Fairfax in the late sixteenth century to display his great interest in heraldry. A remarkably colourful heraldic frieze wraps around the majority of the room, above the wooden wainscoting, displaying twenty-two trees representing all the ancient territorial divisions (wapentakes) of Yorkshire. Webb reports that 'in the leafy, sometimes blossom-filled branches, some 450 shields are emblazoned with the arms of Yorkshire nobility'. It was amongst these historic and grand surroundings that Anne grew to maturity. Doubtless, it would have been difficult not to develop a sense of her own importance and entitlement, given the historic name and privileged line that she had been born into.

Nevertheless, although Anne's father drew an income from his estates, as a Roman Catholic he was barred from public office and therefore from a lucrative means of supplementing his finances. Ever ambitious for more funds, Charles Gregory did create some stress and anxiety for himself by continuing with risky investments. He sank a whopping £11,000, the equivalent of £1.3 million today, in the cargo of a ship called the Amable Maria which sailed between Cadiz and Lima. He also had an interest in a wine importing business, as well as an insurance brokership in Antwerp.

During the 1750s, Anne may have spent some time in London with her father and sister as he leased a house in Kensington for the winter season. Prior to 1750 they may have lodged with a succession of distant relatives and acquaintances. Each spring the family would travel north to Gilling, where they would remain during the summer, going on occasional outings to Knaresborough and Harrogate to sample the waters. Lord Fairfax was drawn to the entertainments that towns afforded and could neglect his country estates. There are numerous letters between him and his frustrated estate managers who urge him for decisions on the business of his land holdings.

Not only was Lord Fairfax in financial and medical danger, he was also in peril due to the religion which he was born into. In 1745 England was invaded by a rebel army led by Charles Edward Stuart, who based his claim to the throne on his descent from the Catholic King James II. Called the Jacobite rebellion, taking their name from Jacobus, the Latin for James, Charles Edward Stuart believed the King George I and King George II of Hanover in Germany had usurped his throne. The threat to the British crown was very serious as there had already been an uprising in 1715. For several months the nation held its breath as the British army engaged the Jacobite forces in a series of battles and skirmishes. Supporters of the rebellion were diverse and not only found in Scotland, but also in England and Ireland and had its allies in the Catholic monarchies of Europe, including France and Spain.

The outcome of the 1745 uprising was decided when the Jacobites made a strategic retreat to their stronghold in the Scottish Highlands. By the spring of the next year, they suffered a crushing defeat at the hands of one of the brothers of King George II, the Duke of Cumberland. While Charles Edward Stuart managed to escape and flee to safety in France, the battle was so bloody that the Duke was ever after called 'the butcher of Cumberland'.

Following the defeat, the government and monarchy sought to repress the Jacobite movement, which was forced underground, but not before executing approximately fifty fighters accused of treason. They were marched from the Castle Prison to the Knavesmire where they met their death. The heads of the ringleaders were then spiked on Micklegate bar as a warning to all others who tried to overturn Hanoverian rule. Fortunately, Anne who had been made timorous and shy due to the tragic circumstances of her family life, was no longer at school at the Bar Convent. Otherwise, she would have been faced with the horror of the heads every day.

King George II believed that Jacobite supporters were predominantly Catholic and therefore decided that anyone of the Catholic faith was to be barred from public office and positions of authority. Catholics were made to swear an Oath of Allegiance to the Crown and only Protestants could succeed to the throne. Despite these measures, fear and suspicion of the Jacobites persisted for several decades after the rebellions and Catholics became second-class citizens in their own country.

Lord Fairfax may have not been as discreet as possible in his sympathies for the Catholic movement and he was warned on more than one occasion by the Archbishop of York, Thomas Herring, that he needed to be more circumspect in the practise of his religion. A rumour had been circulating that he was harbouring troops at Gilling Castle in preparation for an uprising in the 1745 rebellion. Hugh Aveling records that the matter turned out well because the archbishop decided that he had 'taken the matter too highly'. The charming Lord Fairfax drank to the king's health with the officer of the militia who had been sent to interview him and the incident fortunately ended amicably.

Another strain on Lord Fairfax's finances was his decision to pay for the education of some of his distant relatives. In the 1760s he put the two sons of his friend Sir Edward Gascoigne through school in France, causing him some worry and vexation. He felt obliged to take control of their education as had been named co-guardian with three of his fellow aristocrats. One of his nephews, Francis Bredall, was put through Lambspring College at the Viscount's expense.

Bredall was then set up as an apprentice apothecary in York. Living with his only surviving daughter after having lost two wives and eight children to smallpox, it is not surprising that both Anne and her father developed a preoccupation with their health. Bredall was just one of the relatives of the father and daughter who preyed upon their vulnerability. Not satisfied with having been trained in a profession by Lord Fairfax, according to Webb, Bredall then went on to exploit the 'somewhat neurotic obsession with illness and disease of Fairfax and his daughter'.

After having just taken up an apothecary's post in London in 1734, he sent the Viscount his first, but not last obsequious begging letter, which reads as follows:

'Uncle…I beg the favour to let me have a new suit of clothes which my master thinks I stand in need of & likewise of gloves and a pair of buckles and if you think it proper to favour me with a little pocket money I shall reckon it among the favours you have done me'.

For forty years he was happy to ply the aristocratic father and daughter with all sorts of dubious medicine, then bill them for it. Take for example:

The Stomatick tincture Yr Lordship	*2s.6d*
Purging potion with manna Miss	*1s. 0d*
Horse Balls.	

In 1753 between July and December he doled out seventy different items over the course of fifty-six days. Some of his remedies have names which are quite frightening, such as 'compound purging potion for Thomas', one of the servants. As well as ministering to all the household servants, he provided Anne with ' a pott of lenitive elictuary'. It is to be hoped that Anne felt better after this as 'lentive' simply means soothing. It is anyone's guess was 'elictuary' means. Unfortunately for Anne, Bredall was not the only distant relative to prey upon her vulnerability in an attempt to extort money from her. Towards the end of her life, the devious and scheming Nathaniel Pigott would crawl out of the woodwork.

By 1753 Lord Fairfax was in his fifties. With his wife and most of his young family dead, Webb describes his emotional state with compassion:

'He was desolated by this great tragedy and fearful for the future of his estates in the absence of any surviving male heir. With little left to live for, he became resolved to devote the remainder of his life to the well-being and happiness of his only surviving daughter, Anne'.

Lord Fairfax was keen to find a suitable husband for Anne. The portrait of her from 1740 by Philip Mercier in which she sits alone, shows her in an elegant yellow satin dress with a pretty pink rose at her bosom. The background is a pastoral idyll and she has three sheep to her right. In her left hand she holds a crook and is presented as a shepherdess to emphasise her youth and innocence. Her hair is darker than in her portrait with her sister and this time she stares directly at the viewer with her large brown eyes. Her skin is beautifully pale, and she has a small smile playing about her mouth. She would have been an extremely good catch for an eligible bachelor. The three paintings by Mercier all disappeared from the family collection over the passage of time, only to reappear in a North Country sale in 1985. York Civic Trust was able to acquire the portrait of Anne with the help of generous donations. The stunning picture currently sits above the fireplace in her bedroom at Fairfax House, her yellow dress complimenting the yellow wallpaper decorated with exotic birds and foliage.

At the age of twenty-four, Anne became engaged to be married to Thomas Clifton of Lytham, who had been visiting Gilling Castle from time to time during the 1740s. However, the relationship between them did not meet Lord Fairfax's approval and was not allowed to proceed further. In April 1749, Fairfax wrote to his friend, Sir Edward Gascoigne:

'I would not omit to let my dear Bart. know immediately that I have had the great Esq. of Lytham a week at Gilling. I am glad I know him. I cane but say that if I had not seen him before it was at an end it might have give one now and then some uneasiness thinking I had been more hasty, and I have the satisfaction that your God daughter is now more chearfull than ever I knew although I have said nothing to her, by, which as Mrs Forcer tells me, she does not doubt that it is at an end. I bless God for her perseverance as I think there could not have been much happyness for her to have been expected...'

It seems that Anne was relieved that the tentative relationship was Clifton was at an end. There is also a hint that Lord Fairfax found him somewhat arrogant. The Mrs Forcer referred to in the letter was a distant relation of the family who acted as Anne's companion and possibly surrogate mother, as she appears to be more knowledgeable of Anne's state of mind on the matter than her father.

Six years later Anne's father proposed that she married William Constable of Burton Constable. Perhaps this was an attractive proposition to her father as the two previous intermarriages between the families had helped to restore his financial stability. The expectation would be that if Anne bore a son, he would eventually inherit the estates and change his name to Fairfax. The wedding plans were coming together apace. A trousseau of bridal garments and linen had been created for Anne and a special license for the event had been obtained. The date was fixed for the middle of June of 1755 and the two families travelled to London in readiness for the occasion. However, Lord Fairfax began to develop serious doubts about William Constable's commitment to the Catholic faith.

Shortly before the wedding took place, William wrote a long letter to Anne in which he admitted that he had 'only been to prayers on two working days'. Upon reading this confession, Lord Fairfax was deeply worried. For him, his faith was central, superseding even his concerns for his estates. He believed that William and Anne were completely incompatible if William did not attend Mass regularly. Anne was told by her father to write to William to receive assurances that he would become more diligent in his religious practice. However, Lord Fairfax felt that he did not receive a satisfactory response. Almost at the last minute, Anne's father cancelled the wedding and whisked Anne back to Gilling Castle.

In an explanatory letter to William, Lord Fairfax is full of apologies as he does not wish to offend the important Constable family. He is careful to lay the blame at the door of Anne, stating that she should have let him know her misgivings earlier. He explains to Constable:

'You are good in excusing Miss. I am sensible since I came home, as I told her, she was to blame to be always on that topic after so many assurances you had given her, especially as a man of honour. If she in the least ever doubted it, why did she let things go on so far and not acquaint me with it until almost the last, which was very wrong in her. But I found I was not mistaken in my judgement that it proceeded from your mentioning in one of your letters to her of your having been but twice at prayers on working days, so from that time gave me continued uneasiness on that score, as well as to now if you had been regularly on days of obligations...'

Webb argues that Anne would have accepted her father's decision because she was 'timorous and compliant'. However, he suggests that 'knowing what we do about Anne's nature, it is more than likely that she had her own dark thoughts about her involvement with William. One can almost hear her silently pleading, "for goodness sake father, get me out of this awful predicament – I can't possibly go on with it"'.

Perhaps the thought of marriage and all the upheaval that it would bring to her life was too much for her. After all she had seen her exhausted mother die after bearing eight children and therefore perhaps marriage was not the romantic and attractive proposition to her that many women were trained to believe in. Webb concludes that:

'Her concerns were probably not just about religion. Her whole sheltered upbringing and convent education would have been quite inadequate to prepare her for such a drastic step into the unknown as marriage'.

Perhaps she was happy to continue her privileged life as her father's only, and therefore favourite child. She had Mrs Forcer for company and a good friend in the sister of Viscount Fauconberg, Mary Bellasis. Maybe Anne felt that her life was complete, and safer, without marriage.

Webb also hints at a darker side to William Constable that she may have become aware of, which may have deterred her from entering into such a binding commitment with him:

'Could it be also be that in her meetings with William she had become vaguely aware of certain other of his alleged propensities which are probably best left unexplored in the context of Fairfax history?'

It has been impossible to confirm what William Constable's 'alleged propensities' were. He is renowned for having an interest in science and natural history, creating a cabinet of curiosities which is now in Hull City Museum. He also redesigned the gardens of Burton Constable, his ancestral home and is the subject of a book by Elizabeth Hall called 'The Plant Collections of an Eighteenth Century Virtuso'. It seems that he was put off marriage for quite some time after his debacle with the Fairfaxes, eventually marrying Catherine Langdale in 1776.

As regards Anne and marriage, Weber concludes that she simply wasn't the marrying kind:

'What comes through very clearly in any study of Anne's life and character is that she was definitely not the marrying sort. She probably breathed a great sigh of relief when the tumult subsided...'

In 1755 an earthquake devastated the city of Lisbon and the total destruction of the metropolis shook Europe. Webb believes that:

'It is likely that 25-year-old Anne Fairfax was in London with her father at this time. The experience and the memory of it would have made a deep impression on her delicate mind, already made unstable by the recent loss of all her family'.

The fact that Anne outlived all her siblings, went on to make some very important decisions both during and after her father's death, was able to defend herself from a predatory relative and leave her estate to whom she wished, suggests that she was made of far stronger stuff than Webb gives her credit for.

Lord Fairfax's relationship with his religion gives us an interesting insight into his character. Webb repeatedly describes him as 'obstinate' and having an 'inflexible and uncompromising nature'. Because of the 'overriding importance he attached to his religion, he always found it very difficult to find a chaplain who would respond wholeheartedly to his wishes. He got through no fewer than seven chaplains in twelve years before eventually finding one, Fr Anslem Bolton, who was prepared to serve him with the single-minded obedience which he considered his due'.

Father Bolton was to become a very important person to Anne Fairfax in the latter part of her life, showing that she was equally as devoted to the Catholic faith as her father. Perhaps both Anne and her father used their faith to help them through their numerous bereavements.

In 1760 Lord Farifax spent £2000 on purchasing a property on one of York's most ancient streets. By this time York was full of the townhouses of the aristocracy who went to the city to enjoy the entertainments on offer for the winter season. As York was suffering an economic depression due to the decline in trade brought about by the silting up of the River Ouse, as well as the ongoing restrictive practices of the Merchant Adventurers that ensured only those who acquired the status of Freeman of the city could trade, the city fathers decided to turn York into a fashionable metropolis to tempt the northern gentry out of their boring country estates. The journey to Bath or London took days over treacherously rutted roads and so the corporation of York decided to capitalise on the sociability and love of gaiety of the gentry and upper classes.

The delights on offer included a range of plays at York Theatre Royal, fine gatherings and dances at the beautiful Assembly Rooms, one of the first neo-classical buildings in the country, as well as horse racing at the Knavesmire. Lord Fairfax is on the list of subscribers to the Assembly Rooms and would have enjoyed dances there. Anne had more solitary character than her father and was content to stay at home, not as tempted by York's glittering social scene.

One of the oldest and grandest streets in York, Micklegate, was already packed with the elegant Georgian townhouses of the gentry and aristocracy. Sir John Bouchier had snapped up the imposing Micklegate House with its grand sweeping staircase overlooked by a fashionable Venetian window. Blake Street and Petergate were equally as densely inhabited by the affluent and the fortunate. By the late 1750s, Lord Fairfax decided that he wanted a permanent base in the city, and probably struck on a property in Castlegate because there was no other fashionable site large enough left in the city. The property that he lit on was extensive enough to allow him to fulfil all his ambitions and provide him and his daughter with all the most modern amenities.

Castlegate, another ancient York street, was not the most desireable area of the city. Contiguous with the prison complex dominated by the ancient Clifford's Tower, prisoners would be forced down the cobbled lane in carts, after which they would meet their deaths at Tyburn, adjoining the Knavesmire. Twenty years earlier in 1739, the notorious highwayman Dick Turpin bought himself a new suit so that he looked his best before the crowds which gathered to witness the spectacle of his transportation to his place of execution. Radiating down from Castlegate to the River Ouse were the three notorious Water Lanes, the homes of the most destitute in the city, which by the next century would become a maze of squalid courtyards where a criminal underclass operated.

Nevertheless, Castlegate's lack of prestige did not deter Lord Fairfax who employed the foremost architect in northern England, John Carr, to remodel his townhouse to such spectacular effect that by 2003 it would be described as the 'finest townhouse in England' by Simon Jenkins' in his compendium, 'England's Thousand Best Houses'.

Although Lord Fairfax had had plenty of practice overseeing building work, such as his remodelling Gilling Castle twenty years earlier, Fairfax House was to be a much more ambitious project. The receipt for the insurance of the house taken out in 1761 shows that the complex comprised a washhouse and laundry behind the main building, a stable in the yard behind the house and a coach house on the opposite side of the road. A little later on, Farifax decided to buy the house next door, which he partially demolished to create a carriageway to the outbuildings at the rear. The plans that he envisaged for the property were radical.

The complete renovation of the interior involved the cutting out of new windows and bespoke iron balusters were made for a beautifully ornate staircase. As the new building work progressed, a substantial quantity of woodwork that was no longer required was advertised for sale. Records in the archive show that the 'necessary' needed to be made more comfortable by altering the platform that it sat on. The doors to the most important rooms were to be made of prohibitively expensive mahogany. However, Lord Fairfax made the economical decision of using the original pine doors for the least impressive rooms. One of the mahogany doors in the main saloon on the first floor was a false door, showing that Fairfax was determined to have a perfectly symmetrical entertaining room that showed that he was at the height of fashion.

The housekeeper, Mrs Pyatt, and the butler were provided with beds, although he had to sleep in the pantry. More servants were housed in a service wing, which has since been demolished. Clearly, security conscious, the windows were protected with steel bars projecting into the window jambs, of such strength that some exist to this day. Lord Fairfax did not wish to be awoken one night by 'house breakers'. Originally the front of the house was protected by railings and double gates, which were lost when Castlegate was widened. Anne and her father enjoyed meals by their cook, Martha Brown, who along with Mrs Pyatt, was fastidious in her purchases and payments.

During the winter season, a skeleton staff of servants was brought in from Giling Castle and the monthly provisions of food are estimated to be at around £75, the equivalent of £10,000 today. No wonder Lord Fairfax's funds were always stretched.

Guiseppe Cortese, an Italian stuccoist resident in Wakefield, was employed to create the beautiful white plaster designs in the hall, which can be admired as one descends the stone cantilever staircase. While most of the inhabitants of the city at this time had to obtain water from the rivers Foss or Ouse, or from wells, Lord Fairfax and Anne enjoyed a piped water supply. Had it not been for this modern convenience, servants would have had to go out into the street with buckets. The water originated from the only pumping station in York, housed in Lendal Tower. The engine was worked by two horses that sent the water through wooden pipes to some of the favoured streets of the city. However, it was impossible to satisfy the full demand for water and so each half of the city was supplied on alternate days. The wooden pipes leaked so badly that the engine was often stopped for long periods.

The Fairfaxes' new house probably enjoyed just one tap in the kitchen or scullery, with servants dispensing water around the rest of the house. Viscount

Fairfax also needed a good supply of water for another of the indulgences that he had afforded himself. Across the road his brewhouse needed copious amounts of water to ferment the beer that in those days was safer than the unpurified and unfiltered water. The Viscount enjoyed alcoholic beverages and he had his own wine merchant in London called James Underhill, who sometimes had great difficulty in meeting the Viscount's exacting standards. According to Webb, when totalling up the Fairfax wine bill, they consumed 'prodigious quantities'. After writing a letter of complaint to his merchant about the poor standard of a batch of burgundy, he received the following obsequious apology.

'I am heartily sorry to hear that the Burgundy I have sent your Lordship has proved so very bad. When it went from hence it was thought exceeding good by everybody that tasted it, and I faithfully assure your Ldsp that if I had thought it would not have proved good, I never would have sent it to your Ldsp'.

Clearly Mr Underhill did not wish to lose this highly lucrative customer. Records show that the minimum consumption for the Viscount and his daughter was one bottle of port and three bottles of sherry per day. It is a wonder that both of them lived well into their sixties.

The fireplace in Lord Fairfax's library featured a Greek key pattern and panels of marble from Sienna in Italy, which the prolific architect John Carr used in other mansions. On the ceiling of his library, Lord Fairfax commissioned four portrait medallions of writers and thinkers of the day – John Milton, Joseph Addison, John Locke and Alexander Pope, a clear indication of his literary taste and sensibilities.

After two years of remodelling and construction, Lord Fairfax complained of the huge sums he was spending on the house. In 1762 he wrote to his London banker, Mr Wright, 'my Daughter's house, which is just finished and paid for, drains me of all my money'. Clearly, the house was intended as a legacy for Anne, although after two failed engagements and the fact that she was by now thirty-six, it is unlikely that it was intended to form part of her dowry.

Estimates suggest that he spent in the region of £8000 on the refurbishment, the equivalent of over £800,000 today. Lord Fairfax was evidently completely broke. He wrote to John Mayer in 1763, a friend who had acted for him in the purchase of the house four years earlier to see if he could borrow some money. Mayer was not forthcoming. 'My Lord, I am very sorry that I have not at present any spare cash, and to procure that sum for so short a time will be next to an impossibility; but as I am morally assured of the money for the wood being paid next Monday, it may answer your Ldsps expectation'. The sale of wood was again to come to the Viscount's financial rescue.

When his grand oeuvre was complete, Lord Fairfax decided to throw a lavish party to inaugurate his new townhouse and celebrate his sixty-third birthday at the same time. It was such a celebrated event that it was reported in the York Courant on April 19, 1763. It read:

'Last Thursday, being the Anniversary of the Birth of the Right Hon. Lord Viscount Fairfax, his Lordship gave an elegant Entertainment and a Ball to above 200

Gentlemen and Ladies at his magnificent new House on the Castlehill in this City, which is just finished.'

Clearly, Lord Fairfax and Anne were the modern equivalent of York's very own media celebrities and invitations to the ball would have been highly sought after. Lucky party guests arrived over a period of several hours. Once gathered they were entertained with music and dancing. For such a huge party, the guests were fêted by a spectacular buffet.

Around the same time, Anne's father hosted a more informal and intimate gathering for approximately seventeen of his close friends and relatives. Invited to the select dinner were his nephew Francis Bredall, the quack apothecary and his wife. The house was graced with the presence of Lord Fairfax's friend, the 5th Viscount Fauconberg of Newburgh Priory, his wife, Lady Fauconberg and his sisters Mary and Catherine. Anne would have been particularly pleased by the attendance of Mary and Catherine, as she was to become firm friends with Mary during her time in York.

Lord Fairfax's inner circle also include Gerald Strickland of Sizergh Castle near Lake Windermere and his wife, Lady Gascoigne. The Gascoignes of Yorkshire were represented by Sir Thomas Gascoigne and his sister Mary. Lord Fairfax had overseen Sir Thomas' education, along with that of his brother. Unfortunately, Edward Gascoigne was not at the celebration as he had died the previous year. This had enabled Sir Thomas to succeed to the baronetcy. Mrs and Mrs Stephen Tempest of Broughton attended, as did Lord and Lady Irwin of Temple Newsam, whose ancestor had disastrously married Mary, Queen of Scots. Lord and Lady Buchan were also present.

In anticipation of the vast quantities of alcohol which were to be consumed, Lord Farifax had arranged for a local brewer, John Moyser, to be brought in for five weeks prior to the event to brew up the beer that would be needed to entertain his guests. Three types of beer were brewed – ale, middle beer and small beer. Additionally, his wine cellar must have groaned under the weight of bottles. In winter alone, the Viscount was known to spend over £100, just over £10,000 today, on his predilection for wine. A bill from John Carr for work between June 1762 and April 1763 shows that it was a furious race to finish the house in time for the banquet.

In 1990 York Civic Trust commissioned a recreation of the dinner celebration to commemorate the anniversary of the completion of the restorations of Fairfax House that they painstakingly undertook. The replica banquet comprised of sixty-four dishes presented at the table during three courses. Guests were served by the footman and housekeeping staff. Guests were not expected to sample everything on offer but select those dishes that whet their appetites. The butler would oversee the wines and ensure that everything ran smoothly. This kind of service became known as 'a la Francois' and caused difficulties in keeping all the food warm. If a guest was particularly keen on sampling a dish, he or she would need to ensure that they caught the eye of the waiting staff.

When 4.00pm arrived, the footman Joseph Sturdy escorted the guests into the saloon while they awaited his announcement that 'dinner is served, my Lord'. The gathered nobility would have admired the crimson damask colour scheme, designed to create an appropriate backdrop for the gilded frames of the Viscount's paintings. Three years later, the Viscount and his daughter changed the design of the room to a pale blue 'sky mixed' damask. The large sofa and set of eight small armchairs and the two larger ones were re-upholstered and new curtains were added to the windows. The walls, doors and fireplace were trimmed and defined by a decorative gold stripe called a 'fillet'. Webb suggests that the expensive redecoration, just a few years after moving in, were a 'whim on the part of Anne Fairfax', or may have been a desire to keep up with changing fashions in the 1760s.

The guests then descended to the dining room where the meal would begin with warm French rolls from the kitchen. Wine was not usually placed on the table so that consumption could be controlled. Should a guest wish their goblet to be topped up, one clever strategy was to propose a toast to someone's health. It is likely that there were numerous toasts to Anne and her father to thank them for their hospitality and the achievement of having completed such an ambitious project. There must have been considerable toasting at the Viscount's celebration because records tell us that thirty-four bottles of wine were consumed, washed down with forty-eight pints of ale. In 'An Illustrated History and Guide to Fairfax House', the author writes that:

'...in Georgian times, a Dining room was considered an extremely important dynastic statement. Fairfax clearly recognised this concept and lavished a great deal of attention on this room'.

Because of the varied nature of the dishes on offer, guests could choose which beverages to consume. However, it was usual to begin with champagne if this was on offer. It is likely that the Viscount was conservative in his seating arrangements and had his guests sit in order of rank with the mistress of the house at the upper end of the table and the master at the lower end. Seating the guests in the new mode of alternating men and women probably didn't appeal to his traditional nature.

According to York Civic Trust's catalogue of the banquet entitled, 'Pyramids of Pleasure', after taking their seats the guests would be presented with 'a dazzling display of wealth and importance. Created silver plates would be flanked by matching knives, forks and spoons all similarly engraved and the napkins when provided were usually placed on the left hand could be folded several ways. Knowing the Viscount's passion for French rolls however, it is likely that the footman would have used a double fold and wrapped up the bread in an attempt to keep it warm. This method would also allow the Viscount's monogram to be displayed to advantage'.

Lord Fairfax used Monsieur Seguin, a French confectioner who had been resident in York for over thirty years, to supply the sweetmeats. His shop window in Petergate would have displayed marvellously fantastic sugar work creations that took the breath away of all those who passed by. Fairfax then employed the chef, William Baker, to create a spectacular confection, covered in sugar paste or chocolate. Animal heads were often the choice of showpiece and he may have ordered a mock boar's head or something equally as surprising and conversation-provoking.

Whatever Anne and her father's menu choices, the feast cost a small fortune with the 15-guinea bill totalling more than the housekeeper, Mrs Pyatt's wage for the whole year. Guests were provided with two water glasses with a delicate engraved flower pattern, one for rinsing their fingers after eating the deliciously sticky sweetmeats. In 1763 Lord Fairfax purchased blue and white 'Liverpool' china from Anne Baker, which could have been his chosen tableware for the feast. The cutlery may have displayed his armorial bearings to the assembled guests. The Viscount had an impressive collection of sliver totalling 4,000 ounces. Having paid £100 for a 'large silver waiter', it is likely that he may have wanted to show this off at the banquet too. Presiding over the whole affair from his portrait above the mantelpiece was one of the Fairfax's heroic ancestors, Admiral Robert Fairfax, who had died in 1725.

It is likely that half an hour after the banquet finished, guests would have repaired once more to the saloon where drinking and toasting would have continued. All of Viscount Fairfax's guests shared his same religious faith, so there may have been reference to the political situation of the day. Although as ladies were present, it is unlikely that the conversation would have turned onto matters of business, as women were not thought able to understand the complexities of such subjects.

At the end of the evening, Anne would have retired to her bedroom which was decorated in the latest fashion – a yellow mock india paper had been chosen for 'the misses Bedchamber'. This refers to wallpaper which was block printed with a repetitive design and which had been imported into the country by the East India Company.

The following morning, Anne would have descended the staircase holding onto the iron baulustrade which has been described as 'a positive tour de force by Leeds-based eighteenth-century ironsmith Maurice Tobin…' The ornate wrought iron was dotted with gilded rosebud motifs. Her father would have told her that the rosebud secretly symbolised the unfulfilled potential of the Stuart, 'Jacobite' cause. The metaphor is repeated in the elaborate stucco work, intended to remind Anne and her father to stay loyal to the one true faith as they went downstairs to embark on their day. Flanked by the bust of Newton to the left and Shakespeare to the right, each surrounded by a flourish of palm fronds and inanimate drapery, the delicate morning light would have been refracted through the Venetian window 'without parallel in Britain' and which 'makes this space an outstanding architectural set-piece', according to 'An Illustrated History of Fairfax House'.

Above the Venetian window, an agitated dragon representing a female devil is thought to represent James II's daughter Mary Stuart, who, by marrying the Protestant William of Orange caused not only the downfall of the Stuart dynasty but also, the last opportunity for Catholic ascendency. While it has taken historians decades to decode the numerous symbolic meanings in the design of Lord Fairfax's grand staircase and hallway, it probably amused him to think that his friends among the Catholic gentry might be able to decipher his artistic riddles.

Mary Bellasis was very excited to be a guest at the formal ball for two hundred guests and wrote to her father a full four months before the event:

> 'The Fairfax's birthday is to be celebrated on Monday 16th...there is to be a great dinner, ball and supper which I don't doubt will be very elegant...Hope your Lordship will order your best dancing pumps to be aired'.

Anne must have had a good appetite because she had dropped some hints to Mary that she would like her to provide a cut of beef that she had once enjoyed while in their company. Mary's letter continues:

> 'Miss Fairfax talks with such pleasure of a chine of yr Scotch beef that I promised to use my interest with yr Ldsp to procure her one against the 16th. I therefore make my humble petition and beg it may come ready roasted...'

To celebrate her arrival in York, Anne went on a little spending spree, visiting Tasker & Routh where she had a riding suit made, among other garments, for the considerable amount of £11 10s and 1d. Perhaps she wore the suit as she travelled between York and Gilling. It is not known whether Anne was a good horsewoman. Perhaps her father had something to say about the enormous bill, as he was shocked on occasions at how much money she could spend.

Even though Anne was able to enjoy the luxury and glamour of her father's York townhouse, this did not prevent her from going through a very tough period in terms of her mental health. By 1763, the letters of her friend May Bellasis to her father, the 4th Viscount Fauconberg of Newburgh in Coxwold, prove that Anne was a troubled soul.

Mary's first extant letter reads:

> 'My dear Lord, Accept my thanks for your kind letter which I received this evening...Miss Fairfax is rather better but still very low and hysterical. Everything affects her, the Doctor proposes her going to Scarborough the latter end of this week to bath in the sea. She seems very desirous I should stay in York with her till she leaves it, which I have promised to do. By the doctor's desire I endeavour to keep her as quiet as possible, & from the many York friends who would willingly attend her, as also to persuade my old love [Mary's affectionate name for Lord Fairfax] that quiet is absolutely necessary for her, but you know some people understand in a Germanic manner'.

By this time Anne was thirty-eight years old and seems to have been struggling to adjust to life in York. Her mother had been dead for ten years and her sister, Elizabeth for nine. It is hardly surprising that she displayed symptoms of depression and was often very tearful. It is likely that her self-confidence was at rock bottom and there is a hint from Mary that her father's response was not as sympathetic as it could be. Mary writes that he understands in a 'Germanic manner', a reference to the fact that he grew up in Germany and also a suggestion that he had a strong, 'no-nonsense' character. No wonder a sensitive soul like Anne clung on to Mary. Both Gilling and Fairfax House were often filled with visitors. Mary was sometimes able to protect and shield Anne from mercenary hangers-on like the Bredalls, who preyed on the Fairfaxes vulnerabilities.

Although it sounds like her father's response may have made Anne feel even worse, Mary reports that still she 'endeavours to exert her spirits before him & he imagines her much better & seems totally ignorant that talking and affected spirits are hurtful in the complaint'. Out of love and respect for her father, Anne tried to put on a brave face in his presence.

Anne's plight really does sound rather desperate when Mary describes witnessing 'the flow of spirits more than I know is natural'. It is clear that Lord Fairfax has no idea what Anne is going through. Mary continues, 'His Lordship seems to be pretty easy about her, as I really do think he does not seem to me to be sensible of her complaint, but *entre nous* who know some secret reasons, I think it a very bad way to be in, humour may fly to the head, as well as other parts'. Here Mary hints at some intriguing 'secret reasons' why Anne is ill and hints that her psychological condition is so severe that it may even begin to affect her physically.

Mary was the third daughter of Thomas Belasyse or Beallasis who had been a Privy Councillor and Lord of the Bedchamber to George II. Webb states that 'Mary had great strength of character but she was no beauty. Despite indifferent health – she suffered very badly from rheumatism – her cheerful character always overcame such disabilities. She was an inveterate gossip and at one time started the 'Tittle-Tattle Gazette...' Although her exact date of birth is not known, she seems to have been a little younger than Anne, in her mid-thirties also.

Lord Fairfax enjoyed hosting guests and during August race week of 1763, Mary stayed at Fairfax House, along with Miss Langdale and Mrs Crathorne, as well as the wife of Fairfax's sponging and ubiquitious nephew, Francis Bredall. Mary with her inimitable penchant for teasing calls Bredall's wife and daughter, 'Madame L'Appocecaire & sa fille'. Having company would inevitably bring disturbance to the household and not have been very helpful to Anne in her sensitive state. Mary wrote an alarming letter to her father:

'I am sorry to say that I think my poor little friend grows worse instead of better. She seems to have (when out of the presence of her father) the deepest melancholy upon her, a thousand wild thoughts, I really think her brains seem much affected. The Doctor has ordered her to go into a Cold-Bath and now proposed her bathing in cold water instead of her going to Scarborough'.

It is hardly surprising that Anne continued to struggle emotionally and psychologically when instead of prescribing therapy, the Doctor suggested a visit to the sea-side and then a very unappealing cold bath. Water therapy seems to have been the Georgian cure-all and not much use to a disturbed mind.

Fortunately, Anne seems to have had a true friend to console her in Mary Bellasis, who continues:

'Really I am quite unhappy about her, she so earnestly presses me to stay with her & seems to have greater confidence in me than in anyone else, that with yr Ldsps permission I think I must stay with her till she is something better...I have a melancholy scene here, this is a time to show friendship...I have wrote you a melancholy account, but this is only between you and me...'

Anne Fairfax's mental anguish continued into November when Mary wrote to her father at the end of the month:

'I was with my little friend in Castlegate this morning. She had the headache violently yesterday and looks very ill today, her fingers are not yet well, indeed I don't think she is in a good way, she has been very little out since she came to York'.

Anne is clearly someone who does not resort to company and socialising to take her mind off situations but prefers to be quiet and safe at home. The attractions of the York social scene, the premier hub for the aristocracy in the north of England seem to have held little consolation for her. Towards the end of 1764 Mary went to London where she spent the winter at her family townhouse in George Street and she lost contact with the Anne Fairfax temporarily. It is not known how Anne pulled herself through her depression, but somehow she made it through, despite the cold baths.

Fortunately, Christmas was on its way and it was customary for Lord Fairfax to celebrate in style. As early as November 23rd he received a bill for killing game which included woodcock, snipe, hair, partridges, pheasant and three larks. In total there were sixty-nine birds and this was just one of several food bills. Clearly, he was envisioning quite a feast. Fairfax House would have looked even more beautiful during the yuletide season, decked out for Christmas. Columns were decorated with entwined evergreens, mantelpieces were heavy with the bounty of the garden. The family portraits were venerated with a garland of greenery draped around the frame.

However, despite an enjoyable first Christmas in York, by 1766 Anne Fairfax had not only to contend with the psychological maladies set in train by the loss of practically all her family to smallpox, she herself contracted the deadly disease. Lord Bellasis' steward, Richard Chapman wrote to him with the news on 1 February:

'I heard this day that Miss Fairfax is extremely ill of the smallpox at York, is very full and in great danger, they are expected to be at height tomorrow'.

The letter suggests that she was covered in blisters and that the fever was to reach its peak by the next day. However, just over two weeks later, by 18th February, the York Courant was able to report with relief that she was out of danger:

'It is with pleasure that we can inform the public that the Hon. Miss Fairfax is now happily recovered from the smallpox'.

It is hard to imagine whether Anne would be pleased or disappointed that her personal suffering was reported to all and sundry in the north of England.

Worrying about the health of his only surviving daughter, Lord Fairfax's health seemed to suffer also. In July 1766 Mary Bellasis' sister, Anne Talbot, wrote to her father that Lord Fairfax was at Harrowgate taking the waters and was in a bad state of health. She feared that he would not live much longer. Fortunately, she was mistaken and he soldiered on for another eight years.

Although Anne recovered from smallpox, there is no record of whether she was left with any permanent skin damage. However, there is evidence that she continued to be psychologically scarred. On 22 August Doctor Dealtry wrote to her father, who was staying at Gilling:

'I saw Miss Fairfax the other night and her a little [hurried?]; upon enquiry she had not been very well before she came to York, and though she was careful not to increase her complaints, yet I thought it advisable for her not to return to Gilling so soon as he intended or wished. I think she may come on Monday or Tuesday & that your Ldsp will rest satisfied that it is owning rather to my precaution than to any degree of hazard there is in her complaints...I do not think her disorder was quite hysterical, yet a little so'.

It sounds like Anne was prone to suffering anxiety and panic attacks, understandable under the circumstances. Dr Dealty's letter also reveals that Lord Fairfax trusted her enough to be on her own at Fairfax House in York while he was away at Gilling, showing that they were not completely inseparable, so she was capable of leading a life independent from her father at times.

By 1768 Lord Fairfax decided that Anne stood a good chance of recovering from her psychological problems if she were sent off to France with her chaplain, Father Anslem Bolton. Their itinerary was to include stays at a convent in Cambrai, which Lord Fairfax had links with. Helen Gascoigne, a family friend, was the Mother Superior of the convent. In those days this journey could be not only highly uncomfortable over rough and dangerous roads, the North Sea crossing to the Continent was notoriously unpredictable.

Nevertheless, Anne's socialite father was convinced that a change of company and surroundings would be beneficial and invigorating to Anne. In April Lord Fairfax accompanied his daughter and her chaplain to Dover and then went to London for a while before returning to Gilling Castle in June. Not averse to making money, the Viscount was to let out his house in York and part with his servants.

The pair were to journey to Lille and then onto Cambrai. Father Bolton's letter to Lord Fairfax reveals that Anne was finding it difficult to settle into life on the road:

'We found at Calais an English coach with which Miss Fairfax seems much better pleased than ye French post-chaises. Ye hire of ye coach was rather high, but as she is so very timorous, I hope yr Ldsp will think it reasonable enough as Miss Fairfax does at present'.

Thus far Anne Fairfax has been unfairly portrayed as demanding and 'voluble in her discontent' with Webb writing that 'one pities the servants who had to minister to her querulous complaints'. Although, her desire not to get into a French coach that she deemed dangerous was clearly so annoying to Father Anslem that he felt the need to report it to her father, it is quite understandable, given that it is highly likely that she had an exaggerated instinct for survival after all that she had been through. There has been little sympathy displayed for Anne by those who have written about her before. She is repeatedly described as 'neurotic' with all the negative connotations that the word carries in an age when mental health conditions were ignored in the interests of maintaining a stiff upper lip.

The writer of 'Fairfax House, An Illustrated History and Guide' treats her slightly more kindly when writing that she 'was a troubled young woman and seemingly difficult to please'. As the only surviving child of Lord Fairfax's nine children, it is highly likely that she was somewhat indulged. However, sending her to mainland Europe the year after recovering from smallpox, was hardly treating her with kid gloves.

At first Anne was understandably unhappy in France. Father Anselm reported that 'she proposes seeing some more places after a little rest here and after that to return speedily to her good and tender parent…I assured her that ye arms of ye best of Fathers would be open to receive her and restore her all desireable comfort. This pacified her for the present and ye more speedy her return ye better'. Although Webb interprets Anselm's attitude to Anne as a 'tiresome burden', she was strong enough to take up the issue herself with her father when she wrote to him on the same day:

'My Lord, I hope this will find your Lordship in perfect health, we arrived at Cambray last night, I can't say I like the conveniences, I shall go to two or three places more, except I find more contentment than I have done so fare, hopes to have the comfort of seeing my good Parent in a very short time, hopes you will excuse the great expense I have put you to, I beg your Lordships blessing, and am, My Lord, your Lordships most dutiful child, Ann Fairfax'.

Both Anne and Anslem refer to the physical discomfort that she is in. After growing up in the relative luxury of Gilling Castle and then enjoying the advantages of the 'finest townhouse in England', it must have been hard for her to 'rough it'. She is also quite clever, reminding her beloved father that this trip is costing him a lot of money and suggesting that maybe he is not receiving the value for money that he expected. It would appear that tugging on Lord Fairfax's purse-strings was an effective way to make him sit up and listen and was possibly a contributing factor in his decision to recall her home.

Two days later Anne wrote again an anguished letter to her father:

'With your Lordships leave I think of staying about a fortnight, I hope I shall have the comfort of hearing from you before I leave Cambray, whether your Lordship would have me go to Spaw or no, I cant say God knows I am any better, I am in hopes spaw may be of some service after I have seen two or three places more, if your Lordship would be so good as to accompany me there it would give me great comfort, Mr Bolton desires his best respects to you, he would have whroat but he is not well…I beg you will be so good as to send me some money…'

Suffering from homesickness, she asks her father to meet her at 'spaw', which was in Brussels. Again, we see the Georgian obsession with water as the potential cure for all ailments.

By May 15th Anne was still at the convent in Cambrai and she had not been able to settle. She sent a desperate letter to her father:

'Give me leave to return to your Lordship my most grateful thanks for your kind and affectionate letter and good advice which you are so good to give me, God only knows what is best for us and certainly I ought to wait with patience his order of providence, and trust in his goodness that spaw will be of service to me, and by suffering with resignation for a time hope to recover for your Lordships and my own comfort. I design going to Bruxelles and trying if I can like it better where there is an our own apartment for I cant say dining at the common table is agreeable…'

For someone whose knocks in life had made them timorous and shy, collective dining in a hall with complete strangers must have been a trial for sensitive Anne. However, it was not the case that she was an Englishwoman alone amongst the French, for her own correspondence and that of Father Bolton reveal that there was a community of English Catholic daughters lodging in apartments at both the convent at Cambrai and at Brussels. Anne sends the best respects of Miss Gibson to his Lordship. Bolton refers to the fact that Anne is staying in the apartment of Lady Barbara Radcliffe who is returning soon and is the reason for her wishing to go to Brussels. The reason that she wants to go to Brussels is because 'there is an apartment ready for her with Mr Mannock & the two Miss Pigotts', who were the daughters of Lord Fairfax's nephew, Nathaniel Pigott, who later turns up in Anne's life like a very bad penny.

Although Anne was finding it difficult to settle at Cambrai, this did not prevent her from planning further adventures. According to Bolton, after staying in Brussels for a while, she intended to go:

'to Liège or Aix la Chapelle to drink ye spaw waters in case she cannot have the good at Bruxelles. She is going to have a footman, a sober middle aged man who understands little English, can speak French, German and Flemish and has lived in an English family here for some time. She was afraid of this being too expensive but after having considered that both her own convenience and ye title of her person demanded she should have a footman, she consented to hire one by ye month who is obliged by ye agreement to do everything he is commanded and attend her in her tour and residences. Mr Moore, who paid ye Honble Miss Fairfax a visit here with her cousin, Mr du Vivier, will arrange any money she wants to draw from Mr Wright [Lord Fairfax's lawyer]'.

Despite the cost incurred by hiring a footman, Lord Fairfax did not demur and by the 7th June she had arrived in Brussels where she stayed with the Dames Benedctines Angloisses. In his letter to her there Fairfax seems anxious about her:

'I hope your received my last [letter] having been in pain not to have heard from you or some of you before now but hope in God you are all well'.

The religious faith of both father and daughter are evident in their letters. Lord Fairfax repeatedly refers to the grace and providence of God. He has accepted the bill for her travels and tells her that his banker, Mr Wright, has paid her previous bill and that he has left 'an order with him to pay all your bills so that if Mr Dillon let you have any money you have only to give him a Draught upon Mr Wright'. Accessing money on the Continent was a complicated affair before the days of credit cards and traveller's cheques. Lord Fairfax, who could be lavish with money, was happy to finance his daughter's trip in the hope of helping her to overcome her demons. He ended his letter, 'I send you my blessing and embrace you with all tenderness. I am, my dear, your most affectionate father, Fairfax.'

However, as time progressed he began to complain repeatedly about the exorbitant postal charges. Born in 1700, Lord Fairfax was as old as the year in 1768 and Anne's travels abroad began to cause him some anxiety. On June 20ᵗʰ he wrote:

'My Dearest Jewel, I own your letter and Mr Bolton has afflicted me much but I hope Providence will me grace of true resignation, as you are the only comfort I have in this world, but are not to expect our will, but his Holy to be done in all things, and hope he will give us grace of true resignation in all he is pleased to send us, if we doe, we may hope through his mercys to enjoye that happiness in the next that he has prepared for us. It is I and not you that deserves all this.'

Here we have evidence of his love and affection for his daughter, as well as his profound religious faith. It seems that both Anne and Father Bolton were ill because he finishes his letter by stating that he will 'goe tomorrow to Dr Dealtry to acquaint him the contents of both your letter and shall write to you again.'

As we have seen, Anne was often keen to shield Lord Fairfax from her true feelings, perhaps because she did not wish to upset him. By now she must have been really desperate to get home because she had written to him about both her own and Father Bolton's maladies.

Lord Fairfax's next letter to Anne shows how he was prone to worry about her:

'My eassiness in not hearing from you gave me much uneasiness and trouble. I own both your letters have me uneassie to find you are no better, as I fear, as well as the doctor that by your unsesasinees it affect your Blood that it cannot get a right circulation…'

The extent to which he placed his faith in his religion is revealed as the letter continues: He tells his 'dearest jewel' to:

'resign yourself to his Holy Will, consider how many suffer much more, and let me beg of you to submit to his holy will, that when you find the come upon you, throw yourself at the feet of the cross and beg he will give your Grace to bear all he send you with true resignation to his holy will, and his will be done and not ours, we are not comed into this world to have ours, but to follow and bear his cross, which he did for our examples. Therefore it you submit to his Holy Will with a sincere desire to do it, he will not leave you to yourself and you are not spared of his mercy'.

Lord Fairfax's resignation to God's will must have been a great comfort to him in his bereavements and he tries to help Anne with the divine prop that he has used to bear his sufferings. He also points out to her that there are a lot of people a lot worse off than she is. He ends his letter emphasizing how materially privileged they are:

> 'You seem to fear you will be miserable in this world, you have no occasion to fear that, God of his goodness has given us much more than we deserve, if (we) should loose it for his sake, his Holy name be blessed, but otherwise there is not the least apprehension so hope you will be easie on that score'.

It is not known whether her father's words were a comfort to her. We know today that words are sometimes not enough to cure depression. However, Anne seems to have rallied somewhat because when Father Bolton decided to return home, Anne preferred to stay on. In a surprising volte face, Lord Fairfax then attempted to persuade her to return also after having one last all-curing bath.

> '...but consider as Miss Gibson and Mr Bolton are coming away how they will bear with your uneasiness, therefore I hope after you have tried his last prescription Bathing may be of great service, it would not be better for you to come over and trye it and you may live as retired with me than in any place, but I leave all this to you'.

He holds out the prospect of a little relaxation to tempt her to return home. After Father Bolton left on August 4th, Lord Fairfax sent a further two letters to Anne on 7th and 20th, despite the extortionate costs of postage. In her absence he had consulted a doctor about her symptoms who had advised that she should return to England as soon as possible. 'I desire you will not hesitate but come without delay. You may be assured everything will be done what is agreeable to you...the comfort to see you is the greatest comfort in this world.'

It seems that although Anne had found the strength to remain in Brussels without the support of Father Bolton, it was her father who made the decision to recall her because he was missing her. Previously, he had been content to lay her maladies in the lap of God to minister to. Perhaps his consultation with a doctor was a pretext to get her home. The postscript to his letter shows that he also had fiscal concerns alongside the spiritual and the medical. He wrote, somewhat surprised:

> 'I find by Mr Wright letter today, besides the Bill of fifteen you gave Mr Bolton, you have drawn on him for fifty pounds more. As Mr Bolton tells me you had thirty five pounds when he came away, I canot imagine you could want another fifty, since especially as you are at Cambray. If you was at Spaw it would be another thing...Not that you shall want for anything.'

The equivalent today of the fifty pounds that Anne had drawn down is approximately £4,362. Lord Fairfax must have taken this into consideration when he recalled Anne to England. We have no record of how Anne managed the journey home without Father Bolton. From his letters to Lord Fairfax we know that the passage from Dover would have taken nine hours. Despite being prescribed endless baths, Anne does seem to have a strong constitution, evidenced also by the fact that she made a full recovery from smallpox.

Money concerns would plague Lord Fairfax until the end of his days. Webb states that, 'as ever, financial matters were the Viscount's main concern. His family commitments and building activities were becoming a considerable drain on his by no means unlimited resources'. He continued to finance his expenditure with the sale of wood from the forests on his numerous estates and from the collection of rent from his sometimes disgruntled tenant farmers.

By 1770 Mary Bellasis had returned from London and was back in York. It is from her correspondence that we learn that Lord Fairfax is dying. In an undated letter she wrote that '...Lord & Miss Fairfax arrived in Famille yesterday. I am to dine with them this day, by all accounts I fear the old peer is in a very weak way'. The following year she wrote again stating that she hoped to stay at Fairfax House for the August race meeting. By the autumn of 1771, the Viscount's health was deteriorating rapidly. On 26th October 1771 she wrote to her father:

'I think Miss Fairfax much better than she has been for some years. Can't say the same for the old peer, who seems to be quite on his last legs. The day I dined there he fell asleep immediately after dinner and slept the whole time we stayed in the parlour. Afterwards we played at cards which seems to the thing that most amuses him and keeps him awake. His speech is bad, as is his memory, and the weakness he has had for some time increases, and makes him really offensive as he takes no care to keep himself clean. I went out with the other morning; it really was horrible and made me quite sick'.

Mary paints a picture of the Viscount suffering some of the symptoms of dementia. Although Anne seemed to be in better spirits, it must have been terribly difficult to see her beloved father ailing in this way. Mary and Anne would sometimes pass the time by going for a walk around the city, ending up upon Manor Shore, which is now the Museum Gardens. Sometimes Anne would grow tired and 'retire into the house' while the garrulous Mary would sit and talk to the old housekeeper of Mrs Prior's house at the north end of Lendal, who she had made the acquaintance of, no doubt striking up a conversation with her on one of her walks.

In her letter Mary reveals a secret about Lord Fairfax's health that no-one dare reveal either to the aging Viscount or to his only daughter:

'The old peer looks worse every day. I can scarce understand one word in twenty that he says. Complains more of the swelling on his side which increases in size. As a secret between you and me, Atkinson tells me its cancerous but seems to think he will scarce live long enough for it to become very painful or nauseous. He has not told him or Miss Fairfax what the complaint is, as he says nothing can be done to relieve it and it might alarm them about an ill which most likely thinks he will not live to feel'.

Despite the dubious medical ethics of this amateur diagnosis and the failure to inform both the subject or the next of kin, it does sound particularly worrying.

However, by November, Lord Fairfax seemed to be rallying, 'Our old friend the peer looks rather better than he did, but now complains of a pain in the other breast'.

It seems that Lord Fairfax was desirous to spend his last days at Gilling Castle, his ancestral home, the tower of which dates back to the fourteenth century. Mary wrote to her father asking him to send a coach for her to collect her when they decided to make the move:

'Lord and Miss Fairfax propose leaving York tomorrow morning and going to Gilling. This resolution is but just taken and its too late for any note I can send you to arrive at Newburgh time enough for your coach to come to York early enough. I therefore propose going with them to Gilling and desire you will be good enough to send over the coach there in the evening. I own I think she had better remain in York a little longer as I think he very little better. But his Ldsp seems to be in a hurry to go to Gilling. Indeed, she will be quieter there for it's the fashion of this house to admit company whether sick or well'.

A steady stream of visitors to Fairfax House while the 'old peer' was in such a poor state of health, cannot have been helpful to Anne's fragile nerves and solitary nature. No wonder they wanted to retire to the country. However, it was not to be and it is likely that the Viscount was too ill to travel on the notoriously pitted roads. However, Mary Bellasis does seem to have been both a practical, as well as moral support to the family:

'I wish I could give yr Ldsp a good account of my nursing, but really I think he grows worse instead of better. Such wild and melancholy imaginations convinces me that the brain at times must be greatly affected. I wish a [?] humour is not got up to the head. Dr Dealtry was here last night. I had a tete â tete with him on the subject. He seems uneasy about her. He was sent for last Sat to Scarboro on a melancholy affair. Sir Woolstan Dixie, a young man lately come to his estate is gone quite mad and cut his throat. The doc says he may recover the wound but there is little likelihood he ever will his senses. I hope nobody will mention this affair here as I know it will affect her. I really feel greatly for the poor old Lord should she continue in the way she is in, it will be a terrible affair'.

Anne Fairfax does not appear to have been coping with the imminent death of her father well at all. She was definitely struggling to come to terms with the enormity of her loss and we can but wonder what her 'wild and melancholy imaginations' were. Although Anne was able to show great physical resilience, she was extremely sensitive to external emotional stimuli. However, it is clear that her behaviour is beginning to test the patience of her sensible friend who is now anxious as to how Anne's reactions could affect the dying lord. It seems that Anne could lash out at people when she was anxious. Mary reports that 'the Bredals are in great disgrace with her. It is impossible for them to please her. If they go out its wrong; if they stay at home it's the same. I wonder they don't return to their home. You may judge by this, my dear Lord, that all goes ill'.

Francis Bredall had been creating dubious medical concoctions for the Fairfaxes for decades and perhaps Anne realised he was using them. However, instead of banishing the family from the house, she chose to behave in a petulant way towards them to display her displeasure and disapproval. Perhaps she did not have the authority or the strength to tell them to leave. Besides a major family fallout would be the last thing that she would need as she watched her father die. Nevertheless, the lingering presence of the Bredalls was clearly trying for everyone, including Mary. But as Weber explains, 'It is easy to guess why the Bredalls were reluctant to leave with all that profitable illness about.' Unfortunately, Francis Bredall was not the worst predatory relative that would cause problems for Anne in her later years.

Fortunately for Anne, Mary was her one comfort, 'She is never contented but when I am with her. If I retire into my own room she follows me immediately. They talk of leaving York next Sat or Monday, but except she is better I have no notion of his going to Gilling. She now baths every other morning. As soon as I hear anything of their leaving York I will inform you.'

After having had it impressed upon her that bathing was the cure for all maladies, it is hardly surprising that Anne took up bathing with such avidity towards the end of her father's life. Her behaviour does sound somewhat compulsive and her histrionic outbursts must have suggested to Mary that she was on the verge of a nervous breakdown, just as he had been before she contracted smallpox in 1763. However, as Lord Fairfax's health continued to deteriorate, Anne was able to call on inner reserves of strength that led to her being ultimately able to cope with his death with dignity and composure.

The Christmas of 1771 was not going to be the jovial affair that it had once been at Fairfax House. On 14th December Mary paints a sad portrait of Lord Fairfax's lengthy decline:

'Our old friend the peer looks sadly. I can scarce understand one word in ten that he says, neither can he scarcely hear what is said to him. His spirits are quite gone and the weakness he has had upon him for above twelvemonth with regard to his water grows worse every day. Neither is his appetite so good as it used to be. Mlle seems very well.'

By the 11th of January of the following year, Lord Fairfax was facing death with bravery:

'Lord Fairfax continues very ill, there is no expectation of his recovery as the stoppage remains altho every method has been tried to relieve him. He seems perfectly well resigned and still cheerful. My little friend is much afflicted but more composed than I'd have imagined. I am with her all the day and think myself happy if I am of use to her…'

Mary's father, Lord Fauconberg, fearful of the effect that Lord Fairfax's death may have on Anne invited her to go stay at Newburgh Priory. Although grateful, Anne found the inner strength to stay with her father at Fairfax House until the end.

'…she is most sensible of your goodness to her but that she proposed remaining in the house here. Indeed she seemed most extremely pleased and grateful

for your friendly attention to her. She keeps up under her affliction with more composure than I could have imagined. I am constantly with her...'

Perhaps Anne remembered her father's advice to her while on the Continent and placed her faith in the will of God. Lord Fairfax died towards the end of January and was buried at Gilling on the 27th January 1772. Almost immediately after her father's death, Anne retired to Gilling Castle in North Yorkshire. By April she had found a buyer for Fairfax House in the form of Mrs Thornton who was the owner of the pump house inside Lendal Tower that supplied the house with running water. Anne wanted to complete by May Day but the sale was held up because she was trying to organise for a charitable donation of £3 a year to be made from an allowance out of the purchase money. Anne's charitable donations and endowments were extremely important to her and later in life she would embark on a lengthy and anxious legal battle with her cousin, Nathaniel Pigott, be able to have control of her own money.

Webb explains that:

'Trouble was already brewing for Anne even before her father's death. Lord Fairfax had deliberately left his daughter in the care of the trustworthy Father Anselm Bolton, but had unwisely made no provision for the ultimate disposal of his estate. This played into the hands of Anne's wily relation, Nathaniel Pigott, who had designs on the Fairfax Inheritance'.

Nathaniel Pigott was the son of Viscount Fairfax's youngest sister, Alathea. In 1723 she had married Ralph Pigott and lived at Whitton in Middlesex. They were another staunchly Catholic family and had had business dealings with Lord Fairfax. Ralph Pigott had acted as conveyancer to Fairfax in the purchase of property. He had also lent a large sum of money to Charles Gregory's father, William, which Lord Fairfax had to pay back in the form of an annuity of £50 every 1st January.

In 1752 after her husband's death, Alathea left England for Brussels with her three children. The two daughters were at the Benedictine convent there when Anne Fairfax visited in the 1760s. Alathea's daughter, Rebecca, later became the Abbess there. After going to school in France, Nathaniel went to Brussels where he met his wife, Mathurine de Beriol in about 1737. They returned to England and were living in Isleworth in the 1750s, whereupon they set their sights on Anne Fairfax's dwindling fortune.

Somehow Nathaniel had cajoled, persuaded and pressurised Anne into signing a deed which gave him legal control over her financial affairs. He had probably reminded her that he was one of her last living relatives and therefore due to receive the inheritance anyway. Therefore, why not let him bear the financial strain of the estate and let him take control of her affairs. He probably presented the notion as not only the morally right thing to do, but also the convenient course of action. Anne was growing old and didn't need to be bothered with complicated financial affairs. He would take care of things for her, just as her father had done while he was alive.

We can only speculate as to how he came to convince her, but the artifices of a conman do not seem to be beneath this unpleasant character. He probably saw her vulnerability now that her father was dead and insidiously played on every weakness that he discovered in her sensitive character. After she put ink to parchment, immediately she regretted what she had done. She realised that she would not be able to make the bequests to her friends and charitable donations that she so wished to leave. In a final show of strength, she mustered up the courage to take him to court to get the deed annulled.

The stress of this ongoing legal battle must have been enormous, not to mention having to deal with the unscrupulous and highly disagreeable Nathaniel Pigott. Testament to Nathaniel Pigott's cunning is the vindictive behaviour he displayed to Anne's chaplain, Father Bolton, who as Anne's loyal supporter had unfortunately become embroiled in the affair.

First of all Pigott began a smear campaign against him, accusing him of being a drunkard. Next he impugned his commitment to his religious vows and accused him of sexual relations with Anne. In the late 1770s this would have been a deeply disturbing allegation for Anne also. Unfortunately, his malicious venom was taken seriously and Father Bolton had to face an inquiry. Fortunately, Bolton was eventually exonerated, but not before he had spent some time in prison. Pigott's devious ploy of removing Father Bolton from Anne's side and leaving her even more vulnerable to his nefarious influence ultimately failed, but would have been very disturbing for both Anne and her chaplain.

By 10 April 1776 James Preston, the steward of the estate was acting for Anne in London, presenting legal papers. The letter he wrote to her would have relieved some of the anxiety, worry and distress that the case was causing her:

> *'Honoured Madam,*
> *Mr Pigott has appeared to the bill filed against him therefore we may expect his answer during the next term…I have the pleasure to inform you that I have seen the counsel who drew the bill and he has not any doubt but the deed you executed to Mr Pigott will set aside and though there is great uncertainty in the law yet I assure you I have most sanguine expectations in this business.'*

Two months later on the 6th of July, he repeated his assurances as to the success of her case and 'for further satisfaction I have stated a case and sent if for the eminent counsel in London and as soon as I receive the answer to it, I shall immediately wait upon you at Gilling and in the meantime hope this letter may be some satisfaction to you'.

However, by November things were becoming unpleasant. Preston wrote to Anne that 'Pigott avoids explaining how the Deed was obtained and throws out such invectives as, I must say, do not in the least become him, particularly when in the same letter he expresses a wish to be understood, that he has a great regard for you.' In one sentence we are presented with picture of Pigott as a dishonest, foul-mouthed, sycophant.

After this information, Anne decided to write directly to Pigott herself, expressing her feelings about what he had done to her and telling him directly of the consequences of his failure to set aside the deed.

'…I think you endeavoured to take an advantage of me when I was in town in the winter drawing on in to sign the deed which I executed without knowing or considering the effect of it upon your saying that it was only a confirmation of what I had done before. It may be true that I intended to leave my estate to your family but I could never think of excluding myself from charging my estate with the payment of some legacies and amenities which I had left in my will but there is not any notice of it taken in the deed. I must say that this is such treatment I do not think I deserved from you.
I have taken the opinion of an eminent counsel in London and he is very clear that the deed may be set aside. Therefore, if you wish to be upon any terms with me I should presume that you will not put me to the trouble of seeking a remedy by law but that you will deliver up the deed to me that I may make such alterations as I may think proper'.

It seems that Pigott had tricked Anne into signing a second deed that she did not understand the full consequences of. By March 1778 Pigott wrote directly to Anne, a letter both dismissive of her and wheedling at the same time. He uses the classic devious technique of presenting his actions to her as though she was the instigator of them:

'A few hours ago I received your letter of the 24th and see, with great concern and very deep regret, that I am to give up all hopes of a Reconciliation on which my heart was so much set. Be it so, since it is your pleasure. I must submit to what I cannot prevent and sit down with the self-satisfaction of having done everything that honour, friendship and moderation could suggest in order to compass, what appeared to be so desireable. I have the further mortification to find the whole tenour of your epistle how much you mistook the motives which dictated the friendly and ever submissive expressions of my letter of the 12th – expressions which most assuredly nothing but my real feelings and real sentiments of regard for you could have engaged me to pen…'

Anne was later informed by her steward that she must pay the £50 annuity that Pigott had inherited from his father for the loan he made to her grandfather. However, Preston would try to find a way to discontinue having to pay the annuity in future.

Of course, the mercenary and grasping Pigott was reluctant to relinquish the annual payment of the equivalent of £4,300. Anne's lawyer had submitted a bill and Pigott was obliged to answer to it. However, in a classic legal tactic he dragged his heels until the deadline was due to expire. He was playing a risky game because it was within the power of the court 'to grant an attachment against him' for contempt of court. His reticence was beginning to work against him as Preston informed Anne, 'I must say that the unwillingness of Mr Pigott to answer the bill does not set him in a very favourable light but make your case appear the better…'

After persisting with his delaying tactics, on November 21st, 1777, Pigott and his co-defendants, his sons Edward and Charles Gregory were given three more weeks to answer the bill. The letter from Preston to Anne explaining Pigott's defence is very incoherent, testament to how upsetting the case was for him too. Pigott and his lawyers argued that what he had done had not been fraudulent and filed a counter-bill against Anne. The case was clearly taking its toll on Preston who ends his letter by reminding Anne of how hard he was working on the case and that he believed that if it wasn't for his persistence in the matter, the matter would not have proceeded. Clearly, he wanted some recognition for the hard work and anxiety that he was being put through.

Later Preston was dispatched to York where Pigott was now living with the £300 debt on the annuity that Anne owed him. However, unfortunately, this was not the end of the matter. Pigott wrote to her that she owed him even more arrears and in 1780 he sent her a more controlled, yet insistent letter asking for the remaining money. At the same time as the York visit, Pigott took advantage of the opportunity to inform Preston that he insisted that his son should become the incumbent of the vacant position of priest at Ampleforth, which was within Anne Fairfax's gift to decide. Evidently, he was of the opinion that he was in control of the Fairfax estate, despite the on-going litigation.

By January 2nd, 1779 it seems that Pigott was sensing that his case against Anne was a lost cause as the in following letter he pleads for a reconciliation with her:

'Madam

May I hope to be more successful in my application to you this time than I was the last? May I hope that you will not still be deaf to a reconciliation which the sincerity of my friendship makes me most ardently wish and pray for? I repeat it (and nothing but truth makes me say it) that I am attached to you with all the feelings that the nearest relationship and kindred of blood can create ___Why should I say so, if it was not true? Or what benefit can arise to one from a connection of friendship other than what arises from the personal regard and respect that one naturally feels for the nearest relation? in the miserable lawsuit we are involved, believe me, Dearest Madame I have taken no one step but with the greatest reluctance and it will be extremely painful and distressing to me to be driven to measures which however justifiable and necessary, cut me to the soul, on the thought that they are likely to widen the breach between us. Do not be so unjust as to imagine this means to convey any ideas of threatening; nothing can be further god knows from my disposition of mind. I want I wish I prey to be on a footing of friendship with you. I am ready to do anything that can be justly expected to obtain the desirable end - if after all my submission and endeavours to you still spurn me from you, I must and will endeavour to rid myself of foolish feelings about which I shall trouble you no more.

I am very respectfully
Madam your most obedient and humble servant'.

Although Pigott states that he is not threatening her, his letter is still rather intimidating. Pigott then spent a good part of 1782 trying to extract money from from Anne for the historic annuity. The tone of his letters changes completely and he becomes less aggressive and dismissive, yet nevertheless insistent and persuasive that she pay him the £1000 that he believed that she now owed him. She sent a curt response that she would pay him when he had relinquished the deed. It is clear that she is now in the driving seat because she holds the purse strings. She also drags her heels with regard to the appointment of his son to the position of priest at Ampleforth. Nevertheless, his long and sinuous letters must have been upsetting to her all the same.

In March 1784 Anne received a begging letter from Sister Joseph Walmesly asking for help with a building project. Then in May 1785 she received a shocking letter from Nathaniel Pigott's son in which he described a serious fallout with his father that had led to him being written out of his father's will. Edward Pigott was trying to ensure that she did not forget him in her will.

> 'What I am going to inform you of is till now unknown to anybody except the family & I therefore wish it may be kept secret. My father since these first few years has taken the greatest antipathy towards me, which at present is arrived at such a pitch that I have the strongest reasons to be assured he has disinherited me, & which he does not deny. Such an injustice can only be rectified by you, & I hope in case you leave your estates to my brother you will oblige him, by your will to restore me, what he inherits from my father; at present my brother is so disposed by you must well know how little one can rely on momentary sensations. Without entring into any detail, I may add for my own justification and infinite satisfaction that my behavior is highly approved off, by all the rest of the family. When, dear Madam, you consider the contents of this letter and what importance it is to me, I hope it will be an apology for thus troubling you; no answer is required, now would I wish to receive one directed to me here, tho' I am very anxious to know if this is come to hand…I beg my compliments to Mr Bolton.'

This egocentric letter which is distasteful in its reference to Anne's death must have been both shocking and upsetting to her. Five months later she was to receive another letter from Edward Pigott, this time telling her that he and his father had reconciled. However, just over a year later, in December 1786, Edward sent another letter, shocking not only in its mercenary audacity, but in the picture that it paints of his despotic father:

> 'You will I am sure excuse my troubling you again when you have perused this. Last year as soon as my father had apparently made up matters between us, I thought myself in duty bound to acquaint you of it and consequently writ word that he had not disinherited me, in which I was too precipitate as I since know for certain that he left me nothing, during your life & that of the rest of the family but his apparel. This sham reconciliation is since broke through with the greatest violence, his despotism hatred and injustice are beyond conception; my peace & health are destroyed, my Mother (the best of women) has been strongly affected & now is dangerously ill. The whole family implores him to send me away but nothing can induce him to grant the least allowance, his supreme

happiness is to enjoy absolute power. I relate, Madam, these particulars to convince you that I am not activated by trifles or imaginary conjectures; you may be well assured that what I have said is far from being exaggerated; thus circumstanced he probably will deprive me of everything he can, such an injury can be rectified only by you. I therefore hope that, which of us you later favour, you will oblige him to resotore my father's estate to the other as mentioned in my first letter last year for which I shall be forever grateful'.

Not only was Anne deeply entangled with a thoroughly despicable man, his son was equally as unctuous and untrustworthy. By this time she was sixty-one years old and most likely would have enjoyed the last decade of her life a lot more had it not been for the intimidating presence of the Pigott family in her life, trying to wheedle her out of her inheritance.

Anne was forced to be decisive once more when one Christopher Goulton would not give up his position of Court Steward to the ancient Customary Court of the Manor of Ampleforth. He had held the position for twenty years and was reluctant to hand over to James Preston. Due to Anne's short education as a result of her turbulent childhood, she was never a confident writer. Her handwriting lacks self-assurance and is suggestive of someone who was not comfortable with a pen in her hand. The few extant letter that she wrote in the archive having crossings out over mistakes. However, she was clearly proud lady as she often re-drafted her first attempts to make them more presentable. Despite her solitary existence and vulnerability, she could write an authoritive letter when needed and understood that directness was the most forceful way. In February 1774, after redrafting she sent the following letter to Mr Goulton to instruct him to give up his job and hand it over to James Preston.

'I do hereby require and direct you to deliver to James Preston of New Malton in the County of York Esqr all and every, the Court Books, Court Rolls and other papers and writings in your possession belonging to me, & this shall be your sufficient warrant and authority for so doing, & the said James Preston has my orders to pay, & will pay you what, if anything is due to you from my late father Lord Visct Fairfax decd or from myself. Witness my hand this 3rd day of February 1774. Anne Fairfax. Signed in the presence of Francis Bredall.'

It did the trick and James Preston took over the role. He must have gained Anne's high opinion for his work on her on-going court case with Nathaniel Pigott. It is interesting to note that Francis Bredall was still around at this time. His resilient persistence in ingratiating himself with the Fairfaxes was remarkable.

Although the deed that Pigott had manipulated Anne into signing was eventually set aside by an Act of Parliament, she was still forced to pay his annuity every Lady Day (January 1st). Fortunately, in her later years the Pigotts relinquished their persecution of her in pursuit of her money. They must have realized that it was simply a waiting game before they would inherit her estates. Their despicable ambitions were realized when Anne died in 1793 at the age of approximately sixty-nine. However, the Pigotts continued their scheming even after Anne's death, challenging the various bequests that she had fought so hard to make. Clearly, their greed knew no bounds and they wanted all the money for themselves. Fortunately, they were mostly unsuccessful.

Although Webb states that after her father's death, Anne 'struggled on with her life for another twenty-one years', it is not clear that this is an accurate picture of the final chapter of her life. Even Webb acknowledges that in 1773 she was to be found at a spa and this 'could have been just Harrogate or Scarborough, but was more probably the Belgian health resort she had visited before her father's lifetime'. At one point she wanted a change of scene and was about to rent a house in Hayes in Middlesex for eight months. Unfortunately, she reneged on the deal when she found out that the Pigotts were living nearby. After wasting money on the journey and furniture, she fled the place after just eight days. Pigott must have got wind of her presence and ever-ready to turn something to his own advantage, asked to live in the house himself for the rest of the lease. It is likely that Anne paid the owner the rent due and considered herself to have made a lucky escape.

For company she had taken one Miss Ella with her on this trip. She had also enjoyed the company of Mrs Forcer before she died and so at least was not completely solitary in her medieval castle. However, the person who brought Anne the most comfort and solace in the latter part of her life was the loyal Father Anslem Bolton, the man who her father had appointed as his chaplain. In recognition of the esteem that she held him in, upon her death, Anne left Father Bolton thirty-two acres of land in the parish of Ampleforth at the opposite side of the valley to her castle.

Before she died he began building what was to become an elegant retirement home. However, his plans were not allowed to come to fruition. 1793 was a time of extreme turbulence in France with a series of revolutions that culminated in the execution of King Louis XVI and his wife Marie Antoinette. Catholics were being persecuted in the chaos and found themselves having to flee the country. Several Catholic missions made their way to Lancashire and Yorkshire. Moving from place to place in search of sanctuary, the president of the Convent of St Laurence discovered Father Bolton at Ampleforth. Admiring his new house, the head of the convent decided that it would make a dignified home for his religious community.

Understandably, Father Bolton was reluctant to give up the dream home that he had been looking forward to enjoying for the rest of his natural life, free from the intrigues of the Fairfax family. However, the pressure must have been relentless because a mere nine years later in 1802, he capitulated. (It is possible that pressure was brought to bear upon him from higher authorities in the Catholic Church). As a reward for his magnanimous gesture he was granted the grand title of Abbot of Peterborough. Fortunately, he was not forced to go take up his position as the monastery at Peterborough had been dissolved in the sixteenth century by Henry VIII. However, he was not able to live out the rest of his life in the graceful pastures of Ampleforth and ended up in County Durham.

Consequently, it was Father Bolton's house that became the foundation of the religious and educational establishment known today as Ampleforth Abbey and College. In 1929 Ampleforth Abbey bought Gilling Castle and today part of the school is housed there. It is likely that with Anne's charitable bequests, she would have been pleased that her family home and estate are being used for the formation of the next generation.

It is easy to dismiss Anne as the over-privileged timorous, neurotic and spoilt daughter of one of the wealthiest men in eighteenth century Yorkshire. But this is a far too simplistic picture of her almost seven decades in this world. Her childhood was undeniably tragic and clearly affected her for the rest of her life, suffering spells of anxiety and depression. Nevertheless, she was able to overcome these episodes, despite a complete absence of any medical knowledge of mental health issues, combined with a culture that tried to actively suppress and repress emotions.

She was able to inspire genuine friendship and affection from Mary Bellasis, despite the fact that they had diametrically opposing personalities with Mary being a total extrovert. Just because Anne was an introvert, we should not judge her any the less for it. When it was necessary she was able to take decisive action. After her father's death, she was quick to sell Fairfax House and retire to the country. Obviously, she preferred a more peaceful existence to the hustle and bustle of York. Perhaps she spent much of her life trying to please her father, as evidently city life did not suit her. Her ability to bear her own company, rather than surround herself with sycophants, is testament to the strength of her character.

Despite her two engagements, perhaps Anne was instrumental in the decision to remain single, preferring to maintain her autonomy, her money and her health. She must have seen the toll that eight pregnancies over the course of fourteen years had taken on her mother. Perhaps Mary's constitution had been weakened through relentless pregnancies and her repeated confinements made it harder for her to survive smallpox.

Anne's fortitude was put to the test during and after her father's death when she had to manage the complicated affairs of her estates with the help of her faithful steward, James Preston. She did resort to the help of those around her - Father Bolton in particular, but again it is a brave person who is not afraid to receive the help of others. Unfortunately, there were those around her who must have spotted a vulnerability about her and actively preyed upon it. Nathaniel Pigott was the ultimate test of her mettle. Despite his thoroughly unpleasant character and intentions, ultimately she won through, ensuring that she maintained control of her estates until the end.

When Lord Fairfax, the 9th Viscount of Emley died, his title became extinct because, being a woman, his daughter Anne was not allowed to inherit and become the Viscountess. Unlike in some other European countries, British titles cannot be inherited by daughters. In a particularly enlightened moment in 2006, Spain passed the Law of Equality in the Succession of Noble Titles, allowing both wives and daughters to inherit aristocratic titles. Unfortunately, no such progressive act has been forthcoming from the British government yet, and women are still excluded from hereditary rights.

When the Honourable Anne Fairfax died at the age of sixty-nine, the line of the Fairfax of York, believed to date back as far as Anglo-Saxon times, was extinguished with her. Anne Fairfax enjoyed wealth, privilege and autonomy by default. Had any of her four younger brothers lived, they would have inherited the land and title through the law of primogeniture. That Anne was able to lead a financially independent life for her final two decades is a legacy of the tragic childhood she endured and remarkable in itself. All of her father's love and affection were bestowed on her now that she was the only one left. His tender terms of endearment such as 'my jewel' show how precious she was to him. His loss must have been a devastating blow to her, but she lived on, taking control of her life and her destiny. Like many other women of York, her character was forged through adversity and her mere survival against the odds is enough to make her an extremely interesting individual, worthy of study.

CHAPTER ELEVEN

Anne Lister and her Secret Lovers

IN ONE OF the dark, candle-lit rooms of Shibden Hall, Halifax, John Lister pulled back the old wooden panel to reveal a huge bundle of manuscripts, written in a curious, unintelligible script. The year was 1890 and John Lister could not make out the significance of his discovery. When he looked more closely at the sweeping handwriting, he realised that the documents had been written in some kind of code. Enlisting the help of his schoolteacher friend, Arthur Burrell, together they worked on cracking the cipher, made up of what appeared to be a combination of the Greek alphabet, algebraic symbols and even signs of the zodiac.

After guessing that the final word of a sentence was 'hope', they were able to deduce the meaning of the two symbols that represented the letters 'h' and 'e'. With this breakthrough, they were able to eventually crack the code. As the two friends began to decipher the manuscripts, the realisation dawned on them of the enormity of their finding. The thousands of pages were the secret diary of John's ancestor, Anne Lister, who had kept a journal between the years 1806 to 1839. Begun when Anne was a mere fifteen years old, the documents comprised over four million words.

As John and Arthur read the contents of the diaries, they realised that not only had Anne recorded the details of her daily life, including the running of her estate, as well as references to contemporary national and international events, she had also recorded often in shockingly intimate detail, her many illicit relationships with women. In an era when homosexuality was criminalised, Arthur Burrell urged his friend to burn the diaries in order to avoid an enormous scandal about the secret and extensive love-life of his ancestor, who had died a mere fifty years previously.

Fortunately, something would not allow John Lister to see the beautifully scripted record of his ancestor's life go up in smoke, so he returned Anne's diaries to their hiding place. The diaries remained locked away from sight for another forty years or so, until 1933 when John Lister died and the estate of Shibden Hall passed to Halifax Borough Council. Anne Lister's papers were now the property of the town council where they were secreted away once more. As late as 1964, the Halifax Town Clerk suppressed public knowledge of the coded sections as it was not until 1967 that male homosexual acts were finally decriminalised. Meanwhile, lesbian relationships had remained untouched by criminal law, yet were shrouded in secrecy and prejudice.

One hundred and forty-nine years after Anne's death, Helen Whitbread was looking for a research project after graduating from university at the age of fifty-two. Intrigued by Anne's diaries, Helen began the laborious process of cracking the code and transcribing the diaries word for word. The task took a painstaking four years and ended with Anne's diary taking up twenty-four volumes.

As she decoded every word of Anne's crypthand, she uncovered the truth of Anne's lesbian sexuality, as well as her views on men, money, business, and the society that she lived in. Anne's diaries helped her on a journey of self-discovery, during which she worked through her understanding of her own sexuality. The word 'lesbian' did not exist at the time and Anne referred to her sexual preferences as 'my oddity'. Her diaries allowed her to come to terms with her sexual identity and in 1806, when she was just fifteen, she wrote confidently, 'I love and only love the fairer sex and thus beloved by them in turn, my heart revolts from any love but theirs.'

Born in 1791, Anne was the second child and eldest daughter of Jeremy Lister, a soldier in the 10th Regiment of Foot who served in the American War of Independence. Her mother, Rebecca Battle, owned Sklefler House in Market Weighton in North Yorkshire, where Anne spent most of her childhood. Anne's youngest brother died in infancy, while her older brother was drowned while serving in the army. Only Anne and her younger sister, Marian, survived past the age of twenty.

At the age of seven, in 1798, Anne was sent to a school run by Mrs Hagues and Mrs Chettle in Ripon, where she learned to enjoy music and dance. When visiting her uncle James at Shibden Hall, she would receive lessons from Misses Mellin. At the age of fourteen, Anne was sent to the Manor School in York, a boarding school for the daughters of élite families. Housed in the King's Manor, once the residence of the kings of England when in York, and subsequently the seat of the Council of the North, it is there that Anne developed her first relationship with another female.

Anne was a tomboy and it was feared that her rebellious spirit may be a bad influence on the other girls at Manor School. Consequently, she was not allowed to sleep in the communal dormitory. Instead, she was put into the attic room with another girl called Eliza Raine, which is where Anne's first romance began.

Eliza was of Anglo-Indian descent, the daughter of a surgeon employed by the East India Company in Madras. When her father died, she was brought to Yorkshire, along with her sister Jane, and placed under the guardianship of William Duffy, a York surgeon. As the illegitimate half-Indian daughter of an English surgeon, Eliza was an outsider, like Anne. Thrown together by chance, the two fifteen-year-olds embarked on a secret and passionate affair. They corresponded with each other over the summer and Eliza visited Shibden. When Eliza left, it is then that Anne wrote her first ever entry into her diary.

Through her relationship with Eliza, Anne was introduced to the York social scene and her circle of friends widened. However, Eliza began to realise that she had a rival. Isabella Norcliffe was the eldest daughter of a wealthy landowner, Lieutenant-Colonel Thomas Norcliffe Dalton and his wife, Ann, of Langton Hall near Malton. Anne could not resist Isabella's pretty face and she was also attracted to the wealth and glamour of her lifestyle.

By 1810 Anne was assiduously cultivating this new friendship as she was fascinated by the sophisticated lifestyle of the family. Their social confidence and self-assurance impressed Anne, who was newly arrived in the midst of the York social scene. Ambitious and eager to learn the ways of the world, Isabella was ideal for Anne as she was six years older and much more cultured than the younger Eliza. Although, both Eliza and Isabella fell deeply in love with Anne, she did not requite either of their feelings. Eliza wanted to live with Anne as an adult, but Anne was not prepared to settle down. Unfortunately, it seems that Eliza spent a lifetime pining for Anne, eventually dying at the age of sixty-seven after being admitted to Dr Belcombe's private asylum in Clifton.

Meanwhile Isabella and Anne became friends and occasional lovers for the remainder of Anne's life. Again Isabella wanted to become Anne's life-partner, but Anne rejected her. It was a bitter disappointment to Isabella who remained single all her life, dying in 1846 at the age of sixty-one. Although Anne had to keep her lesbian identity secret, this did not prevent her from being promiscuous. As Arthur Burrell noted after he had helped her ancestor, Thomas Lister, to decipher some of the diaries, 'hardly any of them escaped her'. Anne could be charming and persuasive when she wanted to be, and she cunningly developed strategies to seduce the women who she was attracted to.

Fiercely intelligent and highly educated, Anne set herself a programme of study that included Greek literature, algebra, French, mathematics and engineering, so that she could keep up with the men of her day and run her estate. When she wanted to test the water to find out if a woman was open to a lesbian relationship, she would make an allusion to homosexuality in ancient Greek literature, such as the poetess Sappho. She would then observe the reaction of the woman who she was interested in. She would sometimes 'accidentally' touch them and flirt. Anne had such an ability to charm and woo that it is possible that she tried to seduce Isabella Norcliffe's three sisters as well.

It is not entirely known how Anne met the love of her life, Mariana Belcombe, due to the loss of her diaries which cover that period. However, she does refer to the 'blue handkerchief' incident in later entries and so it can be surmised that perhaps Marianne dropped said handkerchief at one of the parties held at Langton Hall, the family home of Isabella Norcliffe, as a ploy to gain the attention of Anne.

Mariana Belcombe was the daughter of Dr Belcome, a York physician who specialised in the care of the mentally ill when he opened his own private asylum in Clifton in 1818. They met in at the Norcliffe's family home in 1812 when Anne was twenty-three and Mariana was twenty-two. Anne was immediately attracted to Mariana and the two women vowed to spend their lives together.

However, Anne's dream of a life-long companionship with Mariana would never be realised. When Mariana broke the news to Anne that she wanted to marry Charles Lawton, a wealthy landowner much older than herself, Anne begged her on her knees not to do it. Leaving Anne heartbroken, Mariana went ahead with the wedding at St Michel Le Belfrey church, York, in March 1816. Mariana tried to persuade Anne that she was doing it for her younger sisters, so that she could use the marriage as a vehicle to meet eligible bachelors and introduce them to her sisters. Anne saw through her excuses and believed that she had entered into the relationship merely for the money, the trappings of wealth and the social prestige that the marriage could afford. But because Anne did not want to lose Mariana, she could do little else but accept the arrangement.

It was the custom in those days for the ladies-in-waiting to accompany brides on their honeymoon. Excruciatingly, Anne set off with the Lawtons and another female companion as they journeyed to celebrate their nuptials. On her return, Anne fumed that what Mariana had done was 'legal prostitution'. To appease Anne, they conceived a plan together. Because Charles was in his fifties and Mariana in her twenties, they believed that Charles would die first. After his death they would unite households and would bring up any children together. Anne had seen examples of unconventional living arrangements between people. Her aunt and uncle who lived together at Shibden Hall were not married, but unmarried siblings. In 1822 Anne visited the Eleanor Butler and Sarah Ponsonby, who lived together for fifty years and may have been in a lesbian relationship. Anne and Mariana could always pretend that they were in a Boston marriage – the cohabitation of two wealthy women, independent of financial support from a man.

When Charles Lawton found out about their plan and their hopes for his early death, unsurprisingly, he broke off friendly relations with Anne. Nevertheless, Mariana continued to see her lover. Mariana was based at Charles' estate in Cheshire, so she and Anne would sometimes meet in York for an amorous reunion. Unfortunately for Mariana, Charles was so upset by her behaviour that he wrote her out of his will, even though she had signed over her income to him. If he should die, then she would be left destitute.

Ultimately, Charles Lawton reconciled with Anne and resigned himself to her affair with his wife, feigning indifference when they slept together in his own house.

He allowed them to travel together and eventually, under pressure from Anne, agreed to leave Mariana a good annuity when he died. Anne and Mariana went on a 'second honeymoon' together and continued to discuss pooling their resources, including the annuity from Charles. All their plans came to nothing because Anne died before Charles, who lived until his nineties.

The relationship between Mariana and Anne endured for approximately twenty years until a dramatic incident changed Anne's attitude to Mariana. Mariana was travelling in her coach from Cheshire to York and planned a stop at Shibden Hall to see her lover on the way. Extremely excited at the prospect of seeing the love of her life once more, Anne wrapped up warmly and strode out to walk the ten miles to meet Mariana's coach as it stumbled over the rocky ground towards Halifax.

The weather was wild and windy as Anne approached the summit of a bleak hill in Ripponden and saw the coach come into view. When it had battled its way to the top, Anne surprised Mariana, her brother, and her servant by bursting into the coach, mud-splattered and dishevelled. Mariana was horrified and embarrassed in front of her companions and Anne sensed her hostility. From that moment something changed in their relationship and Anne's attitude to Mariana was never the same again. Back at Shibden, Anne was devastated once more when in bed together, Mariana confided that she 'would rather die than let our connection be known'. Mariana nicknamed Anne 'Fred', suggesting that she was the more masculine one in the relationship.

Although Anne had to be discreet about her relationships with women, it did not stop gossip about her. In 1817 she took the decision to always wear black clothes, both as a sign of mourning for her loss of Mariana to Charles and to try to stop the disparaging comments that were being made about her femininity. When walking around Halifax and the surrounding countryside, men would sometimes jeer at her and call her names, most famously 'Gentleman Jack'. According to Helen Whitbread, one man even shouted out to her, 'Does your cock rise?' The term 'lesbian' was not coined until 1890 and it seems that Anne was able to conceal her sexuality because to many people she was an eccentric enigma.

Anne was an extraordinary woman, who despite a sexuality that could have led to her being ostracised, was fearless in her determination to run her affairs well in a male-dominated world. One evening when she was walking home alone over the fields she was assaulted by a man who tried to put his hand up her skirt. She beat him off with her walking stick.

Besides women, another of Anne's passions was travel. In 1819 she made her first trip to continental Europe when she was twenty-eight years old. Travelling with her 54-year-old aunt as chaperone, also called Anne Lister, they went on a two-month trip around France. In 1824 she had the courage to go alone to Paris and stayed there until the following year. One of the reasons for her trip was to find a cure for the venereal disease that she had caught from Mariana, which they thought she had contracted from her husband.

The guest house in Paris turned out to be a great place for Anne to meet female friends. She admitted that she engaged in 'errant flirting' with the young and frail Mademoiselle de Sans. It was there that she seduced an older widow called Mrs Barlow by touching her knees and other 'playful nonsense'. Although Anne succeeded in winning Maria's affections, her social standing and financial worth did not meet Anne's aspirations. A social climber, Anne continued her affair with Maria Barlow, at the same time as her relationship with Mariana Lawton, all the while looking for a suitable partner who would allow her to ascend socially.

In 1826 it was decided that Anne would eventually inherit Shibden Hall and she took charge of the affairs of the estate from this point on. Nevertheless, her new responsibility did not prevent her from indulging her passion for travel and in 1827 she went on a trip with her aunt and Maria Barlow around France, northern Italy and Switzerland, returning to Shibden Hall in 1828.

Between 1828 and 1832, Anne was introduced to many people who belonged to the English and Scottish aristocracy through her friend Sibella Maclean and was thus able to gain entry for a time into the higher circles of society. She received invitations to soirées from the likes of Lady Stuart de Rothesay, the wife of the British Ambassador in Paris. She also socialised with middle class people in York, such as Mr and Mrs Duffin, who lived at 58 Micklegate. Mr Duffin was an influential character in the city. He had been appointed Director of the York Dispensary in 1818 and was a member of the Yorkshire Philosophical Society. In 1830 she wrote a letter to Duffins about her ascent of Monte Perdido in the Pyrenees. While in York she would also have socialised with Isabella Norcliffe who lived with her sister in her mother's house at 9, Petergate.

With Paris as her base in 1829, she toured Belgium and the Netherlands and then headed to the Pyrenees where she scaled Monte Perdido, the third highest peak in the range, reaching a height of 3,355 metres. Of the experience she wrote:

"In about two hours hardish climbing up the rock, we …got to the first glacier, so steep that in spite of iron cramps strapped round our feet and long iron pointed sticks in our hands to hold by, it was with some difficulty we got up it. In the next glacier, still worse than the other, one of the Guides with an axe cut little steps for himself and the rest of us, that we could just stick our toes into, and one after another we all got safe over… Getting to the bottom did not give me much trouble – my foot slipped, I found myself sitting instead of standing, and in this way, glided down so nicely that all thought I had done it on purposes – well there was no crevasse near where I was"
(20 Dec 1830 – Mont Perdu – Letter from Anne Lister, Paris, to Mr and Mrs Duffin, York)

She achieved this remarkable feat while in the company of the wife of the British Ambassador in Paris, Lady Stuart de Rothesay, her two daughters and sundry attendants. Lady de Rothesay was probably somewhat mortified when Anne went over to the Spanish side of the mountain, where she was picked up by Spanish soldiers.

'I was off before the rest and made a nice little excursion into Spain where I had the amusement of being escorted by soldiers one day and stopped by a douanier another. …..and in spite of Mina and his guerrillas I am quite safe and never enjoyed anything more."
(10 Oct 1830 – Letter from Anne Lister, Nimes, to her aunt, Anne Lister [senior], Paris)

Anne's adventurous little excursion could have been very embarrassing for the de Rothsays as Spain was in the middle of the Carlist Civil War.

Back at Shibden Hall with her father, Jeremy, and her sister Marian, she was so uncomfortable that she left on a short trip to the Netherlands with her old flame, Mariana Lawton. For the next year she tried to spend as little time at Shibden as possible, avoiding her family, who she probably felt limited her freedom.

Self-education was extremely important to Anne and she was an avid reader. When she was twelve she wrote to her aunt, admitting that, 'my library is my greatest pleasure…the Grecian history has pleased me much'. She later added a Gothic tower to the grounds of Shibden to serve as her library. In 1831 she became the first woman to be elected to the Committee of Halifax Literary and Philosophical Society. She was intellectually ambitious and created a timetable of study of subjects that interested her. She was also socially ambitious and actively looked for a titled woman with whom she could share her life.

However, by 1832 Anne had become disillusioned in her attempts to elevate her social position with a relation with a titled woman and began to court Ann Walker, who was twelve years her junior and twenty-nine by this point in time. Despite her lack of title, Ann Walker was an extremely good catch for Anne Lister. She was the younger daughter of John Walker, a woolen manufacturer who owned properties adjacent to Shibden Hall. When she was nineteen years old, Ann Walker inherited a substantial fortune due to the deaths of both her parents in 1823 and the premature death of her brother in 1830.

The serious nature of the relationship between Anne Lister and Ann Walker is attested to by their decision to take holy communion together on Easter Sunday in Holy Trinity Church, Goodramgate, York. After the ceremony on 30th March 1832, thereafter they considered themselves to be married. Two years later they went on honeymoon to France and Switzerland.

Although Anne had lived at Shibden Hall and had run the estate for many years, she officially inherited the ancient manor house upon her aunt's death in 1836. She was forty-five years old. Built in 1420 by the Otes family, the hall was subsequently owned by the wealthy Savile family and later the Waterhouses. In 1612 Edward Waterhouse was forced to sell the property to try to avert bankruptcy and it was at this point that it passed to the Hemingway family, who were cousins of the Listers. By 1614 the tenant was one Samuel Lister, a clothier who contrived to bring the hall into the Lister family by encouraging the marriage of his sons to their cousins. A cunning streak seems to have run in the family because five years later the Listers owned the property.

Another of Anne's passions was Shibden Hall. She wrote to her aunt in 1820,

'You know that as far as place is concerned, every ambition and every wish of my heart are in the welfare of Shibden where in so long a series of generations, we have lived with that unblemished respectability which I cannot think of without a feeling of honest pride, nor ever remember without a sentiment of deep and heartfelt gratitude to my uncle who has done so much towards its support. I am daily more and more sensible of this, and more and more anxious to shew that his kindness to, and confidence in myself, are neither unappreciated not undeserved'.

The legacy that Anne received on the death of her aunt included not only the rent from the farms on the 400-acre Shibden estate, but interests in properties in the town of Halifax, shares in both the canal and railway industries, mining and stone quarries. However, despite her investments, Anne was cash poor. After Ann Walker agreed to live with her at Shibden, Anne persuaded her to give her money to help her transform the timber-framed manor house from a 'comfortless house' to a far grander property. She employed architect John Harper to terrace the south lawn and she opened up a Norman-style tower at the west end of the park to install a water closet. She landscaped the gardens creating a cascade and an ornamental lake. She also had a tunnel dug under the building so that her servants could move about without disturbing her, with the additional benefit of affording her more privacy.

By 1838 she had itchy feet again and set off on another trip to the French Pyrenees, where she achieved the remarkable feat of becoming the first amateur hiker to scale the 3,288 metre peak of Vignemale, the highest mountain in the whole range. She clearly needed an outlet for her boundless energy and dynamism.

The following year she embarked on a longer trip with Ann Walker and two servants. This time they travelled in Anne's carriage through France, Denmark, Sweden and Russia, arriving in St Petersburg in September and Moscow in October. With a reluctant Ann in tow, they set off to the Caucasus in February of 1840, travelling across the frozen river Volga. Few Europeans had visited the area, let alone western European women, and their arrival was viewed with curiosity. When she travelled, Anne did not just visit the typical tourist destinations, but entered lesser-known sites such as orphanages, factories, prisons and mines. She stayed in all types of accommodation from grand hotels, private mansions, roadside inns, hovels, monasteries, mountain huts and even her own carriage. She seems to have enjoyed the thrill of danger on her trips and was in Paris during the July revolution of 1830.

It was while she was on her last trip that she died. While travelling with Ann Walker, she caught a fever. She wrote her final entry in her journal in September 1840 and six weeks later she passed away in Georgia at the age of forty-nine. Somehow Ann Walker found the strength to organize for Anne's body to be embalmed and brought back to England. After seven months of travelling, Ann Walker finally arrived back at Shibden, so that Anne's body could be laid to rest with her family in the parish church at Halifax. Anne's obituary in the local newspaper read that she was a:

'respected and lamented lady, whose benefactions to our charitable and religious institutions will long be remembered, and whose public spirit in the improvement of our town and neighbourhood is attested by lasting memorials...'

She kept the Shibden estate within her family by leaving it to her paternal cousins, but left Ann Walker a life interest in it. Fourteen years later Ann Walker died after being declared insane. She spent some years in the care of Dr Belcombe in York before dying in her childhood home of Cliff Hall, Lightcliffe, in West Yorkshire.

More than forty years after her death in 1882, the Leeds Times reported on a dispute over the ownership of Shibden Hall and stated that 'Miss Lister's masculine singularities of character are still remembered.'

Anne Lister and her Secret Lovers

In 2018 a blue plaque was erected on the wall of Holy Trinity church, Goodramgate, York, which described Anne Lister as 'gender-nonconforming'. This wording offended a section of the population who believed that the term seemed to obscure her sexuality. An online petition was started and the group behind the memorial relented and changed the wording. A rainbow plaque now honours the woman who has been described as 'the first modern lesbian'. It commemorates her 'marital commitment' to Ann Walker and reads:

'Anne Lister 1791-1840 of Shibden Hall, Halifax
Lesbian and Diarist;
Took sacrament here to seal her union with Ann Walker.
Easter 1834'.

Anne Lister was a fascinating individual who was far from perfect. There were several unpleasant aspects to her character, such as her social snobbery and her blatant attempts to exploit other people both sexually and financially. Although she was of the gentry, not the aristocracy, she did not like the nouveau riche who had no lineage making money from mills in the industrial revolution. An overbearing person at times, she forced some of her tenants to vote the way that she wanted in the general election. However, as a woman she was unable to vote, so perhaps she was trying to exert her influence in a patriarchal society that excluded her. Politically she was a conservative who wanted to maintain the status quo of the gentry owning the land, a situation that benefitted her. Clearly, she did not believe in a meritocracy and was happy to enjoy her inheritance, while resisting other people's desires for a better life.

She could be calculating in her relationships, evaluating the pros and cons of embroiling herself with different lovers. However, it is impossible not to admire her ability to flout convention and refuse to be cowed in a man's world. She was a successful businesswoman, administering an estate. Not only was she cerebral and thoughtful, able to educate herself through reading, but she was athletic and physical. She scaled two of the highest mountains in Europe. She was an accomplished horsewoman who could drive her own horse and six.

Not only did she leave 7,720 pages of diaries, she left letters and several travel journals that are full of information about her daily life from her clothes to tooth-pulling to the employment of Bessie, the leech-woman to come and bleed her and her family. She wrote about social events, politics, workhouses and the labour troubles caused by mechanisation. Her writings are an invaluable source of primary information about an important area of Yorkshire during the Industrial Revolution.

Nevertheless, it is her often shockingly candid and explicit descriptions of her feelings and sexual encounters with women that have completely changed modern ideas about the history of lesbianism. From an early age, Anne had numerous relationships with women, proof that she was not alone in her desires and attractions. Anne's diaries have caused a radical reassessment of preconceptions about women's sexuality, particularly stereotypes about the purported innate lack of female sexual feelings developed in particular during the Victorian age. Her writings consign ridiculous assertions of the absence of sexual feeling in women to the status of myth, where they belong.

In 2011 the twenty-four volumes of her diaries were added to the register of UNESCO Memory of the World Programme. The collection was described as the 'comprehensive and painfully honest account of lesbian life ... They have shaped and continue to shape the direction of UK Gender Studies and Women's History'. With numerous books published about her life, as well as a BBC television series starring Suranne Jones, it is highly likely that Anne Lister would have enjoyed the spotlight that her two-hundred-year-old diaries have cast on her life. When she hid her diaries behind the wooden wainscoting of her parlour, was she hoping for a more enlightened time?

CHAPTER TWELVE

Mary Ellen Best

Forgotten Artist

IN 1838 MARY Ellen Best painted a portrait of herself sitting in the painting room of her rented house in York. The repeated swirls of green foliage in the wallpaper and the matching pattern in the curtains show her astonishing ability to render minute motifs in exquisite detail. The room is cosy with rugs and a grey-blue carpet. The dark blue velvet tablecloth that is draped over one of the tables highlights her ability to capture the luxurious folds of drapery. Light bounces off a wooden rocking chair in a corner and a small, well-behaved dog waits attentively by the fireplace. Over the mantlepiece hang portraits of her family that she has painted and in front of the window, where the light is best, she sits and stares directly at the viewer, while painting at her table.

Dabbing her brush into her palette, she is ready to carefully add colour to her current painting on the easel in front of her. She wears black mourning in honour of her beloved mother, who has recently passed away. On the opposite side of the room, several of her other paintings lie scattered and unframed. As she holds our gaze, twenty-eight-year-old Mary Ellen Best is clearly and confidently telling us that she is an artist.

Ellen, as she was affectionately known by her family, is a unique artist in both skill and subject. As a woman from an upper-middle class family in the early nineteenth century, if she ventured outdoors, she would always need to be escorted by a chaperone. This societal restriction meant that the majority of Ellen's subjects were detailed scenes of interiors. While she took inspiration from the grand rooms of her grandparents' country seat, Langton Hall, seventeen miles north of York, as well as the many sumptuous rooms in the mansions of her social circle, she was equally as fascinated by the kitchens of such homes, where she would paint a servant going about his or her business.

Ellen was intrigued by all types of people and painted the 'freaks' at the travelling fairs which visited York. In 1833 Miss Emmeline, a seven-year-old expert horsewoman who was part of Cooke's Royal Circus became one of her subjects. Eleven-year-old albino, James Heritage, also caught her eye. In May 1834, Isabella Paula, a 'Portuguese Hindoo' travelled to York and attracted Ellen's attention. Isabella was so exotic at the time that she was able to work for a travelling show, showing the lack of diversity in Victorian England.

Not only did Ellen record the interiors of grand houses, but the rooms of cottages in York, sometimes populated by three generations of women. Her 1836 'A Cottage by Firelight, York' is one example of how her work has become a valuable record of Victorian social history. Ellen was ahead of her time when she painted cottage interiors as the subject only became fashionable towards the end of the century when middle- and upper-class patrons realized that many traditional aspects of rural life were fast disappearing.

Ellen was born into a privileged family. Her mother was Mary Norcliffe Dalton, the daughter of Lieutenant-Colonel Thomas Norcliffe Dalton, a wealthy landowner and his wife, Anne, of Langton Hall near Malton. After taking his MD at Edinburgh University, her father took up two voluntary posts at dispensaries, helping poor people access medical care. After returning to York, he gained a paid position as physician in charge of York Lunatic Asylum in 1804. Ellen's portraits of her parents show that they were cultured, refined and made a very handsome couple.

Although Mr Best did not have substantial private means, unlike Isabella's family, he had such good prospects that her parents spent little time in marrying her off to him when she was just seventeen years old. Mary Norcliffe had received a good education, was well-read and was able to write a powerful letter. She could speak French and was interested in natural history.

In 1809 Mr and Mrs Best had been married for just over two years when they had Ellen, their second child, who they baptised at St Mary's, Castlegate. Ellen was born at home in Little Blake Street, York, near the Minster where she grew up with her sister, Rosamund. Although the house no longer exists it is thought that it was either a three or four storey townhouse in what is now Duncombe Place, in the heart of the city.

The Bests enjoyed a comfortable lifestyle and were able to employ at least two servants. Ellen's father made a good living at the asylum, as well as being able to supplement his salary with private patients. He also enjoyed a share in the profits of a private lunatic asylum in Acomb, a suburb of York.

Their social position allowed the Bests to lead a genteel life in York. Although the apogee of York's social scene had been during the Georgian era of the previous century, there were still numerous cultural activities that the family could enjoy, such as the theatre and the Assembly Rooms. With only two factories in York, one producing lead and the other glass, the Industrial Revolution that transformed other

Yorkshire towns like Bradford and Leeds hardly touched York. The population was small, rising from 18,217 in 1811 to 28,842 in 1841. Nevertheless, the city was the centre of social, legal and ecclesiastical life in the north of England.

The small area of the city of York encompassed twenty-four parish churches, along with its Gothic minster. The library had recently been established, with money raised through subscription and one of the sponsors was Joseph Rowntree, senior. In 1827 the York Institute of Popular Science and Literature was founded. Three years later in 1830 the Yorkshire Philosophical Society' Museum and Gardens were created.

Ellen's family was cultured and sophisticated, with an interest in history and was involved in the creation of the Yorkshire Philosophical Society from the beginning. Ellen's grandmother, Ann, helped to kick-start the mineral collection with a donation of ammonite from Langton Wold. Her mother gave natural history specimens and rare medical texts. Her uncle, Norcliffe Norcliffe, gave a piece of oxidulated iron from Sweden.

While the Yorkshire Philosophical Society did not admit female members until 1830, when it decided to try to expand its revenue base, Ellen and Rosamund were frequent visitors to the museum and gardens and they enlarged their circle of friends and acquaintances with their almost daily saunters around the garden.

While Ellen and Rosamund led a privileged life, unfortunately, this did not shelter them from personal tragedy at an early age. The scandal at York Lunatic Asylum broke in 1813 when Ellen was just four years old. Samuel Tuke, a descendent of Mary Tuke, published a book promoting The Retreat, the Quaker asylum that his father had helped to found. In his text he criticised the running of the rival York Asylum. At the same time, a magistrate called Godfrey Higgins published articles in the York Herald claiming that patients at York Lunatic Asylum were being seriously mistreated.

These allegations caused considerable public concern and, unfortunately, many of them proved to be true. Four patients who had been chained to a wall died in a fire in December 1813 and the governors took no action. Many of the governors were Dr Best's own personal friends, and even his relations. However, they left him to bear the burden of responsibility. Dr Best had to defend himself by arguing that although he was the physician in charge of the medical care of the patients, it was the governors who were in charge of the management and day-to-day running of the establishment. Consequently, he argued that it was unfair for him to take the blame for their living conditions.

The strain of defending himself began to take its toll on Mr Best and the bad publicity did not go away. The York Herald continued to be full of stories about the asylum and in the spring of 1814, forty philanthropic gentlemen paid the equivalent of almost two thousand pounds each to qualify as new governors of the institution, whereupon they set up their own enquiry into the running of the establishment. Their investigations revealed that patients were indeed neglected and mistreated. The accommodation was damp, filthy and overcrowded. Inmates were clothed in rags and the food was foul. Patients suffered violence, were often whipped, and some of the women patients were even raped. In March of the same year the final straw came when Thomas Thompson, MEP, visited the asylum and learned that three patients had just murdered a fellow inmate. He also found the cells and the day room in a filthy state.

In Ann Digby's account and analysis of the affair, she believes that it would be wrong to hold Dr Best entirely responsible for the scandal. The asylum had increased the number of patients from 54 to 199 in order to gain more revenue as inflation sky-rocketed in Britain due to the Napoleonic wars. Meanwhile, the governors would not increase the number of domestic staff, who fed and washed the inmates, from the original seven. While Dr Best's predecessor had had the benefit of an assistant doctor, Dr Best had to manage alone.

Nevertheless, it was convenient for all those involved to blame Dr Best and some of his opponents began to accuse him of financial irregularities. Although he was cleared after an inquiry, the mental strain of the allegations and the repeated denouncement of the asylum in the press bore down heavy on him. When Ellen was six in 1815 her father resigned his post on grounds of ill health and the family went to Nice in France. Dr Best took Ellen, his wife and her faithful servant, Elizabeth Anderson. Rosamund was left at home in Yorkshire in the care of her relations.

While in France, in addition to suffering from tuberculosis, Dr Best also underwent acute attacks of rheumatism. On July 30th, 1817, he died at the age of thirty-eight, a mere ten year into his marriage to his wife, his health shattered. Ellen was nine years old and would be too young to understand the details of what had happened, but she would have known that her whole world had shifted on its axis. She would have seen both her parents suffering for three long years and she would have felt anxiety and worry. Away from her adored sister in France, she sent Rosamund paintings and cut-outs as presents. Even at this early stage in her life, Ellen's love of painting was becoming evident. According to family legend, she even made paint brushes out of her own hair.

While in France Ellen became seriously ill also. Her mother wrote home in 1816 that, 'We have been very near to losing our poor little Ellen to a liver disorder, accompanied by jaundice. We had to sit up with her every night for a week, with slight hopes of her getting over it'. After a very troubling time, Ellen and her mother returned home to York in 1818.

At first Mary and her daughters stayed at Langton Hall and then they lived in a succession of lodgings in York. Still the scandal of the asylum plagued them, and the following year Mrs Best wrote an eleven page letter to defend her husband to Lord Landsdowne who had made a speech in parliament about the Lunatic Regulations Bill. In it she wrote that she was certain that her husband's 'valuable life was prematurely shortened by the long, harassing and most unmerited persecution he underwent on the subject of that institution'. She went on to point out that conditions at the hospital had not improved and a further murder had recently taken place, along with dismissals for inappropriate behaviour with female patients. It must have been hard for the whole family not to feel very bitter.

The result of the death of Ellen's father was to 'plunge Ellen and her sister into an almost exclusively feminine environment', according to her 1985 biographer Caroline Davidson. Mrs Best never remarried and instead brought her daughters up with the help of her closest relations and her faithful servant, Elizabeth Anderson, the daughter of a farmer. Mary had two unmarried sisters, Isabella and Charlotte, who lived at the Norcliffe's York townhouse at 9 Petergate. Meanwhile, Ellen's grandparents continued to live at Langton, not far away.

In Dr Best's will he bequeathed his daughters £50 a year so that they could enjoy a 'trifling independence' as Ellen's mother described it. They would not be forced to earn a living, unlike Anne and Charlotte Brontë, which meant that they could maintain their social status as gentlewomen. Neither would Ellen and Rosamund be forced to marry for financial reasons.

In 1820 the financial situation of the family improved still further when Mrs Best inherited £6,250 from her father, the equivalent of £359,000 today. By this time Ellen was eleven years old. While at home, Ellen and Rosamund received some education and knew reading, writing and arithmetic. They would have enjoyed needlework and it is likely that they had some classes in painting.

Henry Cave was an artist and engraver in York who also had a teaching practice in the early 1800s giving lessons at the Manor School and Peaseholmegreen House. He specialised in drawing, still-life, flower and landscape painting, as well as sketching out famous paintings to that they could be rendered in needlework. It is possible the Mrs Best employed Henry Cave to teach her two daughters before they went to school.

In accordance with the custom of their social class, Ellen and Rosamund were sent away to boarding school in their early teens. It was hoped that they would make friends and meet other girls their age who would invite them to their homes where they could meet suitable young men. The first school the sisters attended was in Doncaster and run by Ann Haugh (1876-1849). Fortunately, it was nothing like the boarding school that Charlotte Brontë and some of her sisters were sent to in the Yorkshire Dales. Ann Haugh began as a governess and then later married George Haugh, a drawing master who specialised in portraits. They opened their school for twelve young ladies in 1797.

At the school, the sisters were lucky to be taught by a highly educated woman who had fallen on hard times. When Barbara Hoole was unable to collect her widow's pension because the firm that it was invested with went bankrupt, she turned to teaching out of necessity. She embraced this profession with some gusto as she also published morally uplifting tales for young people, as well as geography textbooks. She held radical beliefs in education for the time (and some would argue the present), namely that education should be fun and that children absorbed facts more easily if they were entertained in the process. Her books were imaginative and enlightened.

At Ann and George Haugh's school, the teaching of drawing and painting took prime position in the curriculum. It was seen as an accomplishment for girls from middle- and upper-class backgrounds to have lessons in drawing and painting. It was believed that this leisurely pleasure was attractive and could lead to finding a suitable husband.

George Haugh (1775-1827) was an accomplished artist who exhibited regularly at the Royal Academy and British Institution. He taught his pupils to draw an accurate outline with a lead pencil, shade their pictures, apply washes of India ink to tint them, as well as the art of drawing in watercolours. According to Caroline Davidson, by the age of twelve, Ellen could draw a 'creditable portrait and by the age of fourteen her market scenes displayed a real flair for composition.' Both Ellen and Rosamund were loyal to their friends and they stayed in contact with Mrs Haugh well after her husband's death.

In 1824 the sisters ventured south to attend Mrs Shepherd's school in Bromley in the south east of London. Miss Shepherd was a pioneer in girls' education. As a disciple of Johann Heinrich Pestalozzi, a Swiss educational reformer, she believed that children should be allowed to develop at their own pace, following their own personalities. Her ethos included the belief that the purpose of education was to make children as independent and self-sufficient as possible. Among their art teachers were Amelia Long and Lady Farnborough, who lived at nearby Bromley Hill Place.

Caroline Davidson argues that Rosamund and Ellen were 'profoundly influenced' by Francis Shepherd and it was thanks to her that they both became 'independent, well-organised and family-minded individuals'. She notes that Rosamund went on to have three of her daughters educated by Miss Shepherd, who often went to stay with her in York.

Ellen finished her formal education at the age of nineteen in 1828 and returned to York, where she lived a quiet, but pleasant life. The sisters would accompany their mother on her busy round of social calls, including visits to their aunts at 9 Petergate. They also went on daily walks around the city. They spent their time making new clothes for themselves and joined their friends on boating parties on the River Ouse. Sometimes they would trek over West Huntington to the family farm of their loyal servant, Elizabeth Alderson, for tea parties. At other times their grandmother's carriage could be heard clattering down the street as it arrived to carry them off for a stay at Langton Hall.

The family became friends with the family of Dr Baldwin Wake who had succeeded Ellen's father as the doctor at York Asylum. They lived in an elegant house in Blake Street. It was at this time that Ellen began to demonstrate her dedication to her art. Although she had left school, she did not stop learning her art. However, she did practically teach herself from now on. She bought 'Art and Artists' by Carlo Doci. Finding that there were limits to what she could learn from books, she began to practise every day between 1829 and 1830. If the weather was good, she would sketch outdoors to learn to draw from nature. If the weather was inclement, she would concentrate on the interior of a cottage or a church. Her renderings of the interiors of Holy Trinity, Goodramgate and St Denys Church, Walmgate show that she was able to recreate the intricacies of stained glass in all their vibrancy and detail. While staying with her close friend, Rose Stovin, she sketched the romantic ruins of Easby Abbey.

The many country houses of the nobility in Yorkshire had impressive art collections. If a visitor presented a suitable letter of introduction to the housekeeper, they would be allowed to visit the state rooms on appointed days. Ellen went on expeditions to study the history of art and the work of great painters which had often been collected by the aristocracy, often on their grand tours.

At Castle Howard she painted the green damask room replete with all the priceless paintings hanging on the walls. At Fountains Hall next to Studley Park she painted the banqueting room. Some of her social circle had very impressive houses and she painted one of the rooms in Howsham Hall belonging to Colonel George Chomley. She was inspired by the seat of her grandfather, Langton Hall and in particular a statue of Venus by Canova that her mother's brother brought back from Italy. Her mother enjoyed their expeditions and was happy to chaperone her on her adventures, when her health permitted.

Ellen was not just interested in recording the grand and luxurious rooms of the middle and upper classes. At Langton Hall she painted the family at the grand dining room table, but also the kitchen table, complete with crockery and cookware while a servant carries a huge, appetising pie. She was intrigued by subjects of all classes. In 1832 she painted 'Miss Mary Kirby of Castle Howard Inn', probably the daughter of the landlords Seth and Ann Kirby. Mary is shown fashionably dressed, holding a fan made of peacock feathers from the Castle Howard estate.

Mary painted houses, cottages, streets, markets, churches, fairs, as well as portraits of family and friends. Her biographer, Caroline Davidson sums up her uniqueness when she explains that Ellen 'was not interested in the usual repertoire of the early nineteenth-century artist: "picturesque" landscapes and views; great moments from history and literature; religious scenes; and portraits of important men and their families. Instead, she recorded what she saw around her'.

It is hard not to accept this fact without considering that this was due in part to the limitations of her education and lifestyle imposed upon her because she was a woman. If we compare Mary Ellen Best's training with York's other foremost artist, Willam Etty, we can see a stark contrast in the opportunities for training that each were able to access.

Born twenty-two years before Ellen in 1878, Etty's rise to prominence as one of Britain's greatest painters, particularly of nudes, is quite remarkable given his humble beginnings. The son of a miller and gingerbread baker, Etty went to London to complete a two-year apprenticeship in printing where he spent his spare time teaching himself to draw from nature, copying prints and paintings. Like Ellen, he also learnt from visiting museums. Eventually, he developed such proficiency that he was admitted to the Royal Academy's Schools of Design, located in Somerset House, London.

The Royal Academy's schools were opened in 1769 to train painters and sculptors. Once admitted, artists would spend up to ten years drawing, painting and sculpting in the 'Antique School' and the 'School of Drawing from Life'. In the 'Painting School' they learnt by copying Old Masters. There were regular lectures on anatomy, architecture, painting, perspective and geometry.

Although Ellen had the talent, as a woman she did not have access to such comprehensive training, as only men were admitted to the Academy Schools. It wasn't until 1835 that Henry Sass' art school in Bloomsbury admitted women students. As Davidson explains, 'the limitations of Ellen's training and its comparative loneliness help to explain why she stuck to watercolours and never progressed to oils'.

Nevertheless, by 1830 Ellen was beginning to sell her art and gain some national recognition. The Yorkshire Gazette reported that the London Society for the Encouragement of Arts, Manufactures and Commerce (now the Royal Society of Arts) awarded 'Miss Mary Ellen Best of this city' their silver medal for 'drawing still-life'. At the young age of twenty-one, Ellen was able to supplement her income of £50 a year from her father's legacy with the sale of her art. Far from being ashamed of the desire to make money, she found that selling her work boosted her morale. She felt that if people were prepared to pay for her art, then it must be good. She was flattered when Reverend Frederick Kendall of Ricall near Selby offered 12 guineas for two of her watercolours in May 1831.

Had Ellen been a man or belonged to a lower social class, it would have been acceptable for her to advertise her work by displaying it in the window of her lodgings. She could also have advertised in the local press. As a member of the upper middle class, none of these options were open to her because if a woman worked then she was no longer genteel. Fortunately, many of Ellen's social connections were enchanted with her work. When she painted a room in Naburn Hall for George Palmes, he went on to order individual portraits of his entire family. The seven portraits took several months to complete.

Other commissions arrived from the Cholmleys of Howsham Hall, the Wakes of York, the Mainwarings of Middleton Hall. Ellen was also commissioned by Mrs Duffin of Micklegate to paint her in her drawing room. This is the same family who Anne Lister wrote her letter about her excursion to Monte Perdido about referred to in Chapter Eleven. Ellen's family was a great patron and her mother alone ordered sixteen portraits. In an age before the advent of photography, there was a great demand for portraits and when someone showed off their portrait collection, others were tempted to follow suit. As a watercolourist, Ellen had a commercial advantage to artists who worked in oil as her paintings were smaller and cheaper. Oils canvases were often large and the raw materials expensive.

The majority of Ellen's commissions were from female clients, who were more family-oriented and had less money to spend on oil paintings. Around sixty percent of her clients were female and were happy to receive their commissions in watercolour. Despite her lack of formal training in anatomy, Ellen targeted the market for small watercolour portraits.

Before 1840 she painted on average around forty portraits a year. She did not always sell her work but would exchange her canvasses or even give them away. She sold around forty percent and gifted the remaining sixty. Mary Ellen Best was part of a small but thriving artistic community in York in the 1820s. William Shinton taught drawing in St Saviourgate, as did Miss De Guandastague in Petergate. Robert Bank painted miniatures in Harker's Yard, Micklegate. A landscape painter called John Brown was to be found in Walmgate and an animal painter, David Dalby, was located outside Micklegate Bar.

Unable to advertise her work openly, Ellen devised a much subtler and nuanced strategy. She made sure that she always had a painting waiting to be framed at Mr Benjamin Evers 'Repository of Arts' at 43 Stonegate. While Mr Evers was framing her work, passers-by could see her paintings and pop in to enquire about them. This was beneficial to Mr Evers as it helped to drum up business for his shop. Mr Evers was very helpful to Ellen as he had contacts with dealers in Manchester and London. Through Messrs Ackermann of London and Messrs Agnew and Zanetti of Manchester, Ellen was able to sell her work in other towns and cities besides York.

Soon she was showing her work in exhibitions. The Northern Society for the Encouragement of Fine Arts in Leeds took one of her still lives to display, along with its other 356 works. It was an important show which attracted national artists. In 1831 she showed two more works in Newcastle – 'A Woman Paring Apples' and 'Kitchen Table'. That same year six of her still lifes were exhibited in Liverpool.

As the selection boards for these shows were all exclusively male, it was quite an achievement to have her work selected.

Her final exhibition took place in 1836 at Mr J Tuite's house in Castlegate, where she showed eight works alongside ten by William Etty and three by Henry Cave. Although she was in illustrious company, Ellen's work was not for sale. Instead, she held the honorary status of an amateur. The exhibition was an ambitious affair designed to put York back on the artistic map. It ran for four months with a total of 422 works on display by 170 different artists. Ellen's portrait of her sister's baby was singled out for praise by the Yorkshire Gazette. This was welcome news as she and her sister had been nursing their bedridden mother for thirteen months.

Ellen's sister Rosamund was also a talented artist and writer. By 1829 it was felt that the antiquities of York were under threat. York Minster was partially destroyed by fire after an arson attack and there was great debate about how to restore it. The bar walls were crumbling and Ellen and Rosamund joined the effort to raise awareness of the problem. Rosamund drew all twenty-four of York's ancient parish churches, accompanied by short descriptions of each. Her work was so good that it was commercially published in 1831. In one of Ellen's rare landscapes of York she documents Marygate in 1830 with a woman feeding chickens on the mud track outside. Perhaps this was her attempt to record the decline of York's precious heritage.

Rosamund's artistic output waned somewhat after she married a solicitor called Henry Robinson in 1830. In the space of twenty years, she bore him no less than thirteen children. With little time to pursue her drawing, she was nevertheless able to write 'A Family Chronicle of Twenty Years in the Life of Mr and Mrs Henry Robinson, 1831-1851'. This record of the daily existence and the important happenings in the lives of friends and relations of the family was lent to Ellen's biographer by one of her descendents. It is with the help of this detailed document that Caroline Davidson was able to piece together the life and works of Mary Ellen Best in her book, 'The World of Mary Ellen Best'.

After Rosamund's marriage, Ellen and her mother proceeded to live together in a long succession of lodging houses. They went from Pulleyn's Lodgings in Blake Street to Brookbanks at 48 Coney Street. After staying there for four years, they moved on to Ellinson's on Lord Mayor's Walk. They were still very close to Rosamund who visited them nearly every day. Ellen was a doting aunt who not only babysat her nieces and nephews but showered them with gifts also.

By this time Ellen was a semi-professional artist with a forthright personality, unafraid to speak her mind, even though she did belong to what was termed 'polite society'. On 1st June 1831 she bumped into the brother of her sister's husband in the Museum Gardens. Thomas Robinson was so shocked when she described his new haircut as 'frightful' that he recorded their full conversation in his diary of 1831 to 1838. In said diary, Caroline Davidson noted that he referred to 'the artist Ellen Best' on many occasions. When he called on his friends he often heard that she had secured a commission for a painting, or that she was engaged on a new portrait.

Although all the great masters worked in oil, there was a strong sense at the time that watercolour was a new fashionable medium. There was more opportunity to experiment with watercolour than with oil and elaborate gilt frames were often used to frame watercolours, in direct competition with oils. The advantage for Ellen in using watercolour was that the materials were cheaper than oils, lighter and more portable. Ellen could practice anywhere, and it would not create too much mess.

Ellen loved to travel and in 1832 she went on a three-month tour of North Wales via Liverpool. She stopped at Conway to sketch the impressive Elizabethan house, Plas Mawr and was inspired by an old palace in Beaumaris. Two years later she went on a more ambitious fourteen-month tour of the Continent. In Holland she visited Rotterdam where she painted an orphanage as she was interested in charitable institutions. She also painted one of the orphan children. Next, she travelled down the Rhine to Mainz, then on to Frankfurt where she stayed for the winter.

In Frankfurt she took the opportunity to see great works of art at the Stadel Institute and studied their collection of old masters. Her painting of one of the galleries in the Stadal collection shows that she had the ability to paint pictures within pictures with such accurate detail that it is possible to recognise her microscopic replicas of the great masters who she recorded in the room.

While in the German city of Stadel, she and her mother lodged next door to a successful wine merchant called Johann Conrad. He had three daughters and she became great friends with Elizabeth, or Lily as she was familiarly known. After finding new lodgings next to the Bavarian Embassy, she painted the portraits of the ambassador, his wife and their two children.

By this point Ellen was at the height of her artistic career and she developed her skills even further in Frankfurt, as well as selling more paintings. She developed a taste for contemporary German art and made the acquaintance of another watercolourist, Luise Frederike Auguste. In total she sold fourteen major works between 1834 and 1835 while in Frankfurt.

In 1835 Ellen and her mother were forced to return to York due to the latter's failing health. By this point, Ellen's enthusiasm for her work was gradually beginning to wane. Firstly, she no longer felt the need to prove herself. Neither did she need the money anymore because her grandmother had left her mother a substantial inheritance. Alongside the additional £350 a year, Mary Best gained a third share in the house in Petergate. Ellen's mother now had the equivalent of £24,000 a year to share with her daughter.

The following year they moved for the penultimate time to Mrs Palmer's lodgings in Gillygate. Mrs Best was so ill that when she moved for the final time to the lodgings of Jackson the Jeweller on Coney Street, she had to be carried in a sedan chair. While Rosamund nursed their mother, Ellen took her nieces and nephews on trips along the River Ouse. Their days out included watching glass being blown, laughing at the Punch and Judy show, and cowering at the wild beasts at the Whitsuntide Fair. The Martinmas fair brought giantesses and albinos for them to ogle.

When Ellen's mother died in 1837, after a long and painful illness, Ellen inherited an income of £156 a year to add to the £50 from her father's bequest. She now received the modern equivalent of £14, 000 a year. With her wealth Ellen could afford to rent a substantial house in York, employ two servants and buy whichever books and prints took her fancy. She was also able to satisfy her lust for travel as much as she liked. Although she continued to sell her work privately, she did not use dealers or exhibit any more.

As a sign of the high regard that she was held in by her mother, Rosamund recorded in her family chronicle that just before Mary died, she had requested that Rosamund name her most recent child, Ellen, in honour of the artist. Her mother 'fervently prayed that [the child] might prove all to [Rosamund] that Ellen had been to her'. Ellen now decided to move to 1 Clifton to be near to her sister who had set up home at number 4, where she was happy to help Rosamund with her burgeoning family.

However, that same year, perhaps to take her mind off her grief for her mother, Ellen left for Rotterdam on July 4th with Elizabeth Anderson as her chaperone. She spent two months in Holland where the difference between English and Dutch culture intrigued her and she took every opportunity to record her impressions. Caroline Davidson records that her sketch books are full of 'colourful costumes, enormous straw hats and scenes of industry in cottages'. Ellen was impressed with Holland and loved the neatness and order, as well as the cleanliness of the inhabitants. She discovered several excellent charitable institutions which were run by women.

The following year she set off for Germany, visiting Brunswick and Magdeburg. It was on this trip that she became engaged to Johann Anton Phillip Sarg, a German schoolteacher and amateur musician. At twenty-nine he was six months younger than Ellen. It was a whirlwind romance which surprised some of her friends, although it is possible that Ellen may have met Johann on a previous trip with her mother. His brother and sister-in-law owned the elegant Hotel Russischer Hof, where she may have even stayed. We know that Ellen was charmed by the building because she painted the entrance.

After teaching at the most exclusive girls' school in Frankfurt, Johann was working full time at the hotel, organising concerts and musical entertainments. Perhaps her good friend Lilly Eckhard played a part in the match as Ellen asked her to be a bridesmaid at the wedding. However, due to Johann's financial means, some of her friends disapproved of their union. Thomas Taylore Worsley wrote to his sister that it was 'not a desireable match but all seems to be settled and it is to take place about January'.

In the 1839 self-portrait that Ellen painted as wedding gift to Johann just before her marriage, she wears a rich gold-coloured gown, with a tight bodice and bare shoulders. Her rich brown hair is in a formal up-do complete with plaited bun. She has captured the detail of her drapery and the sumptuousness of the material is evident. She holds a small wooden framed painting on her knee and a paintbrush in her other hand. She stares directly at the viewer and is unafraid to show that one of her eyes is slightly lower than the other. She is still beautiful, and she clearly still identifies as an artist.

In 1840 Ellen took Johann to meet her family in York and they were married at St Olave's church. They proceeded to honeymoon at another of Colonel George Cholmley's houses at Whitby Abbey. After their marriage, Ellen painted her husband's portrait. He is shown holding the self-portrait that she gave him in December 1839, just before their marriage. By this time Ellen had perfected the technique of painting a picture within a picture, as demonstrated from her paintings of the galleries of museums and grand houses. In Johann's portrait he has glossy, dark chestnut hair, just like his wife and his face is of a similar shape. Together they would have made a striking couple.

While in York they had some complicated bureaucratic business to complete so that Anthony, as Johann came to be known, could draw funds from his wife's annuities on the Continent. To access her funds, he had to renounce his Nurmeburg citizenship and transfer his household to York in order to become an official citizen. He therefore spent much of his time in the city compiling official documents, as well as trying to persuade the Lord Mayor to sign them. After Ellen found a new tenant to take over the rent of 1 Clifton, they arranged for all their possessions to be sent to Germany.

They left York on March 10th 1840 and lodged in Nuremburg for fifteen months. By this time Ellen was already three months pregnant with their first child. That year she painted eleven interiors and twenty-one portraits, at the same time as learning German. The following year they moved to Frankfurt and rented an apartment in the city centre. Wanting more space alongside peace and quiet, they then moved to a substantial villa in the suburbs with a large garden. By 1843 they had three children – Frank, Caroline and Fred.

Anthony had no need to work and they enjoyed socialising with the Eckhard sisters among others, and Ellen stopped selling her paintings after her marriage. Nevertheless, Ellen continued to regard herself an artist and still aroused curiosity in Germany, just as she had done in England.

When they returned to York for a visit in 1845, Rosamund described Ellen's four-year-old son, Frank, as spoilt in the family chronicle. Over the years Ellen painted all her children, with several of her daughter Ann surviving. She also painted her husband with his friends. He appears relaxed reading the paper or playing cards, very much the leisurely gentleman. In a surviving self-portrait of 1845/46 Ellen no longer depicts herself as an artist. Her cheeks are a little plumper, and she has a kind face. She wears a pink day gown with a delicate lace collar and bow. She no longer holds the viewer's gaze directly, but looks at us obliquely, with a hint of sadness in her large, almond-shaped blue eyes.

In 1845 the Sargs had a brief flirtation with life in Belgium. However, despite the excellent railway connections in Malines, they felt isolated due to their inability to speak Flemish. Combined with a desire to give Frank a good education, they returned to Germany in 1846.

When Ellen was forty the family moved to a delightful villa called Remaier Hof on the outskirts of Worms that they bought for £1250, the equivalent of £100,000 in today's money. Anthony made wine on a small scale and raised money to restore the local thirteenth century church. Finally, they settled down and lost their zeal for travel.

In 1851 they made a brief visit to York because Rosamund's husband, Henry Robinson was ill. Approximately ten years later, it seems that Ellen had given up painting. Her last known work is a vase of three glorious delicate pale pink roses, surrounded by dark-green leaves dated to 1860. Ellen was fifty-one years old.

Six years later the Sargs sold their house and went to Darmstadt to retire where they lived in a succession of lodgings. They wanted to be near their daughter, Caroline, who had met an army officer. Her sons had gone to Latin America where

he had to flee for his life to Amsterdam in 1679. With the restoration of Charles II to the throne, the Act of Toleration was passed in 1689, which allowed open worship by dissenting groups, such as the Unitarians, the Congregationalists, the Baptists, the Presbyterians and the Quakers.

Lady Sarah's Unitarian faith was based on the idea of unity or oneness with God. It rejected concepts such as original sin, predestination and the infallibility of the Bible, placing emphasis instead on using reason to interpret the scriptures. Freedom of conscience and freedom of the pulpit are the core values of the tradition to this day. In 1692 Lady Hewley built a brick meeting house in St Saviourgate for her community to worship in. Lady Hewley's chapel is unusual in its cruciform transept.

In 1697 on the death of her second husband, Sarah Hewley inherited a vast estate, out of which she financed the construction of almshouses on Tanner Row, intended for nine elderly widows of dissenting ministers, with one poor man to act as chaplain. In her will she set up a trust that would also provide for poor and godly preachers and their widows, as well as godly persons in distress. Five young men at any one time, who were destined to enter the ministry of the church, were to be educated with the funds from her bequest also.

In 1710 Lady Hewley died with the instructions that her 'vile body' be disposed of cheaply and without ceremony. She was buried alongside her husband and her two children, Wolrcych and John, who had died in infancy. Five years before her death she planned the Hewley Trust to care for nine single or widowed women who were over fifty-five years old, with her vast estates providing the income. The manor of West Ayton where Captain Cook was born had been purchased by her father and by 1877 comprised of 1,095 acres of farmland. The trust also benefitted from income from estates in Knaresborough, Braycrot, Killinghill, Coneythorpe, Brearton, Sussacres and Arkendale.

One hundred years after her death in 1830, Lady Hewley's trust found itself embroiled in a lengthy court case that ended in a House of Lords judgment. From 1755 to 1833 the sub-trustees responsible for the hospital were predominantly Unitarian. It was felt that they favoured Unitarian inmates over other denominations. In 1848 the case was finally resolved in favour of the Baptist, Congregationalist and Presbyterian communities. From this point onwards members of the board of trustees had to be drawn from each denomination in order to ensure that a broader selection of inmates was admitted to the hospital.

At the same time as the ongoing legal action, George Hudson the 'Railway King' had been allowed to compulsorily purchase the Tanner Row almshouses for £5,105 so that he could build two tracks for his new railway. A new set of almshouses was then constructed in St Saviourgate on the opposite side of the street to Lady Hewley's Unitarian chapel, at a cost of £1,711.

By 1840 the occupants were transferred to their new homes. In 1849 the statute of Charitable Uses of 1601 was replaced with the Charitable Trusts Act of 1853, which came to be known as the Charity Commission. Thus, Lady Hewley's trust became a charity, administered by trustees, which is ongoing to the present day.

The trustees continued to augment the income of the charity by acquiring two estates near Middlesbrough and another near Guisborough, which contained iron ore deposits. The trustees were able to receive substantial royalties from this purchase. With the surplus funds from the sale of the Tanner Row almshouse site, the 45-acre Whixley Estate was bought in 1840 also.

The original nine poor widows or spinsters over the age of fifty-five were provided with an annual stipend of £6 each. By 1882 one Margaret Taylor added to the income of the charity by leaving an endowment of £90. By 1920 the women were paid £40 a year and to ensure that they were in need of charity, their total income should not exceed £46. By 1946 pensions of 10 shillings or 15 shillings weekly were paid according to means. In this year the building is described as comprising nine stone dwellings, a chapel 'in regular use' and a caretaker's house. It is remarkable that over two hundred years later, Lady Hewley's charitable foundation continues to this day, despite challenges to both its physical and legal existence.

A further three almshouses were set up by women in seventeenth century York. In 1717 Dorothy Wilson left a bequest of land and shares intended for a hospital on Foss Bridge for ten poor women. Originally housed in her own home, the building comprised an almshouse and a schoolroom with a school master's house attached to the rear. It took two years to set up with the house falling into disrepair by 1765, when it was rebuilt. Building work continued throughout the century and in 1805 the schoolmaster's house was reconstructed immediately behind the almshouse. Rebuilding took place again in 1812. Today a stone memorial records that Dorothy Wilson's charity was for the 'maintenance of ten poor women as also for the instruction of English, Reading, Writing and Clothing of twenty poor Boys for ever'. The grand Grade II listed building was modernised in 1958 and converted into two room flats. It is of an unusual orange brick with five bay windows. There is also a memorial tablet to Dorothy Wilson on the wall of St Denys Church, which explains that she founded a school at Skipwith. Of Dorothy Wilson's personal life, little evidence remains.

In contrast, Mary Wandesford was born the eldest daughter of the five children of Sir Charles Wandesford, 1st Baronet of Wandesford of Kirklington, and his wife Eleanor Lowther, the daughter of Sir John Lowther of Lowther Hall. They derived the majority of their wealth from coal mines on their estate in Castlecomer in Ireland. Mary was baptised in the church at Kirklington, North Yorkshire, on 23 June 1655.

In order to pursue her religion, Mary moved from her family estate to the city of York where she rented lodgings near to the Minster. Testament to her religious devotion are the black gilded iron gates of the Minster that she donated.

Having never married, in her will of 1725, Mary left funds for the creation of a 'religious house of Protestant retirement' in York for ten poor unmarried women. Construction of the hospital in Bootham began in 1739 and unfortunately acquired the familiar derogatory name of the Old Maid's Hospital, as well as Mary Wandesford's Hospital.

Opened in 1743 the site was staffed by a steward and a chaplain. Each inmate enjoyed two rooms and an annual pension. The endowment was funded by the bequest of a sizeable property in Brompton-on-Swale and £1,200 of stock in the South Sea Company. Mary entrusted this income to be held in trust by the Archbishop of York, two canons of the Minster and her nephew, John Wandesford, the rector of Kirklington. By enlisting such powerful clergymen into her design, she sought to ensure that the project would succeed. This endowment also funded the salary of a schoolmaster to teach the poor children of Kirklington.

Mary Wandesford seems to have enjoyed drama. She left exact instructions in her will as to how she would like her coffin to be carried into the church at her funeral. She wanted 'six of the poorest unmarried women in Kirklington' to 'have white vales from head to foot prepared for them and white gloves and carry [her] corps into the church…Let the white vales be such cloth as will do them service hereafter'. It is bemusing to consider how the six poor women felt on being approached with this eccentric request and whether the executors of her will were able to recruit suitable and willing candidates for the job.

Further drama pursued Mary Wandesford after death when in 1726 her will was contested by the Duke of Newcastle in the Court of Chancery on behalf of Lord Castlecomer, Mary's nephew who was then a minor. The Chancery court upheld her will and a full decade after her death, the hospital was allowed to be constructed. The court stipulated that only women over the age of fifty be allowed to inhabit the house to ensure that it did not become a home for younger women.

Today Wandesford House is one of twelve still functioning almshouses in York and the only one still in its original building. Built in the classical style, it lies behind a front garden. Listed by English Heritage as Grade II, it is owned and run by Mary Wandesford's Charity. Remodelled between 1967-1968, twelve self-contained flats were created. In 1975 some of the restrictions on entry into the almshouse were lifted, so that single women of any Christian faith and any former marital status are allowed admission. The present chaplain takes communion in the original chapel once a month.

In 1732 Margaret Mason's Hospital was founded in Colliergate with an endowment from the founder's will. It was originally intended to accommodate six poor women. In 1939 there were three inmates who received a stipend of £10. In 1946 it was converted into five bedsits. By 1958 it had become derelict and was closed.

It wasn't until one century later that Ann Harrison's Hospital was set up for eight poor Anglican women over the age of fifty in Penley's Grove Street in deeds of 1833 and 1839. It contained eight single-story tenements of brick and stone with a central chapel, which was used for services until 1900. By 1946 the inmates received a stipend of £2 a month. The original endowment was from a £6479 investment in the stock exchange. It was supported by further bequests from two women and one man.

By the Victorian age, in comparison to the rest of the country, York appears to have always possessed a large number of charitable endowments relative to the size of the city. Between 1820 and 1828 the charitable institutions identified were calculated to be worth more than £5000 annually, or £287,000 today.

In 1885 Mary Wilson founded a home for ten poor women over sixty near East Parade in Heworth. By 1946 the inmates each received a pension of 4s a week. However, it was reported that there was some dampness in some of the dwellings and three of the rooms had been empty 'for a long time'. The premises were placed under a demolition order in 1958 and it was not rebuilt. The endowment is now administered by York Charity Trustees.

Besides the notable endowments left by women for the establishment of almshouses, many other women bequeathed sums to individual parish churches, as noted in 'A History of the County of York', published in 1961 and edited by PM Tillott. One significant woman who made a variety of bequests was Lady Ellen Conyngham who established a trust upon her death in 1814.

The Dowager Countess Conyngham of Mount Charles left the money in her trust to be distributed by the archbishop, dean and recorder of York. Annuities of £10 each were to be paid to six poor women of York aged over fifty and chosen by the trustees. The trustees were also instructed to select ten poor clergymen, whose livings in Yorkshire did not exceed £100 a year. They would then receive annuities of £20 year. She was also concerned about 'twelve poor indigent and distressed widows of clergy' who were to receive £20 also.

To access Lady Conyngham's funds, applicants had to submit a petition and a certificate in writing to prove their circumstances. The Countess also bequeathed investments whose dividends were to be divided between four York almshouses – the ancient St Thomas' Hospital and St Catherine's Hospital, as well as Mrs Middleton' and Mrs Mason's.

Born Ellen Merret in 1725, the future Countess was the only daughter of Solomon Merret of London and his wife, Rebecca Savage. At the age of nineteen she married Henry Conyngham of Mount Charles in 1744. Less than ten years later she became Baroness Conyngham in 1753. Three years later she became a Viscountess and twenty-four years later Countess Conyngham in 1780. The Earl and Countess had no surviving children and when she died at the age of ninety-two, she created a trust whose records are held by the Borthwick Institute of York Univessity and continue up until 1933.

By 1946 there were twenty groups of almshouses in York accommodating one hundred and seventy-seven people and four foundations that were formerly connected with almshouses were still paying pensions to those who met the eligibility criteria. As time progressed there seems to have been some competition between benefactors to ensure that their religious demomination was represented charitably, in particular between the Anglican and the Catholic churches.

Nationally almshouses can be traced as far back as the tenth century with the first one being founded in York by King Athelstan (r 924-7). Today some 2,600 almshouses continue to operate in the United Kingdom, providing 30,000 dwellings to 36,000 people. Many charitable women were involved in the foundation of almshouses that have rescued many men and women from homelessness. It is surprising that the legacy of these women of York is not particularly well known or celebrated at the present time.

CHAPTER FOURTEEN

Prostitutes of York

Contagious Diseases Act

By 1864 THE British government was alarmed at the extent of venereal disease that was spreading among the lower ranks of the armed forces. In response a series of Contagious Diseases Acts was passed, first in 1864 with subsequent Acts in 1866 and 1869. When the public became aware of the full extent of the unprecedented powers that the legislation afforded the police, opposition grew and associations were formed to press for their repeal. The scope of the new police powers included the right to arrest any woman suspected of being a prostitute, in certain ports and army towns of the country. No evidence was needed, only the word of the police officer was sufficient grounds for arrest. New units of plain-clothed policemen were created, specialising in arresting suspected prostitutes. It was hoped by the supporters of the Acts that their provision would eventually extend over the entire country.

Once arrested, the suspected prostitute was registered and subjected to a compulsory medical examination of the genital area, in search of venereal disease. If she was deemed to be infected, she would be confined in a 'lock hospital' until she recovered, or her sentence was finished. Unfortunately, the 'hospitals' were more akin to prisons. The most prominent campaigner for the abolition of the Acts, Josephine Butler, conveyed the sense of violation that the women experienced when she described the forced examination of suspected prostitutes as 'steel rape' and 'surgical rape'.

The first Contagious Diseases Act allowed for the woman to be incarcerated for a period of three months. By the time the Acts were extended in 1869, she could be imprisoned for up to a year. If the accused woman resisted examination, hard labour was added to her sentence. Women who were subjected to the examination found their names and reputations affected, and, according to the historian Hilary Cashman, the Acts had the perverse effect of 'turning them to prostitution by barring respectable ways of life to them'.

The Acts came into force with the minimum amount of publicity, but, once their power and remit were fully appreciated, opposition began to become organised. Due to the fact that the police were able to arrest any woman on the mere suspicion of being a prostitute, the potential for abuse became obvious. Nevertheless, even though the respected pioneer of the nursing profession, Florence Nightingale, opposed state regulation of prostitution, arguing in an 1862 pamphlet that the proposed system of regulation did not result in lower rates of the disease, the Acts still became legislation.

Because Josephine Butler was prohibited from joining the all-male National Association for the Repeal of the Contagious Diseases Acts, in 1869 she set up the Ladies National Association for the Repeal of the Contagious Diseases Acts (LNA). Both associations were supported by the Quakers, Methodists and Congregationalists, who denounced the sexual discrimination and 'Double Standard' explicit in punishing the women involved in illicit sex, but not the men.

Opposers of the Acts also argued that not only was it unfair to punish the streetwalkers and not their clients, but also completely futile in controlling venereal disease, as the men were free to spread it, even to their wives. Abolitionists argued that the Acts promoted not only a moral 'Double Standard' by blaming and punishing only women, but that they would also drive the activity of prostitution underground because diseased women would be reluctant to come forward and ask for help.

The LNA published a 'Ladies Manifesto', which stated that the Acts were discriminatory on the grounds of both sex and class. It claimed that the Acts,

'not only deprived poor women of their constitutional rights and forced them to submit to a degrading internal examination, but they officially sanctioned a double standard of sexual morality, which justified male sexual access to a class of "fallen" women and penalised women for engaging in the same vice as men'.

Today we may wonder how such gender discrimination could ever become legislation. Firstly, the House of Lords Select Committee held an inquiry to investigate the growing problem of venereal disease amongst the armed forces. Evidence was given to the Committee that demonstrated the financial losses incurred by the nation as a result of venereal disease amongst the lower ranks of the armed forces, as well as the danger facing the civilian population – both of which evils were deemed to emanate from the prostitute.

However, in emphasising the need for state regulation of prostitution, advocates of the Acts found themselves in a tricky position. On the one hand they emphasised the dangers facing men who resorted to prostitutes, while on the other hand they tried to play down the harmful effects of the activity on the prostitutes themselves.

In order to achieve state regulation of prostitution the House of Lords heard evidence from a man who had published books on both female sexuality and prostitution. In 1857 Dr William Acton published 'The Functions and Disorders of the Reproductive Organs in Youth, in Adult Age, and in Advance Life: Considered in their Physiological Relations'. In this work he made his attitude to female sexuality explicit and claimed to base his argument on 'abundant evidence'. He proposed that:

"the majority of women (happily for them) are not much troubled with sexual feeling of any kind…As a general rule, a modest woman seldom desires any sexual gratification for herself. She submits to her husband, but only to please him; and, but for the desire of maternity, would far rather be relieved from his attentions. No nervous or feeble young man need, therefore, be deterred from marriage by the exaggerated notion of the duties required from him. The married woman has no wish to be treated on the footing of a mistress'.

Later Acton wrote a book on prostitution entitled, 'Prostitution, Considered in its Moral, Social and Sanitary Aspects, In London and Other Large Cities'. His attitudes and values regarding prostitution were ideal for the House of Lords Select Committee as they played down the negative effect of prostitution on the prostitute herself. Acton painted a shockingly optimistic picture of a prostitute's career. He went so far as to assert that once a woman had ceased to be a prostitute, she could easily reintegrate into 'respectable society':

'Thus ceasing to act as prostitutes by commencing or recommencing a "respectable" career, women who a little time before would have been regarded as outcasts too debased to be spoken to, are admitted into the houses of the refined and affluent classes, are entrusted by mothers with the care of their children, become the attendants and probably not seldom the confidants, of their daughters just blooming into womanhood, and, in short, entering every department of domestic life, have confided to them, at one time or another, the most important or the most cherished interests of a considerable section of society.'

Acton's testimony was ideal for the law lords as he continually denied the nefarious effects of prostitution on the prostitute herself and went so far as to claim that a prostitute often married well after she had decided to leave the profession.

'I have every reason to believe, that by far the larger number of women who have resorted to prostitution for a livelihood, return sooner or later to a more or less regular course of life…Incumbrances rarely attend the prostitute who flies from the horrors of her position. We must recollect that she has a healthy frame, an excellent constitution, and is in the vigour of life. During her career, she has obtained a knowledge of the world most probably above the station she was born in. Her return to the hearth of her infancy is for obvious reasons a very rare occurrence. It is surprising, then, that she should look to the chance of amalgamating with society at large, and make a dash at respectability by marriage? Thus, to a most surprising, and year by year increasing extent, the better inclined class of prostitutes become the wedded wives of men in every grade of society, from the peerage to the stable.'

Astonishingly, Acton seemed to present Victorian prostitution as a career choice for women to use as a stepping stone to a good marriage and respectability. His denial of the negative effects of prostitution on the prostitute herself were ideal for the House of Lords Select Committee which wished to introduce legislation that punished the provider of sexual services, but left the consumer impugn. The House of Lords ignored the injustice of their proposed legislation and looked for ways to mitigate the contradictions inherent in their legislation. They hoped that the public would fail to recognise that the Acts blamed the prostitute for the spread of venereal disease but did nothing to cure her. Ironically, the law lords also ignored the contradiction inherent in the argument that if prostitutes were able to enter respectable society, free from disease, as Acton claimed, then there would have been no need whatsoever for the series of Acts and their enforcement.

Acton was an ideal expert for the committee as he saw the source of the supply of prostitutes as being 'derived from the vice of women'. It is hard not to think that Acton had mysoginistic tendencies, taking into account his description of women in the following extract:

'Natural desire. Natural sinfulness. The preferment of indolent ease to labour. Vicious inclinations strengthened and ingrained by early neglect, or evil training, or bad associates, and an indecent mode of life. Necessity, imbued by the inability to obtain a living by honest means consequent on a fall from virtue. Extreme poverty. To this black list may be added love of drink, love of dress, love of amusement.'

However, Acton's work was full of contradictions. He did acknowledge the dangerous reality of prostitution for many women when he recognised that at least one in every four prostitutes in London was known to be diseased, 'spreading abroad a loathsome poison', with 'broken constitutions, sickly bodies and feeble minds', as a result of their trade. However, Acton seems to have regarded the role of his own sex's part in prostitution as victims, rather than seducers or equal participants.

The fact that Acton was no friend of the female sex can be seen in the following extract when he describes his belief that women who were found in kitchens all day often slipped into the world of prostitution. He argued that they were 'dishevelled, dirty, slipshod and dressing-gowned…Stupid from beer, or fractious from gin, they swear and chatter brainless stuff all day…as a heap of rubbish will ferment, so surely will a number of women thus collected deteriorate…to the dead level of harlotry'.

Acton's views on prostitution were contradictory because he had a contradictory objective. His evidence was designed to alert and alarm the nation regarding the spread of venereal disease, while at the same time stressing the inevitability of prostitution and the need for its recognition and regulation by the state. His evidence presented the tacit view that certain men would always resort to prostitutes and so it followed that such women were performing a service to society. Therefore, it was necessary to outline as un-harrowing a picture as possible of the subsequent fate of the many women who took part in the activity, so that there was not public outrage.

Acton told the House of Lords Select Committee that:

'Horrible as the truth may be, it is we fear indisputable that the ranks of this section of civilized communities are, to a great extent, recruited from the finest women of their order, seduction being the means by which the healthiest and most vigorous are selected. They live an idle life, pass much of their time in the open air, are generally well clothed and well fed, and thus proceed in their career *with a capacity of withstanding the attacks of the disease and of bearing its results, which is denied to their more respectable but poorer and harder-worked sisters. "Notwithstanding", says Mr Acton, "All her excesses (and legion is their name) the prostitute passes through the furnace of a dissipated career less worse from wear than her male associates"'.*

When Acton suggested that the type of woman who chose prostitution was more easily able to withstand venereal disease than other types of women, he was colluding with the House of Lords in telling them what they wanted to hear. His evidence resulted in the enforcement and extension of the Contagious Diseases Acts.

What is equally as incredible as his testimony is the fact that he has been described modern by historians as displaying humanity towards both prostitutes and other 'fallen women'. Alarmingly, his work was resurrected in the 1960s and he has continued to influence modern conceptions of Victorian morality. Although his work fell into obscurity in the 1870s, his book 'Prostitution' was reissued in 1968 with very little challenge to his claim that prostitution was a temporary choice for women, who were often able to reintegrate themselves into respectable society. In fact, Peter Fryer in the introduction to the 1968 edition of 'Prostitution', repeated Acton's assertion that:

'Most prostitutes were transients, who re-entered the ranks of 'respectable society within a very few years: and an increasing number did so by getting married, sometimes "above their class"'.

Fryer continued to uphold Acton's claim that many former prostitutes were able to leave the profession by marrying respectably:

'far from rapidly succumbing to disease and demoralisation...for many women, short periods of prostitution often culminated respectably in marriage or in business...The illusion was shattered that prostitutes sank more or less rapidly to the lowest grade of the profession where they soon died.'

As late as 1971 Steven Marcus published 'The Other Victorians' in which he acknowledged that although Acton had a 'dimmed consciousness' in 'Prostitution', he deemed it a 'very good book' which:

'explodes the popular myth of the prostitutes' downward progress, but demonstrates to the contrary, that most prostitutes sooner or later returned to a "regular course of life" and that even when actively engaged in the activity, being endowed with "iron bodies", they were freer from general disease than all other classes of females'.

Fortunately, a student called Frances Finnegan exploded all these myths and more in her 1979 pioneer study of Victorian prostitution in York. In the 1970's, while completing her doctoral thesis on the development of the Irish Community in York, she uncovered an enormous amount of detailed material in local archives relating to prostitutes, which had been neglected until the publication of her book, 'Poverty and Prostitution, a study of Victorian prostitutes in York'. Records survive in York which paint a shocking picture of Victorian prostitution in the city. Although her research into prostitution was a biproduct of another study, she wrote that she could not ignore the existence of an 'equally deprived and unfortunate group'.

Finnegan's research into the existing records of the lives of Victorian prostitutes in York painted a picture of the devastating effects of prostitution on the prostitute, more akin to the work of William Logan in 1871, who published 'The Great Social Evil; its Causes, Extent, Results and Remedies', after basing his work on local research in Glasgow. He portrayed the wretched life of a Victorian prostitute:

'The average age at which women became prostitutes is from fifteen to twenty. The average duration of women continuing prostitutes is, I think, about five years. The most common termination of the career of prostitutes is by death, and this is to be accounted for by the extremely dissolute life they lead. For the most part they live in a state of great personal filthiness – they have wretched homes – they are scarcely ever in bed till far in the morning – they get no wholesome diet- and they are constantly drinking the worst description of spirituous liquors. In addition to these evils they are exposed to disease in its worst forms; and from their dissolute habits, when disease overtakes them, a cure is scarcely possible.'

The evidence that Finnegan examined in York covered the period 1837 to 1887, ending the year after the repeal of the Contagious Diseases Acts and therefore the end of the compulsory registration of prostitutes. She examined two weekly newspapers of the day – the York Gazette and the York Herald, which gave detailed reports of the weekly Magistrates court proceedings and the Quarter Session of the Crown court, as well as analysing the records of the York Quarter Sessions themselves. She read several Chief Constables' Reports on the Annual State of Crime in York, which were summarised from time to time in the local press and which gave the officially recorded number of brothels or houses of ill fame, as well as the number of common prostitutes and streetwalkers 'at large' in the city. Watch Committee Reports to the City Council also shed some light on the problem of prostitution covered by her fifty-year period of analysis.

Another source of evidence was the applications for charity to the Guardians of the York Poor Law, which detailed the names of those who applied to enter the workhouse. There she identified 252 applications from individual prostitutes who sought relief from the guardians at least once.

Finnegan made a pioneer study of a collection of documents relating to the York Refuge, which was also known as the York Female Penitentiary Society. Opened in 1845, the York Refuge was a shelter for 'fallen women', which continued well into the following century. Between 1845 and 1887, 542 prostitutes applied to enter the York Refuge in an attempt to reform. From the collection of Minute Books, Reports of the Ladies' Committee and the Refuge's Annual reports, Finnegan was able to find the age, background and reason for the 'downfall' of many of the 542 applicants, and often with meticulous cross-referencing of sources, she was able to build some remarkably detailed pictures of their individual lives. Unfortunately, she discovered that many prostitutes were dismissed from the Refuge either due to pregnancy, disease or misconduct, often returning to resume their 'life of sin'.

A further help to Finnegan in her study were documents and photographs relating to York's Unhealthy Area and Slum Clearance schemes which took place largely in the 1920s and 1930s. Many of the insanitary cottages and tenements that were demolished as part of this programme had been occupied by 'women of the town' in the previous century. Although accommodation for prostitutes was often precarious, Finnegan examined the census enumerator's notebooks for the years 1841, 1851, 1861 and 1871. Although it was unlikely that a prostitute would remain in the same residence for very long due to the instability of her lifestyle, Finnegan was able to identify 153 individuals engaged in the activity, 122 of whom were prostitutes by cross-referencing their names and addresses with other sources. Through continual cross-reference, Finnegan noted many repetitions of names in the Poor Law records and in the newspapers, which helped her to reconstruct some of the wretched lives of individual prostitutes in Victorian York.

The result of Finnegan's ground-breaking, pioneer study of the individual prostitutes of York themselves is a depressingly sad picture of 'destitution, drunkenness and disease', far removed from Acton's presentation. She found that poverty was the principal cause of a prostitute's downfall and Finnegan's evidence completely dispels several of the Victorian myths about prostitution. Although Acton and the Select Committee of the House of Lords would have us believe that many prostitutes were of the 'rags to riches' variety and were able to reintegrate into society after a transient flirtation with the profession, she found that poverty was not only a cause of Victorian prostitution in York, but a consequence of it too.

Another myth that she exploded was that prostitution was the exploitation of the upper- and middle-class males of lower class females. While there was obvious gender exploitation due to economic inequality, she discovered that the majority of clients of working-class prostitutes were men of the same class. This is attested to by the criminal records and by common sense. Many respectable, middle class men would not venture into the insanitary and dangerous areas of the city where many prostitutes were forced to operate. Finnegan found that 'as well as supplying the needs of and being exploited by the rich, prostitutes were catering too for their own class, and this aspect of prostitution has been much less emphasised.'

Between 1837, the year of Queen Victoria's ascension to the throne and 1887, Finnegan discovered that 1,400 individual prostitutes and brothel keepers were recorded as operating in the city of York. There were also a further twenty 'infamous' people whose premises were known to the police. Finnegan argues that 1,400 individuals involved in prostitution is likely to be an underestimate of the extent of the activity, as there would have been individuals who did not appear on any records as they were able to act with more discretion than those who had to walk the streets or who became addicted to drink, or who picked their clients' pockets or who entered the workhouse destitute or diseased.

Finnegan argues that although her study provided no evidence of 'kept women', courtesans or high-class prostitutes living in expensive lodgings or brothels, it is likely that they 'may well have existed' in York. 'Such girls as these were apparently rarely allowed to leave their establishments unless in the custody of an elderly servant of the house, or occasionally to accompany a trusted client to the theatre or some other entertainment.'

The York Gazette paints a vivid picture of the growing problem of prostitution in Victorian York. In May 20 1848 it recorded that prostitution was becoming 'much greater than has scarcely ever been known to be the case at any former period'. Eight years later on February 7th, 1856, the Gazette concluded that there were 'few places in the country where an institution like the Female Penitentiary [York Refuge] were more urgently required'.

However, there was an apparent lack of action as four years later in 1860, the same newspaper stated that the streets of the city were swarming with 'these poor unfortunate girls'. The Gazette continued:

'Almost every day some of these poor outcasts were brought before [the Lord Mayor] at the Guildhall charged with disorderly conduct during the previous night. From 11 o'clock at night until 1 or 2 o'clock in the morning these unhappy females prowled about the streets and being affected with liquor they conducted themselves in a riotous and disorderly manner and committed acts which were disgraceful to human nature'.

Other newspapers periodically printed various petitions, letters and descriptions concerning the disgraceful state of the city at night, describing swarms of abandoned females prowling the streets, alongside half-dressed women indecently assembling and causing disturbances at various notorious houses and inns. The main thoroughfares of York were the regular haunt of streetwalkers who 'wandered abroad' from the early evening until far into the night. Judging by the frequency of their appearances in court, they caused much annoyance and embarrassment to the respectable, more fortunate inhabitants of the city

Until 1863 Ouse Bridge was the only entrance into the city from the south or from the train station. Consequently, Ouse Bridge and the streets leading from it - Low Ousegate and Spurriergate - were the favourite haunts of prostitutes who lived in the notoriously squalid Water Lanes and North Street areas. Clients picked up on the bridge could be quickly and easily whisked into the dark and sordid back streets of the Water Lanes area, which once radiated down to the river from Castlegate. It is likely that a lot of pestering and soliciting of unwilling parties went on as they entered the city, as exemplified by the sentence handed down to Mary Smith in 1855. She was given fourteen days for wandering abroad in Nessgate and 'seizing hold of persons and detaining them.'

To some the existence of prostitution on such a large scale in such a historic and seemingly genteel cathedral city may seem paradoxical. However, long before the nineteenth century, certain areas of York had been associated with prostitution since the Middle Ages. Grape Lane, a narrow street near the Minster was referred to in ancient texts with the unsavoury moniker of 'Gropecunt' or 'Grapecunt Layne' because of its infamous reputation. Nearby Finkle Street acquired the nicknames 'Murky Peg' and 'Mucky Peg Lane' as late as the nineteenth century. William Hargrove in his 1818 work 'History of York' recorded that St Andrewgate was a traditional centre of prostitution in the sixteenth century when the church which gives the street its name was partially demolished and converted into a brothel.

There are several reasons why prostitution was a problem in the city of York during the period of study. The fact that York was a major marketing centre for the county was an important reason for the high number of brothels and streetwalkers. Although York was declining during this period from its Georgian zenith as a social and cultural capital, it was still a magnet for tourists and visitors due to the races, its fairs and the assizes. The Assembly Rooms and the theatre attracted both the gentry and humbler visitors, many of whom entertained themselves by drinking and visiting prostitutes.

Between 1831 and 1881 the population of the municipal borough of York increased from 26,260 to 49,530. Nevertheless, it was still a pre-industrial city with businesses not employing more than a handful of workers. Except for the railway carriage and wagon works, opened in 1841, most occupations were carried out in small workshops. Throughout the period examined by Finnegan, women consistently outnumbered men in York. A surplus of unmarried female population and limited opportunities for employment except for domestic service, were two of the reasons why so many women resorted to prostitution.

The largest occupation in the city was domestic service, which dominated the female labour force. From the 1841 census it can be established that 68.5 percent of the employed women in the city were domestic servants or charwomen. Next came dressmaking, needle trades, millinery, school mistresses and governesses. By 1871 the percentage distribution was roughly the same with two further occupations for females added – hotel innkeepers and agricultural labourers. The lack of employment opportunites for women in York, other than domestic service and the needle trades, both of which were notoriously badly paid, were at the time reported to be fruitful sources of women of the streets.

York also attracted prostitutes from other places too. In May 1863 the Gazette reported that Mary Ann Smith, Susannah Pears and Sarah McMany had been sentenced to three days in the House of Correction on a charge of 'wandering abroad with the intention to pick pockets.' All of them had come to York especially for the races. Ann Taylor from Leeds and Mary Ann Brabiner from Nottingham were picked up by the police for soliciting on 30 November 1861. They had both come to York for the Martinmas Fair and were discharged after they promised to leave the city.

Sadly, such visits to York could lead to the downfall of a girl, as was the case of sixteen-year-old Hannah Abbey. When she applied to the Refuge in July 1886, she told the Ladies Committee that she had come to York from the neighbouring village of Bolton Percy for the Gala the previous year. She claimed that she had been 'led astray' ever since. Between 1837 and 1888, 31.7 per cent of prostitutes were born in York, 43.9 percent elsewhere in Yorkshire, 16.3 percent elsewhere in England, 4 per cent in Ireland and 3.3 per cent in Scotland. Therefore, 'the majority of York's street-walkers were immigrants to the city – most of these coming from the surrounding small towns and villages – and that as the century wore on, York's population increased, this tendency became more marked.'

York's position as a railway city also augmented prostitution. In 1870 Margaret Reece of Peter Lane was charged with indecency and stated that 'she was going to the railway station to meet the early trains, her object being to pick up any gentleman whom she could prevail upon to go home with her'. In 1880 Elizabeth Bell and another younger girl were induced by Edward Martin of St George's Terrace, Walmgate to catch the excursion train with him from Leeds to York. He then took them to his brothel, and when the girls tried to leave, he refused to let them have their clothes. He was sentenced to nine months hard labour for keeping an immoral house, procuring and theft.

Although York was a garrison town, the provisions of the Contagious Diseases Acts were never extended to the city. Nevertheless, several of the girls admitted in their applications to York Refuge that they had originally 'gone astray' after 'going to the barracks'. Finnegan suggests that there may have been special, yet unofficial provision for their visits, although there is no evidence of this in any of the surviving military records. Sixteen-year-old Emma Clegg was recorded as having 'been in the habit of going to the barracks'. Elizabeth Ore, also sixteen, was discovered by the Ladies Committee of the Refuge to have been 'induced by a girl who died recently to go to the barracks, and ultimately she left her situation [as a domestic servant] and took to a sinful life'. Similarly, other applicants such as fifteen-year-old Elizabeth Wales were recorded as having been to the barracks.

There were many newspaper reports of prostitutes in the company of soldiers being charged with theft, indecency or displaying drunk and disorderly behaviour. In July 1862 Sarah Johnson and Edward Taylor of the 10th Hussars were charged with being disorderly and assaulting a policeman. She was sentenced to seven days in prison and he was 'dealt with at the barracks'. Prostitute Margaret Dodsworth of Friargate, one of the notorious Water Lanes, was charged with disorderly behaviour in the company of soldiers from the barracks in July of 1867.

The next year Fanny Cass of Walmgate was charged with stealing a dress and chemise form the barracks. Ann Hanson and Ann Saunders were imprisoned sixteen months later for attempting to hide private William Bloom of the 15th Hussars who had deserted. In 1878 private John Burns of the 4th Dragoons was sentenced to three months in prison for hitting and stabbing prostitute Annie Dolbin 'when she was talking with another soldier'.

Not only privates, but occasionally officers were reported as being in the company of prostitutes, though the infrequency of these reports suggests that they had recourse to more discreetly run brothels. Even members of the aristocracy were reported in the press as associating with prostitutes in York. Lord Marcus Beresford and his companion W.W. Hope Johnstone of the 7th Hussars were both aged twenty-two and single according to the 1871 census. On 19th October 1870 the Gazette reported that they had been fined twenty shillings for disorderly behaviour in the company of two prostitutes. On this rare occasion, the prostitutes were not named.

During the mid nineteenth century much of the neighbourhood between the barracks and the city centre contained numerous working-class terraces, which housed many of the city's prostitutes. Disturbances became so common that in 1885 the Chief Constable decided that because Fulford was such an important district due to its 'proximity to the Barracks and the numerous prostitutes residing in the neighbourhood' that a new police station at Alma Terrace would open.

Unfortunately, his action did not have the desired effect because as late as 1887 the Ladies' Committee of York Refuge reported that young girl applicants continued to cater to the needs of the barracks. Ann Elizabeth Medd, seventeen and from Malton, admitted that she had spent one month in a brothel in Ambrose Street, one of the terraces near the new police station.

Even the wife of the Archbishop of York, the Honourable Mrs Maclagan, was alarmed at the relationship between soldiers and prostitutes. In her appeal for more funds for the York Association for the Care of Young Girls, it is reported that she stated:

'In making a special appeal to the wives of the officers she said God forbid that she should dare to say that soldiers were worse than other men. She did not wish to think that for a moment, but they were much more attractive, and there was a glamour about a scarlet coat which turned the heart of a weak woman. She must honestly tell them that out of the cases that were brought to their rescue home, by far the larger proportion had been tempted and had fallen from the barracks.'

It appears undeniable that the presence of the barracks contributed to the comparatively high demand for prostitutes in the city of York. Nevertheless, Finnegan's study of prostitutes in York provided overwhelming evidence that the main cause of prostitution in the city was the extent of poverty of the area.

The vast majority of the applicants to the York Refuge were in a state of extreme destitution and had already spent some time in the workhouse. Many had begun their working lives in domestic service. The work included relentlessly long hours, was physically punishing, tedious and repetitive, as well as extremely poorly paid. Hannah Simpson applied for admittance to the Refuge in November 1882 when she was nineteen and an orphan. She had been in domestic service, in the workhouse, and living a 'sinful life' for some months.

Annie Short, aged twenty-three was recorded in March 1884 as having been brought up in the workhouse, spent a short time in service, returned to the workhouse, left of her own accord and had 'led a bad life ever since'. She had also been imprisoned 'three or four times in the Castle'. Nineteen-year-old Elizabeth Hansome came from a very large family in Carmelite Street, a slum terrace in Hungate. She had been employed in several domestic country situation but had at times lapsed into a 'disreputable life', the last time for more than six months. In 1863 she was picked up in Hull for begging and imprisoned for twenty-one days, before being sent to her mother and applying to the York Refuge. The Ladies' Committee of the Refuge reported that Dinah Matthews applied to be admitted in 1863 and that, 'the girl has been in service since she was nine years old, but frequently left her situations and when not required to sleep at them, resorted to a house of ill fame in Green Lane instead of going home as her parents desired'.

William Logan, temperance reformer and author of 'The Great Social Evil' (1871), investigated the problem of prostitution in Dublin, Edinburgh, Aberdeen, Inverness, Greenock, Paisley, Kilmarnock, Liverpool, Newcastle Upon Tyne, Hull, Leeds and York, as well as a number of smaller towns in England and Scotland.

He visited hundreds of brothels and notorious houses, interviewing thousands of women. He recognised the principal cause of women resorting to prostitution was the limited conditions of female labour, which sometimes resulted in near starvation wages, followed by seduction, overcrowded and squalid housing conditions, bad parental example, disagreements between daughters and parents or stepparents and lack of education.

The irony was that if a girl or woman left domestic service, became a prostitute, and then applied to the York Refuge, if she was fortunate enough to be accepted for being 'reclaimed', she would be trained in laundry work and in plain sewing and then 'placed' in service after being 'reformed' after her two years in the Refuge. Unsurprisingly, many of the inmates returned to their old ways and 'vicious courses'. A few however, managed, against incredible odds, to regain their 'character' and make their way back into society. Finnegan's study of the records of York Refuge shows that a very small proportion of them even succeeded in marrying.

Fifty percent of the prostitutes and forty percent of their clients were from outside York. The vast majority of the girls came from the surrounding towns and villages. Elizabeth Ashton was nineteen and from the village of Hovingham. After living with her father and stepmother, she had been sent into service in Malton. There she was seduced and became pregnant, giving birth to a stillborn child. Her stepmother had treated her unkindly and she had run away, ending up in 'a disreputable' house in Walmgate. She soon became ill and went to the workhouse, there being told by the medical man that her recovery was doubtful. 'She became alarmed and began to read the Bible'.

Ellen Wilson from Pocklington had originally left home after the re-marriage of her father. She had spent two months in a brothel in Hull and had then made her way to York, where, being entirely destitute, she had slept rough and then wandered about until a policeman took her to the workhouse where she lived for three months. She was described by the Ladies' Committee as being 'very ignorant, and without education of any kind'. Eighteen-year-old Fanny Briscome originated from Green Hammerton. In her 1862 application it states that she had been in service, had taken to the streets and ended up destitute in the workhouse. Margaret Dohele was a twenty-two-year-old servant from Ashton-under-Lyne. After prostituting herself in York for nine months, she had been 'reduced to begging in the streets for subsistence'.

York was a dangerous place for both young, gullible and naive men and women. The annual Hirings at Michelmas were recognised as a fruitful supply of prostitutes for procurers. The problem became so notorious that when the recruitment fair was opened at the Merchant Adventurers' Hall in Fossgate, the York Society for the Prevention of Youthful Depravity, founded in 1860, provided accommodation and refreshment for servants attending the Hirings, in an attempt to keep them out of harm's way. Later the York Association for the Care of Young Girls continued this practice until the close of the century. The danger and excitement of the Hirings was recognised by the mistresses of the York Association when they noted that 'to many of the girls the attractions of the Market place still prove irresistible'. Female servants were vulnerable to the snares of procuresses and male servants to the attention of prostitutes who were also pick-pockets.

The size of the problem of the exploitation of young people is attested to by the existence of a society whose aim was to prevent 'youthful depravity'. Its claimed in its second report that its most important objective was to gain 'not only the cooperation of the City Authorities, but the vigilance of the Police force, in order that decency and external propriety may be preserved in the streets'. It also campaigned for 'the adopting of judicious means for obtaining reliable information respecting the agency employed in ensnaring young people, and the places frequented by immoral characters; and when other means have proved unavailing, the taking of proceedings in law, or otherwise, for the suppression of immoral houses and the punishment of offenders'.

Its objectives suggest that the police sometimes turned a blind eye to child exploitation and prostitution. Unfortunately, child prostitution did exist in York. Finnegan's study uncovered the cases of five fourteen-year-old girls. However, there was no evidence of child prostitution in York to the extent uncovered by rescue workers in other provincial towns of the period. For example, in 1857 the 'Report on Female Prostitution' stated that in Liverpool alone, there were at least 200 'regular' prostitutes under the age of twelve. Nevertheless, Finnegan asserts that 'it is obvious that by the eighties there were houses in the city containing very young prostitutes, and some of these, when applying to the Refuge, mentioned houses in Hungate and Walmgate which seemed to specialise in girls of their age'.

In 1884 Mary Jane Sutherland applied to York Refuge. She had been in service for a short time in a public house in Hull and had associated with 'bad' companions. Her parents lived in Scarborough and she had come from there the month before with 'a woman who took her to a house in Walmgate'. She had been rescued from the brothel by the police and she had been to the refuge at Aldwark House before applying to the York Refuge in Bishophill. She was fourteen years old.

From the reporting of magistrates' court proceedings in the York Herald and York Gazette, the unfortunate link between prostitution and crime cannot be denied. While Finnegan's study debunks several myths about Victorian prostitution, it also bravely faces the truth of the matter which was that 'prostitutes themselves were exploiters'. There are frequent mentions of thefts in houses of ill fame, brothel robberies and prostitutes picking their clients' pockets. While there were aristocratic and middle-class users of prostitutes in York, 'prostitutes frequently exploited both physically and financially raw working class youths – gullible hobbledehoys and foolish young farm labourers fresh from the countryside…' Seventy-three per cent of all men recorded as associating with prostitutes belonged to the working class or the poor.

The frequency of cases reported involving working class men may have something to do with middle class clients being reluctant to press charges, so as not to affect their reputations of 'respectability'. However, if a man felt sufficiently aggrieved, he would press charges regardless of his class. Perhaps this is evidence of the 'Double Standard' – the Victorian concept that men who used prostitutes were only a indulging a natural inclination and so clients did not feel the sense of shame that prostitutes were made to feel. However, it was poorer clients who pressed charges more frequently, probably because they cared less for their professional reputations, often for having been robbed before actually transacting their business.

Some prostitutes worked in pairs for the purpose of robbing their clients. In March 1856, an unnamed man accompanied Ann Harrison and Ann Cooper to a notorious house in Petergate, kept by the latter. Here he was relieved of five-pound notes, seven sovereigns, some silver and a purse. As was often the case, the Gazette afforded the client anonymity, while the prostitutes were publicly named and shamed.

Street-walkers were also occasionally in league with male accomplices, sometimes their husbands, who were referred to at the time as 'bully boys'. Robert Lappish, a farm servant, had travelled to York from Church Fenton in November 1839. He was walking over Ouse Bridge early in the evening when he was accosted by two women, one of whom was prostitute Hannah Harrison. He accompanied them towards the Water Lanes. However, before they got very far, he noticed that his money was missing. On 'giving the alarm', he was struck by a man who suddenly appeared out of the darkness.

Prostitutes in York 'stole from their own class, the poor, as well as the rich; and like their own seducers, were quite unscrupulous regarding the youth, inexperience or gullibility of the green, but nevertheless willing victims they lured into the back-street brothels or yards.' Finnegan believes that her study of criminal proceedings 'reveal the mutual basic contempt with which [prostitute and client] each regarded the other'. She argues that prostitutes may have justified their criminal activity to themselves because 'they may well have felt that through no fault of their own but poverty, or possibly seduction and birth of an illegitimate child, they had been driven to the streets, condemned by society and forced to make a living in the most degraded and dangerous manner'.

Through the course of the analysis of the records, it emerged 'there was a submerged class of petty criminals in York, an underworld of disreputable beer- and lodging-house keepers, fences, thieves and thugs who assisted the prostitute in her work'.

Another clear link that became apparent was between prostitution and alcohol. In 1845 there were 118 recorded houses of ill fame known to the police. By 1865 there were three beershops and two coffee houses that were said to be disreputable. A large number of publicans and beerhouse keepers were charged with harbouring prostitutes, or allowing persons of notorious character to assemble on their premises. The Green Tree in the Water Lanes was kept by the Gibsons who used the premises as a lodging-house and brothel. They provided the workhouse with various destitute and diseased prostitutes when they no longer had use for them. Various licensees of public houses in the Water Lanes used prostitutes as barmaids with the landlord receiving a share of their takings. In February 1857, the landlord of the Crystal Palace in Swinegate was charged with allowing the unlawful assembly of twelve prostitutes on his premises. In response he quipped to the magistrates that if the police had arrived half an hour earlier, they would have found twenty-four.

One of the most notorious public houses in the centre of the city was the Punch Bowl in Stonegate. In the 1880s the publican was charged with keeping a disorderly house and twenty-four 'immoral characters were found on the premises'. Mary Megginson ran the most notorious of all the beerhouses on the corner of the

First Water Lane and King's Staithe. In January 1860 she was charged with allowing prostitutes on the premises after the police found fifteen abandoned girls and five convicted thieves alone in one room. In Mary Megginson's beerhouse, clients would meet 'ruined girls' and then accompany them to the houses of ill fame in the Water Lanes, often in the squalid Cross Alley.

As a great deal of soliciting took place in pubs, large amounts of alcohol were consumed in brothels and houses of ill fame, at the clients' expense. Prostitutes used drink to disarm their clients and extort additional funds from them. Unfortunately, many prostitutes were alcoholics themselves and it has been difficult to establish from the evidence whether alcohol was a cause or a consequence of prostitution. It is likely that the answer is that it was both.

Prostitutes often earned commission on drinks which their clients bought in certain beer-houses, pubs, and other notorious establishments. The link between drink and prostitution is well illustrated by a case in 1857. In October that year an unnamed gentleman went into a riverside public house on the King's Staithe, and was served beer by prostitute Mary Kilgarry. Prostitute Mary Ann Lockett then served him more drink, after which he accompanied them both to a brothel in one of the adjacent Water Lanes, where there were also 'two or three other females'. He was then robbed of three pounds, and though the police afterwards found Mary Kilgarry and her associate Alfred Bethany (in whose trouser pocket the missing purse was discovered) in bed together in another house in the Water Lanes, all three were discharged through lack of evidence.

Margaret Barrett was a particularly shocking and sad case of a prostitute addicted to alcohol. The Gazette described her as 'a ruined character' who was frequently before York magistrates on charges of prostitution and of being drunk and disorderly, as well as theft. She had contracted syphilis, was a vagrant and eventually became a violent convict. For more than twenty-five years she staggered from one conviction to another, appearing in court on fifty-tree separate occasions. By 1887 she had served various prison sentences totalling nine years. As time progressed, her prison sentences became increasingly more severe. As an alcoholic her stints in prison and the prison regime must have been torture for her. The sentences she received seem particularly merciless. The last on record was two years hard labour for receiving a stolen bottle of brandy. Surprisingly, Finnegan found that Barrett seemed 'to have been pursued with extraordinary zeal' while certain other women 'who might otherwise have appeared at court on a charge of prostitution enjoyed police protection and were only arrested if a complaint was filed against them.'

Of the 603 prostitutes arrested, thirty percent faced at least one charge involving drink. Seven percent of those convicted for drunkenness had been charged on ten occasions. Twenty-four-year-old Elizabeth Eden was admitted to the workhouse with delirium tremens. Other prostitutes were so affected by drink that they tried to kill themselves or had breakdowns in police cells. Margaret Thompson, a 'woman of immoral character' was arrested for drunkenness in November 1870 and tried to strangle herself in the police cell by tying a handkerchief about her neck. Ann Dixon made a third attempt at self-strangulation in the police station in September 1843.

In 1865 Jane Garbutt was charged for the twenty-second time with being drunk and disorderly. Catherine Fowler of the Water Lanes made her fifteenth appearance before the Bench in 1864. Ann McDonald, formerly from Glasgow, received twenty-two convictions. In January 1877 she was apprehended for lurching down Walmgate with 'a sickle in her hand' flourishing it above her head 'alarming persons who came near her'. Julia Gray was sentenced to one year's imprisonment with hard labour in September 1877 for prostitution and indecency. She had no fixed abode, had had at least fourteen previous convictions and was obviously a hardened drinker. Unfortunately, such women were recognised by rescue workers as the most difficult class of prostitutes to reform - ' being generally regarded as unhelpable'.

Several women were repeatedly convicted for offences combining drunkenness and prostitution. Some were re-arrested and returned to jail on the same day or the day after their release. Julia Walker attempted suicide in the police cells after her re-arrest only one day following her release from prison.

The addicted and degraded individuals received little sympathy. In a pamphlet entitled 'Notes on Work Amongst the Fallen' circulated in Rescue homes and Female Penitentiaries, the Report recorded that:

'*after a debauch, the effects of which have hardly passed off before they are at liberty to repeat with impunity the offence for which they have so frequently been convicted…these habituals look upon the gaols as national Sanatoria, in which they can sojourn for a brief period without performing any but the most perfunctory work – their condition, in many cases, not admitting of labour'.*

York Refuge in Bishophill admitted fallen women for two years, but habitual drunkards and alcoholics were rejected. The main purpose of 'Notes on Work Amongst the Fallen' was the circulation of an up to date, strictly confidential national 'Cautionary List' which contained the names and descriptions of prostitutes already dismissed from homes for being especially troublesome. Matrons of homes were strongly advised to reject any applicants on the lists, many of whom had alcohol problems.

William Logan was convinced that the major reason for women taking to and remaining on the street was drink. In contrast, another reformer named Tait, in his book 'Magdelanism', regarded drink as a consequence of women taking to the streets, as much as a cause. He believed that many women 'first formed their habit of intemperance, and subsequently resorted to a life of prostitution in order to procure the means of satiating their desires for stimulating liquors'. J Miller in his 1859 pamphlet 'Prostitution – Its Causes and Cure' powerfully described the vicious cycle that alcoholic prostitutes could fall into:

'*By and by the unfortunate grows a hardened prostitute; and then, what made her so, keeps her so…Drink then becomes the necessary to maintain the prostitution, and prostitution must be continued to provide the drink. Terrible reciprocity'.*

The Cautionary Lists circulated to rescue homes are interesting also because they contradict another myth about Victorian prostitution originating in evidence given to the House of Lords Select Committee. Their Lordships are recorded by Nield in 'Prostitution' as having stated:

> 'The fact of a girl's seduction generally warrants her possession of youth, health, good looks, and a well-proportioned frame – qualifications usually incompatible with a feeble constitution.'

However, the Cautionary Lists, circulated to Homes throughout the country in an attempt to prevent unmanageable or deceitful girls from re-entering refuges, present a less flattering picture. Girls are often described as having irregular or flat features, crossed eyes, bad or chronic complexions and unpleasing countenances. Matrons of Refuges, street missionaries and other contributors to the Reformatory and Refuge Union's quarterly 'Notes on Work Amongst the Fallen' refer repeatedly in the 1880s and 1890s to the increasing number of half-witted and simple fallen women who were in need of care, many of whom were coarse featured and generally unattractive. Far from being drawn from the most desirable and attractive women as the House of Lords Select Committee would have society believe, most prostitutes were drawn from the most vulnerable and under-privileged class of women. Some of the descriptions of the women suggest that today they would be classed as having special educational needs.

The relationship between the prostitutes and police of Victorian York was an interesting one, as illustrated by the case of Inspector Turner who was the leaseholder of six cottages on Stonebow Lane, which were notorious brothels, which he in turn leased from the church. The scandal broke in 1855 when Inspector Turner was reported by Mr Charlton of the Watch Committee and the case was brought before the council. The Gazette reported that Mr Charlton, declared that there was 'a great evil and disgrace that should be looked into'.

At the enquiry it emerged that Inspector Turner had been the leaseholder of the the cottages since he had first entered the police force in 1836. The cottages had been sublet to prostitutes and used as brothels for some considerable time, even though the properties had never been recorded in the Chief Constable's Reports on Crime in York as houses of ill fame. Nor had any of the occupants on any occasion been brought before the magistrates. The Gazette reported that the inquiry went as follows:

> 'After having established ownership of the properties, Mr Charlton visited one of these places himself and met with a young woman who was the mistress of the house and who, the moment he entered, shut and locked the door. (laughter). The fact is, that it being known who is the landlord of the houses and what is his position in the city it is required that these places should be conducted in a peaceable manner. (laughter) However, he obtained what information he wanted and then he wished to make his exit but he was told that he could not go yet as there had to be a lookout to see that the coast was clear and when that was the case he was allowed to depart'.

Alderman Evers piled in stating that,

'During the time in which he had acted as magistrate the circumstances referred to came under his own observation and he spoke to Turner and remonstrated with him on more than one occasion'.

Inspector Turner pleaded extenuation stating that he had made attempts to 'keep his tenants respectable, had frequently discharged disreputable tenants and had some of his cottages standing empty in consequence'.

He then offered to discharge his tenants or sell the cottages for the remainder of the lease, if the committee so wished. However, the pressure was too great to bear and he resigned the following week, promising to let the properties to respectable tenants only, until such time as he could sell the lease. With this promise he was able to keep his pension.

However, it appears that he did not sell the lease. According to the accounts of the Watch Committee, five years after he resigned, in October 1860 J Turner was required to 'attend…to answer charges against him of letting his houses situate in Stonebow Lane to prostitutes'. Even being brought in front of the Watch Committee had little effect on J Turner's attempts to find respectable tenants as the 1861 census shows that one of the cottages was occupied by Thomas Simpson, his wife and three unmarried female lodgers. Mrs Simpson was a brothel-keeper and her three lodgers were well-known prostitutes.

A letter from a concerned parishioner of St Saviours three years previously, published in the Herald, sheds some light on why J Turner may have been reluctant to evict his tenants:

'I have found…that in a great many instances the owners of such property let to that class of persons that generally pays a greater percentage than be paid by a mechanic earning a livelihood by honest labour'.

The letter also outlined the problem with evicting brothel-keepers from one part of the city only

'Seeing that an effort is being made to dislodge from one part of the city persons keeping disorderly houses, allow me to remark that unless such efforts meet with co-operation throughout the city, it will merely tend to the whitewashing of one neighbourhood by the blackwashing of another.'

The writer of the letter also highlighted the problem that the church and those with civic responsibilities were turning a blind eye to the problem:

'On reading the 10th Annual Report of the City Mission, I find it stated that the moral and spiritual state of the Hungate and Layerthorpe districts is fearful and that there are 28 houses of ill fame therein. In one parish that I reside in there are 6 houses belonging to the church and one belonging to a gentleman who is a member of the jail committee. These seven house are of the worst

description to be found in our city and scarcely a week passes that the police report contains an account of some robbery committed therein...so dangerous has the road become that few people venture to pass through it at a late hour of the night.' (Herald, 20th November 1858)

The writer of the letter was right to be anxious about the extent of the problem of prostitution and also the extent of police corruption with regard to prostitution. Unfortunately, Inspector J Turner's situation was just the tip of the iceberg.

While soldiers from the barracks were frequently recorded as associating with immoral women of the town, a shocking fact uncovered by Finnegan was that one in every six identified clients of York prostitutes was a policeman. This number was only exceeded by labourers. This high proportion of policemen found to be patronising brothels is hardly surprising as they possessed powers, the opportunity and the knowledge of the trade, generally denied to other men.

In August 1846, Police Constable Boyes was fined one week's wages and cautioned for absenting himself from his beat and being found drunk in a brothel. The following month, having repeated the offence in a house of ill fame in Aldwark, he was immediately dismissed. Three months later, Police Constable Clark was reported for being off his beat at four o'clock in the morning and found reposing in a brothel in the same street. He also lost his job. In October 1849 PC Whitwell was fined one shilling a week from his pay for ten weeks for having been found in the 'City Arms public house in Walmgate while on duty, and having indecent intercourse with prostitute Isabella Ogram in a passage in Castlegate'.

Two years later PC George Franks was dismissed for drinking, smoking and visiting prostitutes in a brothel in Wentlock Street at three in the morning. William Horbury, George Armitage, Thomas Rainsdale, PC Maude, PC Pinkney, PC Dacre, Constable Duffy and Constable King were all recorded as being the clients of prostitutes, several of whom lost their jobs.

Constable Duffy's case illustrates the abuse of power that some police officers committed. He was summoned before the Watch Committee in 1866 after a complaint was made against him by Mrs Smith, wife of William Smith of the Shoulder of Mutton beerhouse in Water Lane. She alleged that he had entered the house and asked for a glass of ale, stating that he had no money. When Mrs Smith pointed out that he had just been paid, he replied, 'I have no money, but I will pay you another time. You had better, it will be better for you.' She supplied him with a drink, then he demanded the loan of half a crown 'to go and get a sweetheart with'. Since it emerged that Duffy repeatedly frequented the house, 'which is one of ill fame', he was dismissed.

Policemen's use of prostitutes could account for lower figures of recorded incidents of prostitution as, understandably, police officers who used prostitutes may have been reluctant to take into custody those with whom they consorted on such intimate terms. Perhaps some girls enjoyed police protection and so there are no records of them among the 1,400.

The case of Harriet Mottley of North Street is an interesting one. She was charged with the theft of twenty pounds from farmer and innkeeper John West. The Gazette reported that Mr West maintained that 'they were both upstairs together, but the prisoner said there was no upstairs, and the Chief Constable (who knew the house well) stated that there was no upstairs, only two rooms in the house, one of which was entered by going downstairs.' The case was dismissed on the evidence of the Chief Constable, and she remained otherwise totally unrecorded.

It seems that some prostitutes' activities were ignored by the police, unless a charge was brought against them, while others appear to have been somewhat hounded by the police. A group of residents of the Bedern area of the city petitioned the owners of the accommodation, in this case the Anglican church, to clean up the area. A letter was sent to the Ecclesiastical Commissioners and can still be found in the Minster Library Archives. It reads:

> 'Your petitioners three years ago, in order to get the whores out of it [Bedern], prosecuted one at great expense to the said Liberty, and with difficulty got evidence and a conviction of one month's imprisonment in the House of Correction – at the expiration of which time she went back in a Cab or Fly, preceded by a band of music and her associates flocked back double in number. The place is in that state that, if crime be committed, the inmates of it dare not give evidence for fear of their lives or property being injured by it.'

The prostitute referred to in the letter was Mrs Sarah Heaton, who in July 1840 was charged for the second time with keeping a disorderly house in the Bedern. Originally she had been one of 16 females removed from a brothel in Aldwark, whereupon she set up residence in the Bedern. According the Herald:

> 'She was followed by several prostitutes, the latter were removed, but she remained and the others returned…and scenes of revelry, debauchery and prostitution were carried on with impunity…at all hours of the night…The cause of the noise and the frequency of the women of the town was the convenient brothel upstairs kept by Mrs Heaton'.

In contrast prostitutes like Margaret Barrett, sentenced to two years hard labour for receiving a stolen bottle of brandy, appear to have been unable to get away with any disorderly conduct. Likewise, Elizabeth Bickerdike appeared in court on numerous occasions and was described as a prostitute and a brothel-keeper. The magistrates reserved some particularly harsh descriptions for her such as coming from one of 'the most disorderly families in the city' and being 'one of the most abandoned and disgusting women in the city'. She received prison sentences for her 'immoral and disgraceful behaviour'. She was a 'woman of immoral character', 'almost beyond control'. Her final recorded charge was for being an idle and disorderly person, a rogue and a vagabond. She received a sentence of one year's hard labour. It is difficult not to compare the judicial consequences of her behaviour with the consequences of the behaviour of the police who used prostitutes.

While it is often difficult to prove whether criminality and alcoholism were the causes or consequences of prostitution, there were several very obvious and very negative consequences for the prostitute involved in the activity of prostitution.

The physical condition of prostitutes was systematically recorded in applications to the workhouse and the York Refuge. Of the 234 destitute prostitutes who applied to the workhouse and were recorded as sick or ill, half of them were suffering from venereal disease. These were listed as 'gonorrhoea, syphilis, V.D or diseased'. Eighty-seven percent of those with venereal disease were in the fifteen-to-twenty-five-year age range. It is likely that the women and girls with venereal disease would have been infected for some time before applying to enter the workhouse. A large number were admitted direct from brothels and houses of ill fame, and although diseased it is likely that they would have continued in their profession until absolutely unable to continue. Even low-class brothel-keepers had no use for diseased prostitutes and rid themselves of such women as soon as they were no longer able to work. In 'The Great Social Evil,' Logan recorded speaking to a girl in a workhouse in Bradford who admitted that she had been a prostitute for four years. She confessed to the matron shortly before she died that:

'The mistress of the brothel was everything to me when in health, but when unwell I was turned out of doors without mercy, and the doctor said that I might have died any moment.'

In York, forty of the named applicants to the workhouse were admitted straight from named brothels. Twenty-four-year-old Elizabeth Baldin came from Mrs Maude's in Kings Court and died soon after being admitted.

Due to the likelihood of their advanced state of infection, the women from named brothels must have been responsible for considerable spread of the disease. Court records show that thirty-one diseased prostitutes continued the activity after a brief stay in the workhouse. Harriet Atkinson was admitted to the workhouse with venereal disease in 1861 and was still walking the streets eight years later. Sixteen-year-old Ann Muldowney had venereal disease in 1859 and was still engaged in the profession in 1863.

The quantity of diseased prostitutes may be an underestimate of the total figure. In 1861 the Law of Settlement was amended to state that all those prostitutes who had lived in the city for less than five years were ineligible for relief and could be removed back to their parish of origin. Returning home a fallen woman with a diseased or swollen body loudly proclaiming her shame may have deterred many infected women from applying for parish relief. In 1865 the period of eligibility for relief was reduced from three years' residence in the city to twelve months. As many prostitutes were drawn from a fairly wide area, it is likely that many would have sought treatment elsewhere or did not attend to their complaints at all.

Another obvious consequence of Victorian prostitution was pregnancy. Fifty-two applicants to York Refuge were rejected for either being diseased or pregnant. Only towards the end of the period under analysis were they recorded as being 'in a terrible state of disease' or 'in the family way'. Previously euphemisms were used such as 'her condition requires that she should leave the Home immediately.'

Of the fifty-two rejected applicants, only thirteen applied to the workhouse, probably due to its punitive atmosphere and regime. The remainder would perhaps have resorted to begging, scrounging, stealing or finding an occasional day's work in occupations of the lowest description. Clearly, many of the destitute and diseased women preferred to scratch the barest of livings than apply to the workhouse. It is highly likely that several died as a result of their lifestyle.

While Acton and the House of Lords believed that seduction was the main cause of a woman's entering the realm of prostitution, Finnegan's study found overwhelming evidence that the causes of prostitution were poverty, overcrowding, poor pay and working conditions and lack of employment opportunities for women. She also found that many prostitutes came from dysfunctional families. The annual report of York Refuge in 1900 reported that many of the inmates of the home:

> 'have had in their parents bad examples which they only too naturally followed; and some have been actually initiated in sin by those who should have been their protectors from evil influences'.

Bad home conditions were likely to include drunken parents, neglected and deprived childhoods, cruelty or frequent quarrels and fights with parents or step-parents, or simply poverty. Many of the girls were described as orphans and 'entirely without friends'.

Ann Boothdale's application recorded by the York Refuge in December 1859 reads:

> 'Her mother is very disreputable, it is thought her drunkenness and evil habits made her husband leave her and go to Australia. The girl seems to have been driven by her mother into sin. She is anxious to be admitted and states it was "contrary to her own wishes" that she has been leading the life she has done'.

Harriet Hardcastle, 17, applied in May 1857 because her mother 'turned her our of doors and this was the immediate cause of her fall. She professes to be thoroughly disgusted with her past manner of life'. Jane Scaife's father refused to have her in the house according to her application to the Refuge in January 1858.

The applicant recorded only as 'Stubbs' in June 1859 said that she left home because she and her stepmother did not agree. She knew a girl who kept a disorderly house and was thus 'led into sin'.

Other types of family breakdown could lead to prostitution. Maria Nettleton had been deserted by her husband. Other women had been widowed. Some women had illegitimate children and were thus already 'fallen women', vulnerable to fall even further into the sordid world of prostitution.

William Logan in 1871 and Frances Finnegan just over one hundred years later found evidence that dire overcrowding and squalid living conditions were a cause of prostitution. Because York's population almost doubled between 1831 and 1881 from 26,260 people to 49,530 and although the number of houses in the city grew from 4,955 to 10,733, there were still numerous complaints of a chronic shortage of cottage accommodation.

Even as late as the turn of the century, Rowntree observed that the very poor were still inhabiting insanitary yards, courts and tenements within the old walled city, or were crowded into closely packed rows of dismal back-to-back slums in the Walmgate and Hungate areas. It is significant then that most of the brothels identified in Finnegan's study were in these areas and 'the vast majority of recorded prostitutes drifted from one miserable hovel to another'.

Finnegan's findings fiercely negate the stereotype of the Victorian brothel being a well-appointed mansion, staffed by accomplished young females and frequented by the dissipated gentry. Instead she paints a picture of 'single rooms in dilapidated tenement yards, whole families of the poor and sick crowded together with appalling sanitary consequences'. Sadly, it was from these same buildings that various degraded streetwalkers were reduced to apply for final admission to the workhouse.

During Finnegan's period of the study, Bedern, once the home of the Vicars' Choral, featured briefly but prominently as a place associated with prostitution. In 1818 the York historian, Hargrove, reported that the former mansions and outbuildings had become the 'sad receptacle of poverty and wretchedness' by being sublet into a vast number of dwellings.

When Laycock reported to the government in 1844 on the state of the city of York as part of his wider enquiry into the condition of large towns and districts, he stated that in Bedern, 'Of the 98 families living there, 67 have only one room for all purposes, 18 have two rooms, and 13 have two rooms or more.'

Until it was colonised almost exclusively by the Irish in 1847, Bedern was a flourishing centre of prostitution. On 16th November 1839, the Gazette recorded that thirteen brothel-keepers were charged with keeping bawdy houses in Bedern in one single day. When reading the letter sent to the Ecclesiastical Commissioners in 1844 by the 'respectable' inhabitants of the neighbouring streets to petition the church owners of the property to take action regarding the behaviour of the prostitutes in the area, the extent of the problem becomes very clear:

'The place called Bedern was the College of the Vicars' Choral, and more or less their residence; and by the ancient Statutes, they ought to reside there, and close the gates every evening at 8 o'clock to keep women out – that they have since leased the property out to various individuals and that in consequence the houses having been erected in the suburbs of the city… nearly all the respectable part of the inhabitants, have left their residences and gone there. That their late residences have all been let off in single rooms, many of them filled with whores, thieves, streetwalkers, etc, thereby bringing great incumbrances upon the Liberty, besides great disgrace and scandal upon the Church of England by the Lessors continuing still to lease the said property after knowing the condition of the place, and that there is no remedy for the evil except by a complete renovation of the place…'

With the influx of the Irish, only one brothel was recorded in the area after 1846. In the decade of the 1830s almost one quarter of all the offences recorded associated with prostitution took place in this tiny courtyard. In 1843 the Chief Constable reported that of the 118 prostitutes resident in the city, thirty three (28 percent) lived in the Bedern.

Five years later in 1849 the Gazette published a powerful letter from a citizen of York describing the pitiable state of Bedern following the second outbreak of cholera in the city:

'The respectable classes in this city can have no conception of the condition of certain localities. Take Bedern for instance and what do you find – filth, misery, drunkenness, disease and crime. Let those who doubt the proof of this assertion examine (if they have the courage) for themselves and they will find that no language can describe the feelings excited by observing the swarms of human beings hording together, without the slightest regard to the decencies of life. Let them for a short time inhale the close and pestilential atmosphere of these abodes of filth, and contemplate if they can without horror man in his lowest state displaying a brutal unconsciousness of his degradation. We need not tell our readers that Bedern is not the only locality in which these scenes of wretchedness abound. Medical men could inform the sceptical of other localities presenting scenes equally disgusting and disgraceful; they can tell of the fetid swarms who crowd the low lodging houses of Long Close Lane, Walmgate, the Water Lanes etc. (Gazette, 27th October 1849)

Even though the prostitutes had abandoned Bedern by the time that the Irish immigrants fleeing the famine in Ireland had moved in, the major centres of prostitution in York – Walmgate and the Water Lanes - were equally as disgusting and wretched.

The Chief Constable's report on the state of crime in the city of 1842 recorded that fourteen prostitutes lived in Aldwark and ten in St Andrewgate. Thus, in the 1840s, the three adjoining streets of Bedern, Aldwark and St Andrewgate housed almost half of the city's prostitutes and the same area accounted for almost half of the city's crime. A number of public houses and beershops in the area, such as Gill's Dram Shop and the Crystal Palace, also added to the infamous reputation of this part of the centre of the city. These premises were not only the resort of pimps, prostitutes and thieves, but were also used as brothels.

Although the Walmgate/Hungate area was cleared in the 1930s, its 'reputation for poverty and prostitution survived well into living memory'. However, according to Finnegan, 'various of the sixty or so squalid little courts and yards branching off both sides of Walmgate and Fossgate were settled by the Irish too, but when this was the case, though drunken brawls and other disturbances were fairly common (and made much of in the local press), evidence of prostitution in them was noticeably absent.' Although the Irish immigrants were desperately poor, few prostitutes were found among their number. Finnegan acknowledges then that poverty solely cannot be the only reason for a woman becoming a prostitute, and a combination of factors, including her own personality, must have contributed to her choice of lifestyle.

Walmgate itself was one of the streets in the city in which offences connected with prostitution, such as soliciting and picking clients' pockets most frequently occurred. The brothels in the area were situated almost entirely in the larger houses of Walmgate itself. In 1843 the Chief Constable reported that of the 118 prostitutes resident in the city the previous year, twenty-one lived along Walmgate and six in the Hungate district. The police reported that several 'loose' women were tending to leave houses of 'general resort' and set up on their own account. Consequently, houses of ill fame increased in the city.

Finnegan's analysis of prostitutes' addresses reveals that by the 1840s thirty per cent of all prostitutes in the city were living in the Walmgate/Hungate area, with most concentrated in Walmgate. By the 1870s this trend was reversed with two thirds of prostitutes living in Hungate. Of the fifty-year period of her study, twenty-seven percent of offences (290 in total) occurred almost entirely around Walmgate.

In 1901 Rowntree described the Walmgate/Hungate area as the 'poorest large district in the city'. Imagine densely packed terraced houses, blocks of back-to-back cottages and insanitary tenements such as Bradley's Buildings and Wide Yard. The houses crowded into slaughterhouses and stables. Also within the districts were piggeries and a cattle market, the beasts of which would be driven up Walmgate. The area housed the city's gas works, dung heaps and even unhealthy grave yards. The dung heaps drained their liquid into the River Foss, which was described by James Smith in his report on the insanitary conditions of York in 1850 as 'a great open cesspool into the stagnating water of which the sewers of near half of the city sluggishly pass...'

Despite its insanitary state and the 'sunless courts' described by Rowntree in 1901, Walmgate/Hungate was the second most important centre of prostitution in York in the 1860s. This was likely due to the vast amount of public houses and beer shops. In 1901 Rowntree counted thirty-nine public houses in the area, twenty-seven of which were situated along the contiguous streets of Fossgate and Walmgate. Therefore, there was one public house to every 174 members of the population. Finnegan concludes that the 'public houses and inns along Fossgate and Walmgate, many of which dated from York's days as a major coaching centre, had an important effect upon the area's link with prostitution'. Finnegan also points to the numerous amounts of yards and passages linking the Fossgate/Hungate areas as playing a role in prostitution in the area.

The three Water Lanes that stretched from Castlegate down to the river's edge at King's Staithe were imaginatively named as First Water, Middle or Second Water Lane and finally Third Water Lane. Of the three lanes only Third Water Lane exists to this day and is known as Friargate. The Water Lanes area was the most notorious criminal district in the city, housing or accommodating the largest number of prostitutes throughout most of the period. Most of the offences associated with prostitution, such as theft, drunkenness and assault occurred here.

In 1818 Hargrove in his 'History of York' described the lanes as so extremely narrow that only Friargate was wide enough to allow a cart to pass down to the River at King's Staithe. Middle Water Lane was the narrowest containing a number of warren-like courts, yards and alleys, into whose dim and foul recesses respectable people and even the police were reluctant to venture. Writers paint a pitiable picture of properties of various shapes, sizes and ages, dilapidated, squalid and unfit for habitation. Tiny cottages in the Lanes were crammed into insanitary yards that contained both stables and piggeries. The larger buildings were split into a bewildering number of hopelessly overcrowded dwellings or used as low class lodging-houses for York's most destitute and criminal classes. Meanwhile, the Lanes were criss-crossed by infamous yards such as Cross Alley and Frairs Alley.

In a letter to the Herald, the rector of nearby St Mary's Castlegate, the Reverend Lawrence wrote:

'There is a real want of light, air, ventilation. Some of the houses are supported by beams, others have huge cracks and holes in the walls. The Lanes, courts and alleys are close and narrow…the drainage is defective, the paving consists mostly of large cobble stones, the surface either soaks in or stands in pools, the ashpits are foul beyond description; in some cases there were gratings immediately in front of the door or beneath the windows from which ascends sewage gas'.

Some of the houses in the Lanes are recorded as simply falling down of their own accord. Laycock in his 1844 reported that the Lanes as had 'no water, except from the filthy river, no drainage and hardly any privies'. He was unafraid to hold back his personal opinion that 'the scum of the country here come and sleep, and there is no discrimination of the sexes'.

Just a few years later in 1848 the desperate housing situation in the Lanes was worsened by the influx of destitute and diseased Irish families, fleeing from the famine in Ireland. Hundreds of men, women and children crowded temporarily into the district, before settling into equally insanitary but less notorious slums.

From the 1841 census the Water Lanes contained 147 houses and 713 inhabitants with an average of five people per house. However, some had considerably more than this. In King Street, one house sheltered 26 individuals. Another housed 15. In 1861 'The Green Tree', a notorious brothel, lodging-house and pub listed 55 residents. When they were no longer required, it furnished the workhouse with various destitute and diseased prostitutes who featured in several court cases.

The residents of the Water Lanes were characterised by their extreme poverty. The censuses record their occupations as beggars, paupers, hawkers, labourers, field labourers, watermen and charwomen. Large numbers of them were in receipt of regular parish relief. In the 1851 census, the vast majority were lodgers and it becomes apparent from newspaper reports and Magistrate's court proceedings that many of the so-called lodging houses where low-class brothels with the head of the household being the brothel-keeper and/or prostitute. Many lodging houses would have combined the residences of whole families, with some part of the premises reserved for 'immoral purposes'.

Between 1877 and 1876, almost one quarter of the offences associated with prostitution are recorded as taking place in the Lanes. The offences included theft or assaults on clients, and the drunk and disorderly behaviour of streetwalkers. The Improvement Scheme begun in 1877 demolished practically all of the most notorious district, Friargate being the only surviving Water Lane. However, The Lanes' destitute and criminal classes were simply made homeless and flocked to other unhealthy and overcrowded neighbourhoods, such as Hungate, Walmgate, Skeldergate, North Street, Aldwark, Swinegate or Wesley Place. Then in the late 1870s abandoned women began to settle in the area around the barracks.

The Lanes were the centre of the city's underworld, where most of the prostitutes were diseased, habitual drunkards and pickpockets. Therefore, it is highly unlikely that local middle-class gentlemen customers would flock to this area for a night on the town, whether they were hardened users of prostitutes or inexperienced adventurers. Only unwitting or drunk visitors to the city would risk their wallets and health in the dingy alleys and foul, disgusting lodgings of the Lanes.

North Street and its numerous yards along the river's edge on the other side of Ouse Bridge to Skeldergate was famed for its number of brothels. By the 1880s, nearby Tanner Row and Wellington Row were acquiring similar reputations. On 21st April, 1868 the York Herald reported that there were ten brothels operating in North Street alone. 'These establishments were probably superior both to the notorious dens of the Water Lanes and to the miserable cottages to which street-walkers took their clients in the Hungate district'. Like Skeldergate, North Street never acquired the criminal reputation attached to the Water Lanes.

The mere fact that hundreds of refuge and rescue societies existed throughout the country is testament to the sheer size of the problem and number of women involved in the activity. Throughout the whole country there were hundreds of Refuges, Homes, Guardians and Asylums established to try to rescue individual prostitutes and fallen women. Finnegan found in her study that all were 'hopelessly inadequate' because they failed to tackle the social, economic and moral causes of the problem. Although she acknowledges that the refuges were the result of the 'sincere attempts of a few middle-class ladies and gentlemen to deal with an appalling situation'.

York Refuge, also known as the York Female Penitentiary at Bishophill was one of five institutions in the city which sought to help prostitutes, although it was the only one that offered 'long-term' help. Successful applicants were taken into the home for a period of two years. In 1869 a Rescue Home for Fallen Women in need of temporary shelter was opened in Skeldergate. The Home for the Friendless and Fallen or 'St Martin's Home' was housed in Trinity Lane. However, forty-three per cent of recorded prostitutes in York during Finnegan's period of study either applied to enter or were admitted to the care of York Refuge.

York Refuge was a charitable organisation which depended on voluntary subscriptions and support. It was established in 1822 with a legacy from Dr Stephen Beckwith, who had spent many years trying to rescue women from a life of prostitution. In 1843 the trustees of the Refuge bought his former house in Bishophill, along with two cottages in the same street. They also built a laundry to provide a training ground for the inmates. The donors consisted of clergymen and dissenting ministers. The Society was run by a president, a treasurer, a secretary and a committee, which elected and paid a matron and an assistant, as well as a medical officer. They also made arrangements for the religious instruction of the inmates. Helping with the administration of the Refuge was a Ladies' Committeee which presented a monthly report and was responsible for the moral and religious improvement of the inmates. The Ladies were to help the Matron to find suitable situations for the women who had successfully completed the two-year internment.

To gain a place in the York Refuge, the applicant had to meet certain criteria and the inmates who were accepted were deemed the most favourably suited to reform. A former prostitute had to be a 'hopeful case'. An age limit of no older than twenty-five was chosen so that the woman's lifestyle had not become too embedded or ingrained. (Nevertheless, ten women aged between twenty-five and thirty entered the Refuge, so there must have been some pity for them on the part of the Ladies' Committtee). A former prostitute could not be either pregnant or diseased. Between the date of opening in 1845 and 1887, 502 girls were admitted for varying lengths of time and a further 40 made unsuccessful applications.

Finnegan studied three sources – the Minute Books, the Reports of the Ladies' Committee and the Annual reports. Here she found recorded the age, background and reason for the initial 'downfall' of many of the 542 prostitutes who entered or applied to the home between 1845 and 1887. For much of the period too the press published the Annual Reports of the York Female Penitentiary Society.

The fallen women were to be rescued by being instructed principally in laundry work. They were taught how to scrub floors, make bread, do plain needlework and given limited instruction in reading and writing by the visiting Ladies. The Matron conducted family worship twice a day and an inmate was only allowed to absent themselves from this by illness. The Matron was to report weekly on the conduct of the inmates to the Ladies Committee.

The daily routine was tough. The women had to rise at six in the autumn and in winter at seven. They must be in bed by ten o'clock. Inmates were not allowed out of the house, except in the company of a visiting Lady or other trustworthy person deemed so by the Matron. Certain visitors were allowed, such as the father, mother or other near relative, as long as they were 'known as such', but only in the presence of the Matron and at her discretion. No other visitors were permitted. The women were required to were a drab uniform or 'Penitentiary dress' and there was a strong religious character to the institution. It was strongly supported by leading York Quakers and Samuel Tuke, the descendent of Mary Tuke, was the first President of the Society. Various other members of the Tuke, Backhouse, Rowntree and Richardson families served on the both the Ladies and the Gentlemen's Committees. Gradually, this Quaker influence was replaced by an Anglican one and by the end of the period of study, the President was the Dean of York.

Upon admittance to the institution, the women had to sign a pledge that read,

'I am wishful to abandon my sinful life and by God's grace to lead a better. I am willing to remain two years in the Home. I will do my best to conform to the rules and discipline of the Home'.

By 1868 the girls were allowed to attend public services in two neighbouring churches and various non-conformist chapels in the vicinity in the company of the Matron. Elderly residents of the Bishophill area remembered the 'bad' girls as 'sullen and peaky in their grey cloaks and bonnets, marching two by two to church each Sunday.'

Many of the inmates were entirely illiterate or barely able to read or write. Without any training of any kind, they were even ignorant of basic domestic skills. Many were simple minded, most were uncouth and almost all during their stay at the Refuge showed signs of emotionally unbalanced and even violent behaviour. As such, they were hardly suitable for the domestic service or laundry work for which they were being prepared

As the less judgemental influence of the Quakers waned, the more condemnatory influence of the Anglican church would have placed an additional strain on the inmates who were subjected to fierce and daily indoctrination. They were constantly reminded of their own guilt and shame. Although this policy was well-intentioned, it is likely that it did more harm than good, resulting in many cases of girls running away or being dismissed. Finnegan found that letters from former inmates showed that many had been 'reduced to spiritless demoralised creatures obsessed with religion and their past sin, entirely lacking in self-confidence or self-respect and betraying a morbid and desperate dependence on the women who had lately ordered their lives'.

It seemed beyond the understanding of the administrators of the Refuge that women 'desperate to turn from a life of prostitution were in need of courtesy and kindness rather than recrimination.'

In the 1849 Annual Report, it states,

'One of the inmates [called Winter] has been confined several months to her bed, and is fast declining in a consumption; she came into the Refuge an orphan, very destitute, and very ignorant in June 1848. She was apparently in robust health, but in a few months time her health gave way when her mind became awakened to her sinful state.'

Unfortunately, Winter died the following January 'in a hopeful and peaceful state of mind, expressing a simple trust in Christ and exhibiting great patience under her suffering'.

Besides receiving money from donations and subscriptions, the Refuge was funded by the proceeds from the laundry work that the inmates carried out. The Assistant Matron was a laundress whose task it was to instruct the girls in the art of washing, starching and ironing. The work was exhausting, particularly for many of the girls with poor constitutions, who contrary to the proponents of the Contagious Diseases Act were not robust sexual automatons, but weak and sickly children. It wasn't until 1851 that the Refuge bought a wringing machine to help the poor girls to cope with the amount of laundry being taken into the home. In 1857 it was decided that 'the pressure of work should be lessened to afford more time for other instruction'. Despite this concession, the Refuge was competing with other commercial laundries and the many other washerwomen in the city.

As time progressed, the rules began to be interpreted a little more leniently. By 1868, trusted inmates were allowed out occasionally alone to run errands for the Matron. Gradually a kindlier attitude was adopted towards many of the girls, many of whom were fourteen or fifteen years old. More time was spent on elementary instruction in literacy, listening to religious works and plain sewing. Towards the end of Finnegan's period of study the women were even granted treats and rewards for good conduct.

Nevertheless, Finnegan's examination of the weekly Visitors and monthly Minute Books reveal evidence of many petty jealousies, squabbles, bullying incidents and constant bickering. In 1858 there were only two inmates due to the rest either having run away or being dismissed. In 1875 the Ladies' Committee requested funds for an additional member of staff so that the 'girls should never be left without supervision, and especially at night'.

Amongst the papers relating to the Refuge that Finnegan was allowed access to there was an anonymous letter dated 1900 that was sent to the Refuge Committee. It paints a shocking picture of life in the Refuge:

> *'Last night Bishophill presented a disgraceful scene and one of two girls that had run away being dragged along the road by three men who safely lodged her inside the door. The street was crowded with men, women and children some of whom passed not very complimentary remarks upon the present management of the institution.*
> *Last week I was passing when a girl got out of one of the front windows from which she had taken a square of glass, and ran away as fast as she could. A workman that was passing said that another girl had run away last week.'*

The unhappiness and poor behaviour of some of the inmates led to staffing problems. One Matron was dismissed in 1853 after allegations that alcohol abuse was leading to poor quality laundry work.

The wall of the Refuge ran down to Skeldergate, just in front of the River Ouse. In 1856, Campbell 'made her escape over the wall. She was brought back by one of the police, but being determined in her wish to leave, was allowed her clothes and go.'

It is likely that many of the girls ran away because they were temperamentally unsuited and lacked the self-discipline necessary to remain voluntarily in such an institution. It is also clear that the discipline, dreary routine and religious indoctrination were unsuited to their needs.

By 1858 the Ladies agreed to a 'more conciliatory management' as they believed this would be more likely to be beneficial in producing 'a softened mind' among the inmates.

Nevertheless, escapes continued and 'over the wall' or 'over the garden wall' became a stock phrase within the institution. Many of the fallouts among the inmates were caused by dormitory accommodation. By 1874 the Ladies' Committee was advocating separate bedrooms for the inmates. Nevertheless, people old enough to remember the Refuge were often adamant that it was a female prison whose inmates were compulsorily detained. Girls who were rude or refused to work were repeatedly confined to the probation ward. There were constant punishments for bad behaviour, stealing and lies. There were various attempts to seclude the girls from the outside world. In 1854,

> *'Some alterations being desirable in the small bedroom windows, it is concluded that they should be made to open only half a pane at the top, and that they should be fresh painted on the outside to form an effectual blind'.*

As late as 1893 the Ladies Committee reported that:

> *'Some men from Skeldergate have been getting on the wall and talking to the girls from the garden and also from the laundry window. It has been going on for some time, but has only just been discovered.'*

From the back bedrooms of the Refuge there was an uninterrupted view out across the city over the river to where the three Water Lanes rose up to meet Castlegate. For many of the girls, the sight of these notorious streets must have had a disturbing effect.

Through analysis of the records, Finnegan found that hardly more than one quarter of the girls admitted to the Penitentiary were actually placed in service. However, she concludes that:

'In spite of these figures, however, which must, to those who appreciated their real implications, have been disheartening, the importance of the Refuge throughout the period was by no means insignificant. It is true that the Society probably rescued and permanently reformed only a small proportion of the total number of prostitutes in the city…Nevertheless, of the 1,246 prostitutes identified between 1837 and 1887, 542 sought refuge in its care and over 500 were admitted. Thus, though the Home was relatively unsuccessful in its primary purpose as it at least afforded many street-walkers temporary shelter and relief, and the opportunity – if they could take it – of entering a more regular course of life'.

Nevertheless, its success rate was not particularly high. Of the 412 formally admitted since its opening in 1845, by 1887 only 142 of the inmates were placed in service after their release. Although the Select Committee of the House of Lords heard evidence that former prostitutes often gained situations as refined ladies' maids or children's nurses, such evidence that exists indicates otherwise.

Finnegan states,

'…those girls who obtained and kept situations as domestic servants were exploited even more than were other "virtuous" women of their class. Their wages were low, even by contemporary standards, and their conditions of work poor and tedious. They were employed largely as drudges by washerwomen, commercial laundries or private families requiring cheap help in a wash-house. One former inmate wrote to the Matron of York Refuge describing a situation at Mrs Hutton's house, which she had left. At 'mrs huttons ther was nothing to your work there a little black hole not room to stir about in it I had a life like a crab'.

Due to the reporting in the press and the physical manifestation of the problem of prostitution in Victorian York, few members of any echelon of society would have been unaware of its existence. Amongst the poor themselves there would have been many neighbours, acquaintances and relatives who would have at least contemplated prostitution as an alternative to destitution and the workhouse.

Prison sentences, usually of between seven to fourteen days, were an occupational hazard for the street-walker, and the frequent absences of these women could hardly have gone unnoticed. Several of those convicted of wandering abroad also had dependent children. The permanent disappearance of younger girls, lured into what initially at least must have seemed an attractive alternative to domestic service or life in a dreary, overcrowded insanitary slum, must have been noticed.

For the vast majority of women in Finnegan's study, poverty was the result as well as the cause of their taking to prostitution, and it was the condition in which they lived while they were engaged in the activity. However, poverty cannot have been the only driver of women onto the streets. If this was the case, then far more women would have taken to prostitution. By the turn of the century, Rowntree demonstrated that thirty per cent of the population was living below the poverty line.

There were many other contributory factors including ill treatment by parents or step-parents; seduction; the birth of an illegitimate child; desertion; widowhood; the need to support dependent children; lack of employment ; being 'led astray by bad companions'; lack of education and lack of living-wage work opportunities. Perhaps several of these factors coincided in the life of an individual prostitute.

Finnegan concedes that 'None of these, however, are necessarily the cause of prostitution in themselves, and even when combined with poverty, need not result in a woman habitually selling her body for a livelihood. However desperate her circumstances, the fact that an individual took to and continued in prostitution, must in the final resort, be seen as a complex mixture of influences on that individual's personality. These, however, cannot be measured in the past.'

Although Finnegan's study dispels the Victorian myth that prostitutes were predominantly exploited by the middle and upper classes, she did find the existence of prostitution on so large a scale in York was fundamentally the outcome of class exploitation. The vast majority of identified streetwalkers took to and remained in the activity because they were part of what was essentially a female under-class created through lack of work opportunities as a result of a patriarchal economic, social and moral culture that allowed for the sexual exploitation of women, at the same time as blaming the women for resorting to the activity.

Finnegan found that while prostitutes were drawn mainly from a destitute underclass, recorded prostitutes' clients on the other hand came from all walks of life, ranging from the aristocracy to the humblest labourer, police constable or soldier. Finnegan's study is compelling in the shocking and depressing irony of the situation when she argues that 'it was the widespread prevalence of poverty – condoned or even worsened by those in whose power it was to remedy the situation and who, while abusing her, were the most vocal in their condemnation of the prostitute and instrumental in punishing her – that was largely responsible for women of the poor taking to the street in the first place'.

Although evidence was presented to the House of Lords Select Committee that contradicted Acton's evidence. The law lords chose to ignore it. Finnegan found that:

'…those who wished to enforce and extend the provisions of the Contagious Diseases Acts sought to present as favourable as possible a picture of the prostitute's circumstances, minimising the harmful effects of her physical health and mental well-being and emphasising her brief and temporary involvement in the activity and the ease with which she could leave it. The fact that this conflicted with traditional and other contemporary evidence and opinion on the subject was brushed aside in a complacent and sanctimonious white-washing

of reality, in order that the legislation which approved and regulated a system so blatantly discriminating against one sex and class, could more palatably be passed'.

Josephine Butler and the Ladies National Association worked tirelessly to campaign against the Contagious Diseases Acts and the meetings she held to raise awareness were often met with dangerous sabotage and violence. Nevertheless, the arguments for the repeal of the Acts that they put forward were very strong. They focused on the sexual discrimination inherent in punishing the women, but not the men involved in illicit sex, calling out the 'Double Standard'. They highlighted the class bias of the acts in the fact that only lower class prostitutes and street-walkers were likely to be detained. They raised awareness of the unprecedented powers of a police force able to arrest any woman on the mere suspicion of her being a prostitute and the obvious abuses implicit therein. They pointed out the hypocrisy of the state recognition and sanction of a vice. They criticised the fact that the Acts did not offer rehabilitation, but brutalised and downgraded the prostitute still further. They argued that the Acts were a futile attempt to control disease through the street walkers and not their clients, who remained free to spread the disease and that they forced diseased prostitutes underground, rather than encourage them to seek help. Finally, they warned that the Acts would become more stringent and extend to an ever-widening female population. Fortunately, their campaign was so successful that the Acts were suspended in 1883 and repealed in 1886. Meanwhile, Finnegan's pioneer study of prostitution in Victorian York draws back the curtain on a shocking and degrading period of history for many women that needs to be acknowledged and learnt from.

Epilogue

Chapter One: Cartimandua
Does Cartimandua deserve to be called a 'quisling', a 'traitor' and an 'adulteress'?

Chapter Two: Roman Women of York
What have you learnt about how the Romans treated women from this chapter?

Chapter Three: Queen Ethelburga
Why do you think that Queen Ethelburga lived in such violent times?

Chapter Four: The Naughty Nuns of the Priory of St Clements
Why do you think so many women 'misbehaved' while in convents?

Chapter Five: Margaret Clitherow
Does Margaret Clitherow deserve to become a saint?

Chapter Six: Jennet Preston
What should be done to commemorate all the women, and men who were killed for being witches?
Should there be a memorial to Jennet Preston at the site of Tyburn on the Knavesmire? If yes, what form should that memorial take? If not, why not?

Chapter Seven: Mary Tuke and Mary Anne Craven
Why did the Merchant Adventurers seek to put Mary Tuke out of business?

Chapter Eight: Elizabeth Montagu and Sarah Scott
Does Elizabeth Montagu deserve a blue plaque outside the Treasurer's House?
Does Sarah Scott deserve a blue plaque outside the Treasurer's House?

Chapter Nine: Women of the Bar Convent
Does Mary Ward deserve to be canonised?

Chapter Ten: Anne Fairfax
Does Anne Fairfax deserve to be described as 'neurotic'?

Chapter Eleven: Anne Lister
Does it matter that Anne Lister wasn't a particularly nice person?

Chapter Twelve: Mary Ellen Best
Should the three paintings by Mary Ellen Best, owned by York Museums Trust, be on permanent display in York Art Gallery?

Chapter Thirteen: Benefactresses of York
Were the benefactresses truly altruistic or did they leave their legacies so that they would be remembered?

Chapter Fourteen: Prostitutes of York
Did the prostitutes of York deserve the consequences of the lives that they led?

Overall
What have you learnt about the lives of women over the course of history from this book?
What role did religion play in the lives of the women?
What other women of York do you think deserve to be written about?
If one woman was to have a statue erected in York, which woman would you choose and why?

Bibliography

Chapter One
Cartimandua

'Cartimandua, Queen of the Brigantes', Nikki Howarth

Chapter Two
Roman
Women of York

'Life in Roman Britain', Birley
'Roman York', Patrick Ottaway
'Ancient Roman Women', Brian Williams
British History Online
Yorkshire Museums Trust Online

Chapter Three
Queen Ethelburga

'Ecclesiastical History of the British Nation', Bede

Chapter Four
The Naughty Nuns
of the Priory of
St Clements

'A History of the County of York: the City of York', edited by
PM Tillott

Chapter Five
Margaret Clitherow

'The Life and Death of Mistress Margaret Clitherow', John Mush

Chapter Six
Jennet Preston

'The Lancashire Witch Craze', Jonathon Lumby
'The Lancashire Witches: A Chronicle of Sorcery and Death on
Pendle Hill', Philip C Almond
'The Wonderful Discoverie of Witches', Thomas Potts

Chapter Seven
Mary Tuke and Mary
Ann Craven

'The Birth of the Chocolate City', Summer Strevens

Chapter Eight
Elizabeth Montagu
and Sarah Scott

'Companions without Vows, Relationships Among Eighteenth-
Century British Women', Betty Rizzo
'Reimagining the Bluestockings', Nicole Pole
'The Letters of Elizabeth Montagu with some of the letters of
her correspondents', pub. Matthew Montagu, Esq

Chapter Nine
Women of the
Bar Convent

'Women in England 1500-1760, A Social History', Anne Laurence

Chapter Ten
Anne Fairfax

'Fairfax of York', Gerry Webb
'Fairfax House York, An Illustrated History and Guide', York
Civic Trust
'Pyramids of Pleasure', Fairfax House, York
'In the Name of the Rose, The Jacobite Rebellions: Symbolism
and Allegiance', Fairfax House, York
North Yorkshire County Record Office, Fairfax papers,
Northallerton

Chapter Eleven
Ann Lister

Various online sources

Chapter Twelve
Mary Ellen Best

'The World of Mary Ellen Best', Caroline Davidson

Chapter Thirteen
Benefactresses of York

'A History of the County of York: the City of York', edited by
PM Tillott

Chapter Fourteen
Prostitutes of York

'Prostitutes of York', Frances Finnegan

Currency Converter
www.nationalarchives.co.uk/currencyconverter

www.ingramcontent.com/pod-product-compliance
Lightning Source LLC
Chambersburg PA
CBHW072134270326
41931CB00010B/1761